The ancient novel, previously relegated to the margins of literary study, has recently taken its place at centre stage. Petronius' *Satyricon*, the oldest surviving work of prose fiction, is in many respects an arrestingly modern ancient novel but the inclusion within it of thirty short poems and two long ones introduces an alien feature in need of investigation. In this study, Catherine Connors draws on recent developments in Latin literary criticism to take a comprehensive approach to the *Satyricon*'s poems, reminiscences of poetic texts, and the figure of the poet, assessing the ways in which they fragment and refashion established literary forms into a new amalgam of prose fiction. This book will be of interest to students of Latin literature, Neronian culture, and the early history of the novel. All Latin and Greek is translated.

Petronius the poet

Petronius the poet

Verse and literary tradition in the Satyricon

Catherine Connors

Associate Professor of Classics,
University of Washington, Seattle

CAMBRIDGE
UNIVERSITY PRESS

PUBLISHED BY THE PRESS SYNDICATE OF THE UNIVERSITY OF CAMBRIDGE
The Pitt Building, Trumpington Street, Cambridge CB2 1RP,
United Kingdom

CAMBRIDGE UNIVERSITY PRESS
The Edinburgh Building, Cambridge CB2 2RU, United Kingdom
40 West 20th Street, New York, NY 10011-4211, USA
10 Stamford Road, Oakleigh, Melbourne 3166, Australia

First published 1998

Printed in the United Kingdom at the University Press, Cambridge

Typeset in Plantin and Greek New Hellenic 10/12 pt   [AO]

A catalogue record for this book is available from the British Library

Library of Congress cataloguing in publication data

Connors, Catherine.
    Petronius the poet: verse and literary tradition in the Satyricon /
Catherine Connors.
        p.   cm.
    Includes bibliographical references and index.
    ISBN 0 521 59231 3 (hardback)
    1. Petronius Arbiter. Satyricon.   2. Petronius Arbiter – Poetic works.
3. Verse satire, Latin – History and criticism.   4. Influence (Literary,
artistic, etc.)   5. Rome – In literature.   I. Title.
PA6559 C83   1998
873'.01 – dc21   98-6743 CIP

ISBN 0 521 59231 3 hardback

Contents

Prefatory note

The earliest witness of the title of the work attributed to Petronius is the fourth-century grammarian Marius Victorinus, who calls it the *Satyricon*. A title in this form would be the Greek genitive plural with *libri* implied. In the manuscripts the title is spelled in various other ways. The form *Satyrica* is preferred by scholars who view it as analogous to the titles of Greek novels such as *Aethiopica*, *Ephesiaca*, *Babyloniaca* and so forth. Either way, punning word-play between *satura*, a gastronomic or literary mixture, and *satyrica*, things associated with lascivious Greek satyrs, was available to readers (see Rose [1971], 1–2; Walsh [1970], 72).

The poem on the Civil War which is performed by Eumolpus at *Sat.* 119–24 is known as the *Bellum Civile*, and Lucan's poem on the same subject is known by the same title or as the *de bello civili*. For the sake of a convenient and clear distinction between them I shall cite Lucan's poem under the title *Pharsalia*. The title *Pharsalia*, which does not appear in the manuscripts of Lucan, would appear to derive from the phrase *Pharsalia nostra* at *Ph.* 9.985 (cf. Statius *Silv.* 2.7.66).

The author is generally identified with Nero's *elegantiae arbiter*, described by Tacitus (*Ann.* 16.18–19). His praenomen is thought to be Titus, rather than Gaius as the manuscripts of Tacitus would indicate (see Pliny *Nat.* 37.20, with Rose [1971], 47–49). Ancient references to the work cite the author as Petronius or Petronius Arbiter. The identification of the author of the *Satyricon* with Tacitus' Petronius was noted around 1571 by Scaliger in his own copy of the *Satyricon*, proposed in print by Pithou in 1577, called into question by Marmorale in 1948, and has been most fully defended in the publication of Rose's monograph on the subject in 1971. See also the brisk overview at Rose (1966a). Smith (1975), xii–xiv, remains skeptical.

The text of the *Satyricon* is cited from Müller (1995) unless noted otherwise. The Latin Anthology contains thirty other poems from various sources which were attributed to Petronius. In his editions prior to 1995, Müller printed as Petronian fragments only five poems from the

Latin Anthology, three of which had been cited as Petronian by Fulgentius, and two which had been anthologized with other segments of the *Satyricon* under the name of Petronius. It is impossible to be certain, but Courtney (1991), 5–11, has argued that twenty-six of the thirty poems attributed to Petronius in the Latin Anthology should be viewed as excerpts from the *Satyricon*, and this is the view adopted here. These poems will be cited by the fragment numbers of Müller (1995), with the numbering from the editions of the Latin Anthology by Riese (1894–1906) and Shackleton Bailey (1982) also given. Translations (literal, rather than literary) are my own.

Acknowledgements

It is a pleasure to thank the College of Arts and Sciences and the Graduate School of the University of Washington for the support which made this research possible. I am grateful to the friends and colleagues in Seattle who have made it such a congenial and stimulating place in which to work. This study would not have arrived at its present form without the generous support of the Department of Classics under the chairmanship of Michael Halleran. On various drafts I have benefited from the advice of James Clauss, Sheila Colwell, Alain Gowing, Paul Pascal, and Sandra Joshel, Visiting Professor in the Department of History; Stanley Whittaker provided valuable assistance in the final stages. Further afield, I extend my thanks to Alessandro Barchiesi, Denis Feeney, Kirk Freudenburg and Alison Keith for their helpful suggestions. I am also grateful for the guidance offered by Pauline Hire and the readers for the Press.

This book had its now distant origins in a dissertation on Petronius' Civil War poem; a thoroughly reconceived treatment of this material appears in chapter 4. The original research was supported by a Rackham Graduate Fellowship at the University of Michigan, and I thank David Ross, Bruce Frier, David Potter, James I. Porter and Patricia Rosenmeyer for their advice. Some sections of the present work appeared in an earlier form in "Beholding Troy in Petronius' *Satyricon* and John Barclay's *Euphormionis Lusinini Satyricon*," *Groningen Colloquia on the Novel* 6 (1995), 51–66, and "Famous Last Words: Authorship and Death in the *Satyricon* and in Neronian Rome," *Reflections of Nero*, J. Elsner and J. Masters, eds. (Duckworth 1994), 225–35.

Finally, I wish to thank my parents for their unfailing support and my husband and colleague Stephen Hinds for all his help.

Abbreviations

AJP	*American Journal of Philology*
ANRW	H. Temporini, *Aufstieg und Niedergang der römischen Welt.* Berlin 1972
BICS	*Bulletin of the Institute of Classical Studies of the University of London*
CA	*Classical Antiquity*
C&M	*Classica et Mediaevalia*
CHCL	P. E. Easterling and E. J. Kenney, General Editors, *The Cambridge History of Classical Literature*, 2 vols. Cambridge 1982, 1985.
CJ	*Classical Journal*
CP	*Classical Philology*
CQ	*Classical Quarterly*
CR	*Classical Review*
CW	*Classical World*
D.-S.	C. Daremberg and E. Saglio, *Dictionnaire des antiquités grecques et romaines.* Paris, 1877
ECM	*Échos du monde classique = Classical Views*
G&R	*Greece and Rome*
HSCP	*Harvard Studies in Classical Philology*
ICS	*Illinois Classical Studies*
JHS	*Journal of Hellenic Studies*
JRS	*Journal of Roman Studies*
MD	*Materiali e discussioni per l'analisi dei testi classici*
MH	*Museum Helveticum*
OLD	P. G. W. Glare, *Oxford Latin Dictionary.* Oxford, 1968–82
PCPS	*Proceedings of the Cambridge Philological Society*
PSN	*Petronian Society Newsletter*
RFIC	*Rivista di filologia e di istruzione classica*
REL	*Revue des études latines*
RhM	*Rheinisches Museum*
TAPA	*Transactions of the American Philological Association*

TLL	*Thesaurus Linguae Latinae.* Leipzig, 1900–
YCS	*Yale Classical Studies*
ZPE	*Zeitschrift für Papyrologie und Epigraphik*

Introduction

Poetry is integral to Petronius' *Satyricon*: reminiscences of poetic motifs and models are in evidence throughout its narrative, a professional poet is a leading character, and some thirty short poems and two long poems are performed by the narrator and others. Why did Petronius spend so much time being a poet while writing this novel? Why do the poems take up so much space in the narrative?

At one level, the reason may be simply the looseness of the generic boundaries of ancient prose fiction. Though certain features recur (or indeed are parodied) from novel to novel, ancient novelists invent, rather than retell, their stories and, as far as we can tell, neither Greeks nor Romans used a generic name for what we call novels. This critical vacuum is probably partly due to a sense that prose fiction operated under fewer constraints than the "named" genres. Novelists can arrange words at will, poets work within the remembered limits of verse. Genre is memory, and novelists' memories can be playfully selective.

Yet the generic looseness of ancient prose fiction is not the only answer. Petronius practices novelistic fiction in a distinctive way: as we shall see in more detail below, there is more poetry in the *Satyricon* than in the other novels which survive. By evoking particular genres or poems, the *Satyricon* exploits and contests the apparatus of literary memory. When Petronius takes up the mask of the poet, and when he makes poetic models visible beneath the surface of his prose, the narrative acknowledges and incorporates the more stylized and traditional structures of poetry within the fluid inventions of fiction in a relatively naturalistic idiom. Now because to modern eyes the Petronian poems often seem detachable interruptions of the lively prose, commentators have treated the poems separately from the narrative, and critics have emphasized disruptive aspects of the verse, viewing the multitude of literary voices which emerge in the text as literary chaos.[1] It is clearly

---

[1] The numerous separate treatments of various poems will be cited in the notes as needed. For critical discussion of the novel as a chaotic mixture of styles, there are good starting

1

right to be sensitive to the disruptive qualities of the novel's poetic elements; yet if we listen carefully to the literary voices echoing back and forth within the novel's fictional space, I think there is more to hear than cacophony. In obvious and subtle ways, the verse is often designed to tell the same story as the prose frame, transposing prose accounts of love and bad luck into a representational register defined by the inherited constraints of poetry. Verse and prose are juxtaposed as rival structures of representation within the novel itself, in effect repeatedly restaging the whole enterprise of choosing to be a novelist instead of a poet, and, with an unfailingly light touch, exploring the consequences of this choice.[2]

Such a fascination with processes of representation and simulation is of course not limited to Petronius' use of verse, and has long been recognized as one of the *Satyricon*'s most notable features. So for example, in a recent study of the practice of still-life painting in various contexts, Norman Bryson has used the *Satyricon* to illuminate the cultural patterns which inform Campanian wall painting. Central to both, in his analysis, are "delight in the exuberance of simulation, and in the power of representation to go past actual boundaries into a more expansive space and ontology." In a Campanian villa one could gaze at a painted illusion of space: Bryson argues that the still-life, natural, architectural and theatrical elements depicted in that space were chosen for their capacity to mark what he calls "elaborately precise transition points between the real and the artificial." He maintains:

... the *Satyricon* is perhaps our best guide to the wider place of such programmes within the culture.... It deals with the way in which the ruling culture understood itself *as* culture, and defined what it took to be the essential moments and processes in cultural production. That definition possesses a highly specific historical form: cultural work is defined as mediation and artifice, representation and simulation. Power is thought to be the capacity to control reality by shifting it from level to level, from a primally given real across a series of distinct thresholds of representation.[3]

It is from the famous Plinian anecdote about Zeuxis' painting of grapes so realistic that birds flew right up to the stage (*scaena*) where

---

points in Zeitlin (1971) and (1971a), which remain full of wonderfully fertile observations; Slater (1990) treats the discontinuous effects generated by the poems with contagious enthusiasm.

[2] On the dynamic processes of choosing a genre, see Conte (1986), esp. 40–52, describing how poetic language differs from non-poetic language, and the discussion of the construction of poetic genres at (1994), 115–20. Of his forthcoming study on Petronius, one chapter (to which I refer below n. 42) has been available to me.

[3] Bryson (1990), 17–59; the quotations are from pp. 51, 56, 55.

it was being displayed that Bryson derives this notion of thresholds of representation, observing that the birds move gradually from what is more real (the sky, and then the space of the theater) toward what is more artificial and contrived (the stage itself, and then the painting).[4]

Though Bryson's discussion centers on visual representations in paintings and in the staged spectacles of Trimalchio's banquet, the concept of movement across thresholds is useful in approaching the *Satyricon*'s verbal strategies of literary representation too. While it is obvious that the *Satyricon* is an artistic invention, not a transparent representation of reality, it is equally obvious that the novel juxtaposes representations in a relatively naturalistic style, closely mimicking the way real people might speak and act, with scenes whose artifice is much more overt. Its imitations of the real are analogous to Zeuxis' grapes in creating the illusion that no illusion takes place; they would include most famously the way the freedmen speak at Trimalchio's banquet, and also such scenes as the tussle over the recovery of the stolen cloak, and arguably even "low" verses of vulgar or popular songs.[5] Even when imitation is at its most transparent the presence of artifice is felt. For a Roman audience, the pleasure of watching a convincing imitation of such "low" discourse comes from the knowledge of the artifice which produces the realistic and raucous illusion. As anecdotes from Phaedrus and Plutarch tell us, an audience enjoys the theatrical spectacle of an expert performer who can throw his voice to convince them that he has a pig under his cloak, but they jeer when they realize a farmer has duplicated the performance without theatrical expertise simply by using a real pig.[6] Petronius' audience might enjoy hearing in the *Satyricon* echoes of freedmen they know, but part of what they enjoy is the knowledge that there is no real pig squealing under this cloak.

Pliny's anecdote about Zeuxis does not end with the grapes: even though the birds were deceived, Zeuxis pronounced himself bested by his rival Parrhasius' painting of a stage curtain so illusionistic that Zeuxis asked for it to be moved so he could see the painting behind: I only fooled the birds, Zeuxis says, but you fooled me (Pliny *Nat.* 35. 65). Like Parrhasius' painting of the stage curtain, the object which divides the artifice of the stage from the reality of the world, some elements of the *Satyricon* flaunt their status as artifice. We might think especially of the rhetorical denunciation of rhetoric at Agamemnon's

---

[4] Bryson (1990), 30–31; Pliny *Nat.* 35.65.

[5] Auerbach (1953), 26–33, celebrates Petronian realism in the *cena* while pointing out its limitations; see too Bodel (1984), a precise analysis of nuances of cultural and historical context in the representation of the freedmen.

[6] Phaed. 5.5, Plut. *Mor.* 674B–C.

school, the elaborate imagery of death and the underworld that per-
meates Trimalchio's banquet, the scenes with Circe or with Oenothea,
and of course the various poetic performances, especially those by the
poet Eumolpus.

The *Satyricon*'s representations of poetic performances and other
overt uses of poetic structures are the primary concern of my study.
Although in some ways Petronius seems to interrupt his novel to
become a poet, I will argue that it makes more sense to understand
his manipulations of poetic forms as part of a whole as integrated and
coherent as the painted ensemble of a room in a Campanian villa: like
the bowls of fruit, theatrical masks, architecture, and landscape in these
painted fictional spaces, Petronius' poems are an integral part of the
fictional space of the *Satyricon*. In analyzing how the poems and poetic
structures function within this fictional space, I do not aim to produce
a comprehensive treatment of the novel. Yet this detailed case study
of one of its most interesting and persistently enigmatic features should
help make it clear that every element of the *Satyricon* rewards the
closest philological and literary critical attention. Only from being
attentive to all of what is vivid, funny, melancholy, puzzling or off-
putting about this novel can we understand what it can tell us about
Latin literature and culture.

After a brief introductory discussion of the role of the verse in estab-
lishing the *Satyricon*'s possible generic affiliations to Menippean satire,
mime, and satiric fiction, I consider four aspects of Petronius as poet:
his epic parody throughout the novel, his use of short, less elevated
verse forms, and his two longer poems on the fall of Troy and the Civil
War. Since epic parody is one of the engines of the novel's plot, the
first chapter offers a comprehensive treatment of epic motifs in the plot
of the novel at large (such as we can tell), in individual episodes, and in
quoted and original epic hexameters. I am especially interested in the
variety of parodic strategies used by Petronius, and my discussions
begin from accessibly broad parodic effects before narrowing down
to consider subtler, more concentrated jokes which rely on a reader's
sharp memories of epic and dramatize the processes of destroying the
epic past and refashioning it into the novelistic present.

In contrast to his practice of directing epic parody at specific targets,
Petronius uses short poetic forms such as satire, elegy, and mime in a
conventional and general way; consequently, looking for precise responses to literary models is not very productive. Instead, my second
chapter looks closely at Petronius' various formal strategies for framing
the short verse in its prose context: the more closely these poems are
read within their narrative frames, the more they show gaps between

the traditional certainties of poetry and the untidy spontaneity of prose fiction. Because one of the recurring themes in the short verse is *fortuna*, the formal analysis of relations between the short poems and their frames extends outward to consider fortune and its relation to the creation of fiction, where the author is *fortuna* as he devises what will befall his characters. In the course of this analysis of Petronius' uses of epic and short verse forms, these first two chapters thus explore the *Satyricon*'s own story of its form, which fragments the epic past and refashions it into the fictional present ruled by authorial *fortuna*.

The strategies of analyzing thematic patterns and formal details developed in the first half of the book are then brought to bear on Petronius' longer poems on Troy and the Civil War. Throughout I discuss what may be called the "poetic" aspects of Petronius' poems, including their evocations of model texts and uses of generic conventions and figurative or otherwise "literary" language. Yet in Nero's Rome, investigations of intersections – or collisions – between the real and the artificial take on a particular ideological urgency, as Bartsch's nuanced analysis of the cultural dynamic of theatricality in the Roman empire has shown.[7] Petronius' use of verse, with its negotiations of the thresholds which divide naturalistic and artificial, historical and timeless, public and private modes of representation, can occasionally illuminate the negotiations of those same thresholds by Nero and his chroniclers. As we shall see, when Petronius retells the tale of the Fall of Troy using representations of repetition, reiteration, and likeness to cast this poem as debased re-enactment of Virgil's *Aeneid*, the *Satyricon* becomes part of Neronian discourses about the power of the distant past in the present. So too in telling the tale of the Civil War from which Augustus eventually emerged as emperor, Petronius explores the effects of the past on the present. Historical memory, which is not inert but continually negotiated and contructed, overlaps with literary memory when the *Aeneid*'s account of Rome's founding by Aeneas and refounding by Augustus represents the present as the culmination of an epic past. When the *Satyricon* repackages motifs and material from Homer and Virgil, and even Lucan, in a contemporary narrative, the novel, like the city of Rome itself, incorporates the epic past into its present. Its vulgarities are far from Augustus' grandeur, but not so different perhaps from Nero's performance in the role of emperor.

---

[7] Bartsch (1994), esp. chapter 2. Her brief discussion of the *Satyricon* emphasizes parallels between Nero's theatrical manipulations and Trimalchio's, pp. 197–9. Rudich (1993), a study of individual strategies of dissent and pretense during the reign of Nero, also has much to offer.

Nero's relation to Augustus might be summed up in his "re-enactment" of Augustus' military triumph: upon his return from Greece Nero makes his ceremonial entrance into Rome in Augustus' triumphal chariot, with placards recording his artistic and athletic victories carried before him (Suet. *Nero* 25.1). Building on the myths which traced the Julian family back to Aeneas, Augustus creates an empire which fulfills a cosmos-ordering destiny arising from the ashes of Troy. As such, Augustus is an epic poet of empire – and Nero is the novelist who parodies him, replacing Augustan constructions of empire's lofty epic destiny with his own debased fictional creations, and eventually, by his death, irretrievably breaking the imperial link with the epic past.

Verse and genre in Petronian criticism

In looking at the *Satyricon*'s poems in this way, as negotiations of Roman literature's thresholds of representation, I am deliberately setting aside many of the questions and presuppositions which earlier critics have brought to them. Because the inserted poems make the novel so different from the novels we have grown up with, they often seem like a conundrum in need of a solution – a cipher carrying a message about Petronius' intentions for the whole *Satyricon*. Are the verses inserted to make the *Satyricon* seem similar to the prosimetric form of Menippean satire? Do they merely show that there was an established form of what Stephens and Winkler (1995, 361) call "criminal-satiric fiction" which mixed verse with prose? What are the implications when characters perform verses or songs which seem to evoke the spontaneity of mime? Unexamined assumptions that Menippean satire regularly engages in serious social critique, and that mime and Greek fiction exist in isolation from discourses of social critique, have made the stakes in this kind of generic argument high, for generic arguments about the *Satyricon*'s verse are often bound up implicitly or explicitly in arguments or assumptions about whether Petronius was a "moralist." Those who see Petronius as a "moralist" tend to bring out his Menippean affinities, and often argue along the way that the moralizing poems censure Roman society.[8] Those who are less interested in the possibility of social critique tend to make connections to mime and Greek prosimetric fiction,[9] and to emphasize how the verse contributes to Petronius' representations of character.[10]

---

[8] With different emphases: Highet (1941); Bacon (1958); Raith (1963); Arrowsmith (1966); Sochatoff (1962) and (1970); and Zeitlin (1971), (1971a).

[9] Sandy (1974), (1994), 140-1; Astbury (1977), Panayotakis (1995).

[10] E.g. Cèbe (1966), 313; Beck (1973), (1979), (1982); Sullivan (1967); Walsh (1974); Wright (1976); cf. Sandy (1969).

Clearly, people keep asking whether or not Petronius was a "moralist" because the *Satyricon* seems such an immoral book. Ever since classical canons began to take shape, the *Satyricon*'s potential for moral instruction, or lack thereof, has seemed in need of comment. Defending Petronius as a "moralist" becomes a way of justifying his inclusion in the canon; asserting that his intentions are not moralizing becomes a way for reader and critic to delimit or to challenge the boundaries of the canon.

The oldest surviving literary critical remark about the *Satyricon* is made by Macrobius in his commentary on Cicero's *Somnium Scipionis*, during a discussion of whether pleasurable fictions can or should provide morally valuable truths.[11] At the end of the *de Republica*, modeled on Plato's *Republic*, Cicero presents a mythologized exploration of the scope of the universe, much as Plato explores life's meaning in the myth of Er at the end of his *Republic*. Scipio Aemilianus has a dream in which he encounters his father and grandfather and learns of the realm within the heavens designated for those who serve the republic well. He is shown the entire world at one glance and hears the celestial music of the spheres of the universe. As a result, he learns to view his own life and human history within this universalizing perspective. The popularity of the theme of the journey to the heavens in comic or Menippean texts may have been part of the impulse which prompted Macrobius to introduce his commentary on the *Somnium* with the categorization of fictions as merely pleasurable on the one hand or pleasurable and edifying on the other. To argue that the obviously fictional qualities of this episode do not undermine the authenticity of its moral lessons, Macrobius aligns the *Somnium* with other fictions which can convey moral truths, such as Hesiod's and Aesop's, and distinguishes these morally useful fictions from others which are purely pleasurable, such as those of Menander, Petronius, and Apuleius.[12] The Christian

---

[11] I concentrate here on texts which refer to Petronius specifically; Morgan (1993), usefully sets out the whole range of ancient attitudes to prose fiction, emphasizing the general distrust and disregard critics display toward it, and demonstrating for the Greek novels that "if no one in the ancient world successfully theorized the dynamics of novel-reading, the instinctive competence of actual readers was, as ever, more advanced than any theoretical analysis," p. 197. See too Bowersock (1994), 1–27.

[12] Macrob. *Comm.* 1.2.8: auditum mulcent vel comoediae, quales Menander eiusve imitatores agendas dederunt, vel argumenta fictis casibus amatorum referta, quibus vel multum se Arbiter exercuit vel Apuleium non numquam lusisse miramur. hoc totum fabularum genus, quod solas aurium delicias profitetur, e sacrario suo in nutricum cunas sapientiae tractatus eliminat. "Comedies such as Menander or his imitators have written please our sense of hearing, or stories filled with fictional adventures of lovers, with which Arbiter occupied himself and in which, remarkably, Apuleius sometimes indulged. This whole class of stories, which engages in producing only pleasure for the ears, a philosophical treatise expels from its sacred shrine into nursemaids' cradles."

Marius Mercator denounces Petronius in stronger terms. To condemn the emperor Julian's writings, he compares them to the mimes of Philistion, Lentulus, and Marullus, adding that only Julian has excelled the talents (*ingenia*) of Martial and Petronius.[13]

Each manuscript source for the fragmentary text of the *Satyricon* is in part a document of reception, revealing at times what its compiler determined to be valuable or dispensable in the *Satyricon*.[14] The exemplar of the O family of manuscripts seems designed to prevent the *Satyricon* from conveying the wrong sort of pleasures. In contrast to the L tradition, which does not avoid obscenity, the O tradition generally avoids the most obscene sections of the story. So, for example, the O class keeps some of the Quartilla episode, but passes over the seductive behavior of Quartilla and her companions and avoids the homosexual axis altogether, apparently patching together several sentences about laughter to paper over the gap.[15] Elsewhere this kind of patchwork procedure has the effect (surely intended) of transforming Eumolpus into something much closer to a respectable *paedagogus*. In the Circe episode, the O class keeps most of the verse, but skips some of the narrative, and eliminates mention of Giton. For the Oenothea section, the O tradition speeds up the action by skipping over some of the narrative, keeps all of the verses, and avoids the obscene details of Oenothea's "treatment" of Encolpius. The question of the *Satyricon's* moral value is obviously at least part of the agenda of the composer of the O excerpts, and a process of intentional fragmentation is used to change the perceived moral content and value of the *Satyricon*. A manuscript or anthology need not be a completely transparent document of reception; it is possible that the compiler of the O excerpts enjoyed the parts he omitted, and indeed decided to omit those very parts on the ground that they created an excessive or inappropriate kind of pleasure.

An attempt to recover morally valuable elements from the *Satyricon* is also evident in the *florilegia*, or medieval anthologies. In France, probably in the twelfth century, someone made a collection of excerpts from the works of almost forty classical authors which is now known as the *florilegium gallicum*.[16] Between selections from Martial and from

---

[13] Marius Mercator, *Lib. subnot. in verba Juliani* 4.1 = Migne, *P. L.* 48, 126–27, 133–34, discussed at Sullivan (1968a), 112–13, Panayotakis (1995), xx–xxi.

[14] On the history of the text see Müller (1995), iii–xxiv, and Reeve (1983).

[15] See *Sat.* 19.1, 20.8, 24.5.

[16] On the four main manuscripts in this tradition, whose archetype is placed in the twelfth century, see Ullman (1928); he lists the authors contained in these mss at 131; see also Rouse (1979). On the Petronian material in the *florilegium gallicum* see Ullman (1930), Brandis and Ehlers (1974).

the *Culex* fell selections from the *Satyricon*. The excerptor assembled some thirteen items of verse, eleven short sections from the *Bellum Civile*, twenty-six short prose *sententiae*, the discourse on decadence in the arts (88.2–9), and the story of the Widow of Ephesus (111–12). The excerpts are arranged generally in the order of the *Satyricon* as it survives today. Whether the person who created the anthology in the form which survives is the same individual who made the initial excerpts from Petronius is not clear; what interests me here is the fact that someone used the creation of discontinuity to implement a moralizing discourse. Like many pagan texts, the *Satyricon* is mined for its worthwhile and instructive nuggets, and these are duplicated and transmitted to subsequent readers. What is ironic and humorous in the *Satyricon* becomes a tame commonplace when isolated in an anthology. Excuses which the characters make to get themselves out of tight situations become slogans to live by, and verse sentiments which were ironically undercut by their prose frames become tidy assertions about the nature of fortune or love.

When the anthologist copied out these pieces of the *Satyricon*, he surgically removed them from their often scandalous or frivolous contexts and created a new anthology text out of these discontinuous bits. Yet the compiler was not being false to the dynamics of the *Satyricon*. The discontinuities which he created correspond to discontinuities that were already deployed for artistic effect within the text. In the *Satyricon*, many of the short poems move the reader from the particularities of fiction to the moralizing universals of maxim and proverb, and stake a claim to memory with their generalizations applicable to situations outside the chaotic inventions of the novel. The recognition that these quotations from the *Satyricon* are perfectly at home in an instructive anthology alerts us to the discontinuous effect they, and some of the *Satyricon*'s other moralizing poems too, already created in their original context.

In the *florilegia*, a text that as a whole (or as a damaged whole) seemed amoral to the pagan Macrobius and probably seemed immoral to Christian monks can be transformed into a source of moral lessons (brief, pointed, pithy, banal, unambitious they may be but they are still by and large lessons) through a process of intentional fragmentation. A more elaborate process of fragmentation and reworking is at work in John of Salisbury's responses to the *Satyricon*.[17] Martin has detailed the ways in which John in his *Policraticus* uses Petronius as a source for striking phrases, moralizing poems, and instructive anecdotes, while

---

[17] A list of John of Salisbury's borrowings from the *Satyricon* is provided at Müller (1995), xxxiv–xxxv.

elsewhere he uses references to Petronius as a kind of private joke among his learned friends. Martin also suggests that in prefacing his quotation of the *Satyricon*'s story of the Widow of Ephesus with a discussion of ways in which fictions can be morally edifying, John may be drawing on Macrobius' discussion of types of fiction, even though Macrobius had clearly said that the *Satyricon* was a purely pleasurable fiction rather than a morally useful one.[18] Here intentional fragmentation of both the Petronian model and Macrobius' comment upon it have been used as a strategy for preserving the classical past.

In the fifteenth century Poggio Bracciolini discovered two separate manuscripts of Petronius. On 13 June 1420 writing from England to his friend Niccoli, Poggio mentioned a text of Petronius, and later he sent Niccoli the manuscript he had found or a copy of it. The value of Petronius is at issue, at least implicitly, in Poggio's letter to Niccoli mentioning his first discovery of Petronius, and here too the point of reference is Macrobius' discussion of fiction.[19] This first text which Poggio found was a manuscript of the O tradition (he later obtained a manuscript containing the *cena*). Even though in Macrobius' terms the story is pleasurable and does not convey truth, for Poggio Petronius is worthwhile.[20] Poggio's approving characterization of Petronius as *gravis versu et prosa constans*, serious in verse and steady in prose, seems just what the compiler of the O excerpts intended.

The rediscovery of the manuscripts in the L tradition, which included far more obscene material, and seem to represent accidental discontinuities rather than intentional excerpts, tipped the balance the other way: Petronius was now a surreptitious classic, not a source of moralizing. Subsequently, in the aftermath of the rediscovery and publication of the single manuscript containing most of the *cena* (H) in the 1650s, the forger Nodot used procedures of supplementation to make the *Satyricon* fully complete.[21] Nodot attempted to prevent any possibility of future "discoveries" by anyone else by filling in every gap

[18] Martin (1979), 73. For the Widow of Ephesus story, see *Policraticus* 8.11 p. 301.14–304.17.

[19] Harth (1984), vol.1. 4 (=Tonelli 1.7).

[20] Indeed, Poggio even praises the virtue of his beautiful young wife with a quotation of a remark addressed by Eumolpus to Giton: *Scribit Petronius Arbiter, "raram fecit mixturam cum sapientia forma."* (Petronius Arbiter writes, "Beauty with wisdom has made a remarkable combination") from a letter to Guarino Veronese, 18 May 1436, Harth (1984) vol. 2. 7 (= Tonelli 6.1), quoting Petronius 94.1 (transmitted in O, *florilegia*, and L).

[21] The forgery is discussed by Collignon (1905), 79-85 and Stolz (1987). I have consulted *Titi Petronii Arbitri, equitis Romani, Satyricon: cum fragmentis albae Graecae recuperatis ann. 1688 nunc demum integrum* (London 1693); other editions are listed in Stolz (1987), 100–02 and Schmeling and Stuckey (1977), pp. 62–65.

in the text, and creating a complete narrative from beginning to end.[22] What he thought worthwhile about the *Satyricon* was its obscenity, and his supplements make it a more explicitly obscene text.

Perhaps because it survives in fragments, the *Satyricon* has seemed especially open to such interventionist readings. These themes are still to be seen in modern critical reactions to the *Satyricon*'s fragmentary text.[23] Some, like the compiler of the O excerpts and the anthologists, construct a Petronius who is a "moralist." This often involves a process of selection which privileges certain discrete moments in the text (often poems) in much the same way as an anthologist might, giving them a kind of moral authority which transcends the characters and situations in which it is embedded.[24] Others argue that the *Satyricon* is not a moralizing reaction to the age of Nero but instead "a sophisticated, scabrous book."[25] These readings, by contrast, often use procedures of supplementation, combining our sketchy knowledge of less canonical genres which survive only in small fragments, especially mime and the racier side of Greek fiction, to fill in the gaps in what survives of Petronius' narrative, and they tend to privilege the ironic framing of potentially moralizing discourse uttered by disreputable characters.

In the last century or so, modern critics have read the *Satyricon*'s verse as an index of its generic affinities, and then in turn interpreted those generic affinities as an index of the presence or absence of moralizing content. In raising the issue of whether Petronius is a "moralist," modern scholarship reflects anxieties about the boundaries which divide high and low, and canonical and non-canonical, literary forms. An interest in such demarcations can already be discerned in the *Satyricon*'s own epic parody and its representations of the composition and performance of literary works. The poems performed by Eumolpus, whose very name (a Greek word meaning "singing well") is a mask designed to signal high literary excellence, and by Encolpius evoke the worlds of epic and other literary forms and insert them into debased latter-day contexts. Now it happens that Agamemnon's verses on education (5), the first verses among the surviving fragments, lay out a survey of the high literary genres. He introduces his verses by describing them as improvised: *sed ne me putes improbasse schedium Lucilianae humilitatis, quod sentio et ipse carmine effingam* ("But don't think I

---

[22] Another short fragment was forged in 1800 by Fr. José Marchena; it is quoted and translated at Rose (1966a), 286–88.

[23] Schmeling (1994) provides a spacious overview of critical interpretations of the *Satyricon*.

[24] So Perry (1967), 193, 205.

[25] Panayotakis (1995), 196.

disapprove of improvised poetry in Lucilius' humble style – I myself will put my thoughts into verse," 4.5). Agamemnon asserts mastery of the whole range of genres by using an informal satirical mode, the *schedium*, associated with improvisation, to describe poetic education and mastery of the loftier genres of philosophy, history, oratory, and poetry.[26] The opening choliambic lines assert that art should be pursued with integrity, not careerist aims. The language emphasizes discipline and control: *prius mores/frugalitatis lege poliat exacta* "first let him refine his character with the scrupulous rule of modest living"; he should avoid the parties of the dissolute (*cenas impotentium*). Agamemnon switches to hexameter (in a move which matches Persius' switch from choliambics to hexameter at the opening of his poetic book), and the terms of control then become literary rather than social. Agamemnon constructs the educated life as a journey through a set of genres, each with their own rules: first (*primos ... annos*) epic, soon (*mox*) Socratic dialogue, then Demosthenic oratory, then (*hinc*) Roman history and poetry. Listing these poetic stages in his *schedium*, Agamemnon spreads out a generic map with tidy borders in a satiric frame; Petronius pulls the map of genre to pieces and patches it together again as narrative. For Agamemnon's ideal poet, a poet's life is lived in the strict confines of one genre at a time; Petronius' characters live in a "lawless" world where generic and social hierarchies and boundaries are constantly being transgressed.[27]

Ultimately, the verse in the *Satyricon* will yield no simple answer to the question "was Petronius a moralist?" Instead, I will show what the verse can tell us about how Petronius uses and transforms the cultural artifacts of literary representation. The chapters to follow will give detailed consideration to the ways in which Petronius represents generic forms ranging from mythological epic motifs, to satire and epigram, to tragedy, and to historical epic. But first, it will be useful here to look briefly at the formal qualities of those genres with which the *Satyricon* has the closest affinities: mime, Menippean satire, and prosimetric Greek fiction.

As we have noted, the similarity of the *Satyricon* to the motifs of mime was remarked in the fifth century by Marius Mercator in his

---

[26] Lucilius called his poetry a *schedium* (Paul. Fest. 335, 335 M), cf. Apul. *Socr.* pr. 1. Sullivan (1968a), 191–92 and Flores (1982), 75–82 discuss ways in which features of Lucilian style may be parodied here.

[27] On the *Satyricon*'s representations of trangressions of established boundaries, see Zeitlin (1971). The discussion of genre and lawlessness in the *Satyricon* in Barchiesi (forthcoming) has influenced me here. Martial's assertion that a *lex* (law) has been given to jesting verses (*carminibus ... iocosis*) allowing them to be obscene (1.35.10) also playfully connects law and genre.

denunciation of the Emperor Julian for obscenity.[28] Recent critics too have discerned mime motifs in the *Satyricon*, and Panayotakis has argued that mime situations and plots constitute structuring devices throughout the novel.[29] Roman mime, which survives only in fragments, seems to have been characterized by lively performances, material which was often obscene, and abrupt endings. Female roles could be played by women.[30] The raucous jokes and sudden surprises at the *cena* and throughout the novel could certainly strike Roman audiences as similar to the plots and dramatic improvisations found in mime. And the spontaneously performed songs, especially at the *cena*, do seem to evoke the world of mime. One of the *Satyricon*'s poems describes how a mime finishes and the actors return to their "real-life" roles; as Slater remarks in his study of processes of interpretation and the manipulation of artifice in the novel, "This poem might stand as an epigraph for the whole *Satyricon*"[31] (80.9.5–8):

> grex agit in scaena mimum: pater ille vocatur,
> filius hic, nomen divitis ille tenet.
> mox ubi ridendas inclusit pagina partes,
> vera redit facies, assimulata perit.

> The troupe performs the mime on stage; that one is called the father,
> this one the son; and that one bears the name of the rich man.
> Soon when the page shuts up the comic roles,
> the true countenance returns, the mimic one vanishes.

In the larger narrative context of the *Satyricon*, the poem calls attention to the artful deceptions of the *Satyricon* as a whole and indicates the *Satyricon*'s self-conscious awareness of its own fictionality.[32] Mime imitated real people, rather than kings or gods, and of all Roman

---

[28] See above n. 13.

[29] Panayotakis (1995). Useful earlier discussions include: Schmeling (1992), Slater (1990), 44, 104–5, 115–16, and throughout his discussion of the *cena*, Ch. 4; Sandy (1974); Walsh (1970), 24–27; Sullivan (1968a), 219–25 (his point that the *Satyricon*'s relation to mime is probably similar to the connections between the novels of P. G. Wodehouse and staged farces is well taken); Preston (1915), 260–65, drawing on Rosenblüth (1909), 36–55; Collignon (1892), 275–81.

[30] On mime in general see Reich (1903), Reynolds (1946), Fantham (1989), Rawson (1993), Panayotakis (1995), xii–xix. Also useful is Nicoll (1931), 80–134. For the fragments see Bonaria (1965).

[31] Slater (1990), 89.

[32] *pagina*, the reading of L and O, is accepted by Müller. In his *editio major* Bücheler (1862) had offered *machina* in the apparatus. Nisbet (1962), 231, prefers that *pagina* be obelized because he objects to mixing a reference to a text with references to actors. He considers *pergula*, a conjecture of Strelitz (1879), 836, which would mean the actors' dressing room. Slater (1990), 13, 89 and (1987a), wishes to retain *pagina* and to argue that the poem refers to book illustrations; Courtney (1991) *ad loc.* suggests that *pagina* refers to the prompter's script of the mime.

theatrical business, the mime is "closest" to real life: a mime actor did not wear the special shoes (*soccus* and *cothurnus*) which comic and tragic actors wore, but was a *planipes*, a flat-foot. Moreover, it seems that mime actors did not wear masks.[33] Like mime, then, the *Satyricon* imitates and caricatures certain types of relatively "ordinary" people in a relatively "transparent" way. The recognition of mime motifs in the Quartilla episode and at Trimalchio's, as well as in the deceptive mime at Croton, sharpens the humor of the text on numerous occasions by bringing a vivid physical imagination to the reading of Petronius' scenes: in effect, two fragmentary contexts, the *Satyricon* and mime, are made to add up to more than the sum of their parts. But epic parody does not seem to have been a dominant feature of mime, and the long poems on Troy and the Civil War do not seem to fit neatly into a mime frame.

The collection of literary techniques which were known at Rome as Menippean satire was also part of the background knowledge which many of the *Satyricon*'s readers brought to the text. Critical studies of Roman satire or of the Menippean tradition, including the influential discussions by Frye and Bakhtin, and the recent study of the form by Dronke, firmly claim Petronius as a participant (albeit an unconventional one) in the Menippean tradition.[34] Courtney connects the *Satyricon*'s literary parodies with the tradition of literary parody in Menippean satire.[35] Coffey, emphasizing the *Satyricon*'s similarities to satire, says that the *Satyricon* "may be regarded as part of the 'alternative convention' of satire, i.e., a mixture of prose and verse, which mocked or censured undesirable social behaviour."[36] Relihan, by contrast, has recently argued that Menippean satires in general undermined the seriousness of any possible moral lessons by their ironic and humorous frames, and that the *Satyricon* in particular, along with the Menippean satires of Varro and Seneca, represents "a transformation of Menippean satire into a parody of Roman satire."[37]

Ultimately, what survives of Menippus is less his own works than what we might call others' reinventions of him. Menippus wrote works of varied literary character, and may have invented the literary form

---

[33] Athenaeus mentions a certain Cleon the *mimaulos*, "the best of the Italian mimes who display their own features," Ath. 10.452 f. Nicoll (1931), 91, thinks that masks may have been worn.

[34] Bakhtin (1981), 22; Frye (1957), 309, Kirk (1980), 11–13, Dronke (1994), 9–12, Sullivan (1968a), 89–91. Frueh (1988) is an extended and rather rigid Bakhtinian reading of the *Satyricon*.

[35] Courtney (1962).

[36] Coffey (1989), 186.

[37] Relihan (1993), 98.

of verse mixed with prose. Varro in turn reinvents Menippus as an adjective to define his own prosimetric works as *saturae menippeae*, inheritors to an eclectic but highly distinct literary tradition. Lucian reinvents Menippus as a fictional character against which Lucian can define his own artistic projects, but uses very little verse.[38] Meanwhile, the clearest surviving example of the Menippean form is found in Seneca's *Apocolocyntosis* ("Gourdification"), which tells the humorous story of the death of Claudius, and the gods' rejection of his bid for deification.[39] The narrative describes a fantastic journey from earth to heaven and ultimately to the underworld, while repeatedly moving between registers of humor and seriousness, truth and fiction, prose and verse. Verse is used some twelve times: verses are produced both by the characters between themselves, and by the narrator; there are quotations and original compositions. The quotations of verse move the action along; if they were omitted, there would be a gap in the narrative. The original verses do not provide anything necessary for the narrative, and create instead ironic discontinuities. They do not rely on evoking a specific model to create their literary effect; thus they are longer than the quotations, which need only be short to remind readers of a memorable context. So, for example, the season and time of Claudius' death are described in lofty hexameter (2.1, 2.4), though the narrator specifies the date and time in prose as well (2.3). A hexameter poem depicts the spinning of a long and glorious thread representing Nero's reign (4); the majesty of the occasion is undercut by the fact that the thread is so long simply because the Fates have been distracted by listening to Apollo sing as they work (4.14–20). When first encountering Claudius, Hercules plays the role of a comic buffoon, frightened, and thinking that he is faced with his thirteenth labor (5.3). After his initial inquiries, Hercules puts on his tragic self (*et quo terribilior esset, tragicus fit et ait*, 7.1) and interrogates Claudius in 14 lines of mock tragic iambic trimeter (7.2).[40]

Over all, it seems that sudden shifts and incongruous juxtapositions (which can be both intertextual and intratextual) distinguished the works of Menippus, Varro, and Seneca. First, the comic is constantly

---

[38] For discussion of Lucian's representations of Menippus, see McCarthy (1934), Branham (1989), 14–25, and Relihan (1993), 103–18.

[39] On the title and the attribution of the work to Seneca (cf. Dio 61.35.3), see Eden (1984), 1–8.

[40] Since Seneca himself wrote a *Hercules Furens*, Hercules' shift from comic to tragic may self-consciously reverse the shift Seneca himself has made in putting on a comic style to compose the *Apocolocyntosis*. Dating of the tragedies is far from secure, but they are often placed in the period before the death of Claudius. See Coffey (1957), 149–51.

balanced against the serious; opinion remains divided as to which prevails. Second, the flexibility and infinite openness of prose is constantly
juxtaposed with the inherited constraints of meter. Varro apparently
even discusses this formal juxtaposition in the *Bimarcus* (*The Two Sides
of Marcus*): in choliambics, a meter known as the "limping iambic"
because the penultimate syllable in its line is long where an iambic line
would have a short syllable, a speaker remarks with self-conscious irony
on the slowness and constraints of verse; in prose someone seems to
celebrate his own poetic achievement.[41] At the ethical level there are
numerous juxtapositions of the virtuous past with the decadent present.
Historically, the mythical past is brought into collision with the mundane present. Intellectually, the pretensions of philosophers are contrasted with witty common sense. The bird's-eye view of the dreamer
or fantastic voyager is contrasted with the ordinary glance.

Part of the impulse to view Petronius within a Menippean framework has undoubtedly been the scarcity and fragmentation of surviving
ancient Menippean texts. Counting Petronius as a Menippean satirist
expands the number of ancient Menippean relatively well-preserved
authors from two (Seneca and Lucian) to three. It would be hard,
though, to maintain that Petronius himself intended his work to be
read narrowly within the Menippean tradition (however flexible and
unconventional the Menippean conventions might have been). Petronius does not mix comic with serious elements in the ways that Seneca
and Varro do. There are threads of parodic treatment of myth in the
Satyricon, especially in the scenes set in Croton, but the gods are
not represented directly. The *Satyricon*'s extended narrative, moving
rather realistically through space and time, seems unparalleled in the
evidence for Menippean satire, and there are no hints of the sorts of
fantastic journeys discernible in Seneca or in the fragments of Varro.
Petronius mixes verse with prose, but as we shall see, the *Satyricon*'s
verse seems more ambitious, more various, more revealing of character, and more complexly integrated within the narrative than what we
see in the Menippean tradition.[42]

The evidence for Greek prosimetric fiction and its possible links to
the form of the *Satyricon* has emerged only recently. With the pub-

---

41 The texts of F 57, 58 (Cèbe 1972, 55, 54) are corrupt but this much seems relatively
certain. The mixing of prose and verse may also be referred to in the *Desultorius* περὶ τοῦ
γραφεῖν (*The Circus Rider's Horse: On Writing*); so Relihan (1993), 60.
42 For further discussion of the *Satyricon*'s differences from Menippean satire, see Barchiesi
(1991), 234–36, Labate (1995), 168–70, Conte (forthcoming), in his chapter entitled
"The Quest for a Genre (or Chasing Will o' the Wisps?): Some Skeptical Thoughts on
Menippean Satire."

lication of new discoveries, it has become clear that there was a wider range of content in ancient Greek prose fiction than is evident in the idealizing stories of true love of hero and heroine in the surviving novels by Chariton, Achilles Tatius, Xenophon of Ephesus, Longus, and Heliodorus. It has accordingly become possible to argue that the *Satyricon* is somehow connected to an established genre of non-idealizing prosimetric Greek fiction. The so-called *Iolaus* fragment mixed verse with prose.[43] It is impossible to determine whether the *Iolaus* (preserved on a second-century CE papyrus) influenced or was influenced by the *Satyricon*, or whether, as Stephens and Winkler formulate the possibility, "the two are unrelated, there being sufficient variety of narrative type available by the first century CE, that both Petronius and *Iolaus* could arrive on the scene independent of each other."[44] References to initiation into the rites of Cybele, and to a *cinaedus* and a *gallus*, are recoverable in the fragment. True initiation as a *gallus* in the rites of Cybele would involve castration; it has been suggested that Iolaus is learning how to disguise himself as a *gallus* in order to get access to someone else.[45] Within the brief fragment there are two instances of verse. The unnamed protagonist addresses Iolaus and a *cinaedus* in sotadeans, the meter elsewhere used by *galli* and *cinaedi*. A second example of verse is a quotation from Euripides' *Orestes* on the value of friendship. Stephens and Winkler translate:

And Iolaus is taught by the mystic all the things that he had learned, and he is a complete *gallus*, trusting of his friend Neikon. "Nothing is greater than an unambiguous [σαφής] friend, not wealth or gold; the mob is a foolish substitute for a noble friend."[46]

In the *Orestes*, when Pylades deters Orestes from committing suicide by suggesting that they plot to kill Helen, Orestes says that "Nothing is greater than an unambiguous friend, not wealth or sovereignty [τυραννίς]." In the new novelistic frame, the praise of friendship is humorous, because Iolaus' situation is so absurd.

The *Tinouphis* fragment too contains a mixture of prose and verse (iambic tetrameter catalectic).[47] The condemned Tinouphis is saved by an executioner's subterfuge which involves an extra-large execution

---

[43] Stephens and Winkler (1995), 358–74.
[44] Ibid., 365.
[45] First suggested by E. R. Dodds in Parsons (1974), 35 n. 1.
[46] Stephens and Winkler (1995), 371. The quotation substitutes "gold" for Euripides' τυραννίς, absolute power. The last sentence is very fragmentary in the papyrus, but it has been restored to give the next line of the Euripides passage, *Or.* 1155–57.
[47] Stephens and Winkler (1995), 400–08; Stramaglia (1992).

chamber and a special brick, devised to allow escape. The event is described first in verse and then in prose: the verses mention the special
brick and report the rescue; the prose gives an apparently fuller narrative of these events, reporting that when the executioner was asked why
he had built the very large chamber (*megiston*), he said punningly that it
was because Tinouphis was a *magos*. Just possibly, the verse gave a
slightly more cryptic, concentrated version of events (exactly how does
the special brick allow escape?) while the prose explained things in a
more pedestrian way.

On the scanty available evidence, there does appear to be a slight
difference between the deployment of verse in the Greek fragments and
in the *Satyricon*. The Iolaus fragment shows a relatively "realistic"
incorporation of verse: the *gallus* speaks in the meter appropriate to
galli, and the introduction of the Euripides quotation is relatively
naturalistic. The *Tinouphis* fragment is suggestive, but so far we do not
see in the Greek fragments the *Satyricon*'s extremely contrived juxtapositions of a lofty poetic version of the action with a more mundane
prose account.

Thus, Petronius' verse has some similarities to what is evident in our
scraps of Menippean satire, mime, and "criminal-satiric fiction," but it
must remain an open question whether one particular generic frame
would dominate over others in the *Satyricon*. Moments of absurd contrast and hypocritical moralizing could evoke Menippean satire, spon-
taneous verse and musical performance could make it seem that the
novel's characters inhabit the world of mime, and some verses (perhaps
connected to especially disreputable characters – as, for example, the
song of the *cinaedus* in the Quartilla episode) could have seemed like
things novelists could have been doing in Greek. Here I draw upon a
flexible approach to the ways Roman authors work with genres out-
lined by Conte, who describes Roman poetry's "tendency to put the
choice of language and of genre in 'dramatic' terms, almost to 'stage'
the problem of the choice of literary form."[48] To switch the metaphor, it may make sense to say that the generic systems which Roman
authors choose to work in are more wardrobe than straitjacket – and
that this is especially true for an author working in the flexible form of
prose fiction. In their determination to clarify the puzzling obscurities
of Petronius' fragmented text, critics often tend to phrase their arguments somewhat restrictively, in terms of what effects the text "would"
produce. But perhaps we can learn more from exploring what effects
the text "could" have. For readers to choose mime or Menippean

[48] Conte (1994), 120.

satire or "criminal–satiric fiction" as a rigid generic frame which "would" have particular consequences for Petronius' exploitation of the mixed forms necessarily conceals what is most inventive and surprising about the verse – precisely because none of the surviving examples of these forms use verse in the same extended and artistically exciting ways that Petronius does. And since the *Satyricon* is so rich and sophisticated and funny a text, and so frustratingly fragmented, it seems a pity to let any of its words go to waste.

1 Refashioning the epic past

During his banquet, Trimalchio tells a peculiar story about the origins of Corinthian bronze (50.5–6):

cum Ilium captum est, Hannibal, homo vafer et magnus stelio, omnes statuas aeneas et aureas et argenteas in unum rogum congessit et eas incendit; factae sunt in unum aera miscellanea. ita ex hac massa fabri sustulerunt et fecerunt catilla et paropsides ⟨et⟩ statuncula. sic Corinthea nata sunt, ex omnibus in unum, nec hoc nec illud.

When Troy was captured, Hannibal, a crafty man and a great slippery character, piled up all of the statues, bronze, gold, and silver, into one heap and set them alight; they were melded together into a bronze mixture. So craftsmen took pieces out of this lump and made small bowls and serving dishes and statuettes. Corinthian bronzes were produced this way from metals all mixed together, neither one kind nor another.

Trimalchio's tale operates against a background of Roman connoisseurship of authentic Corinthian bronze. So, for example, Velleius Paterculus (1.13) uses Corinthian bronze as an index of the difference between two conquering generals, Scipio Aemilianus, whom he describes as cultured (*elegans*), and Mummius, whom he calls uncultured (*rudis*): Mummius was so uncultured that when he brought back bronzes from Corinth he had his shippers promise that if the bronzes were lost in transit they would replace them with new ones.[1] The ability to tell true from fake Corinthian bronze is also of course at issue in Trimalchio's claim that he alone has true Corinthian bronze because he obtains it from a craftsman named Corinthus (50.2–4).[2] Now the story of Corinthian bronze as told by the sober Pliny is fanciful enough: it was said to have originated in Mummius' sack of Corinth; the amalgam of metals occurred accidentally when Corinth was burned (*Nat.* 34.6). On one level, Trimalchio's garbled and completely implausible retelling of the already unlikely story of Corinthian bronze displays his

---

[1] On Corinthian bronzes and the question of authenticity, see further Emanuele (1989).
[2] Baldwin (1973) has suggested that Trimalchio's elaborate tale is partly intended to deflect Agamemnon from examining the plate further and discovering that it is a fake.

foolish and ignorant pretensions, and mocks the connoisseurship of Corinthian bronze.

Yet on another, less literal, level the new version of Corinthian bronze makes perfect artistic sense. Statues are melted down and the resulting metal is transformed into bowls, serving plates and statuettes: the change from the original *statuas* to the subsequent diminutive *statuncula* emphasizes the change of scale.[3] The apparatus of honorific and religious display is converted into the trappings of private enjoyment and consumption. So too, when the *Satyricon* seizes motifs, scenes, and words from epic, and refashions them in its creative crucible, the public literary monuments of Greek and Roman culture are refashioned into fiction, a form more suitable for private enjoyment. Indeed, both the displacement of the origin of Corinthian bronze from Corinth to the fall of Troy, and the adjective *aeneas*, which (despite the differences in pronunciation) seems to have some resonance of Troy's epic hero Aeneas,[4] are recognizable fragments of the epic past jumbled together and given new form in Trimalchio's story. Trimalchio has rewritten the history of Corinthian bronze so that it, like the history of Rome, begins in the fall of Troy, with the additional conflation of Aeneas and Hannibal. This story of Corinthian bronze has a programmatic or metapoetic significance, functioning as a metaphor for the *Satyricon*'s parodic reformulation of epic as fiction.[5]

Perhaps the most concentrated and extreme example of this process of destroying and refashioning epic is the performance of a selection from the *Aeneid* by Habinnas' slave, called Massa, the same word used above for the "raw material" of molten metal from which Corinthian bronze is made. He mutilates the epic material by his poor vocal technique and by mixing in Atellan verses. Then for the first time, Encolpius says, he found Virgil offensive (68.5). Massa follows his offensively imitative performance of Virgil with tiresome imitations of a trumpeter (using a lamp), and a flute player (using some reeds), and some kind of imitation of mule drivers (69.4–5).[6] The motif of one "raw material" offensively imitating many things modulates from performance to food as the next course arrives; it is "much more monstrous" (*longe monstrosius*, 69.7) for in it many different poultry and fish items are in fact imitatively fashioned from pork. Trimalchio says that he himself

---

[3] Juvenal envisions a similar transformation of a statue of Sejanus at *Sat.* 10.61–64.
[4] Cf. Baldwin (1987), 6.
[5] Other approaches to Petronian self-reflexivity are discussed in Barchiesi (forthcoming).
[6] Smith (1975) on 69.5 discusses textual difficulties here; he is skeptical of associating the performance with a putative mime on muledrivers. Because the emphasis here is on imitation (mimesis) Panayotakis (1995), 101–02, is probably right to maintain that connections to mime are likely.

has bestowed the very suitable name Daedalus upon his clever chef (70.1–2).[7] Mentioning the chef's name here may even pick up the Virgilian thread from Massa's initial performance: Massa begins with the first line of *Aeneid* 5 and Daedalus' handiwork is prominently represented in Aeneas' arrival at Cumae at the beginning of *Aeneid* 6.[8]

In the *Satyricon*, epic is constantly being smashed to pieces and refashioned into fiction before our eyes. And, in blithely programmatic gestures like the tale of Corinthian bronze and the performance of Massa, Petronius self-consciously represents that process of fragmentation, refashioning and recognition which constitutes parody. In devising such self-consciously destructive and inventive epic parody, Petronius exploits his audience's literary sophistication, though of course, even without a detailed knowledge of every epic model, the novel is still a good read. Slater puts it this way: "parody so wide-ranging would seem to demand intimate acquaintance with a repertoire equally vast – but in fact parody is often recognizable (and enjoyable) simply as a style, without the necessity of a specific *comparandum*."[9] Still, the more we know about the strategies of ancient parody and the more we can recollect or recover about the specifics of Petronius' parodic targets, the better we can appreciate the peculiar alchemy he works upon them.

In general, parody is slippery to talk about. Though it rarely makes claims to be anything but funny, subtle reactions to model texts can coexist with the obvious jokes: recent approaches to parody, and the richness of parodic texts themselves, caution against reductive interpretations of parody's potential for complexity.[10] Parodic texts produce imitations of their models distorted for comic purposes which can range "from respectful admiration to biting ridicule."[11] Thus parody

[7] Trimalchio then "tops" his account of naming the chef Daedalus by two etymological puns in the next sentence: *et quia bonam mentem habet, attuli illi Roma munus cultros Norico ferro* ("And because he has a good mind, I brought him knives of Noric iron from Rome as a present," 70.3). "He has a good mind" glosses the Greek meaning of Daedalus' name, related to e.g., δαιδάλλω "to fashion with craft or cunning." The Noric iron knives are chosen not just because they are the tools of Daedalus' trade, and not just because the quality of Noric iron was famous (Hor. *C.* 1.16.9, with Nisbet and Hubbard [1970] *ad loc.*), but also for the chance of a translingual pun on words having to do with knowledge: *gnarus* in Latin ("having knowledge") or γνωρίζω, (perf. ἐγνώρικα) in Greek (which can mean "be well acquainted with"). For a man with Trimalchio's feel for language, it would seem obvious that knives-from-Noricum were "etymologically" knives-for-Daedalus.

[8] Saylor (1987) uses the funeral games in *Aeneid* 5 as a framework for understanding the imagery of debased funeral games throughout the *cena*.

[9] Slater (1990), 19.

[10] Hutcheon (1985), Rose (1993), and, with reference to Aristophanic parody, Goldhill (1991), 206–11.

[11] Hutcheon (1985), 16.

is often described as ambivalent or paradoxical: its distortions can be normative, rewarding familiarity with the model text and reinforcing its culturally authoritative position, or they can be transgressive, generating a critical or confrontational challenge to the authoritative position of a model text. Rose summarizes: "Both by definition (through the meaning of its prefix 'para') and structurally (through the inclusion within its own structure of the work it parodies), most parody worthy of the name is ambivalent towards its target. This ambivalence may entail not only a mixture of criticism and sympathy for the parodied text, but also the creative expansion of it into something new."[12] Parodic texts display variety and complexity; equally, their audiences vary in their recognitions of these effects, often knowingly so. So for Goldhill, "The self-awareness of parody provokes a self-awareness in the knowing reader, which incites doubt and a consciousness of duplicity to flourish in the act of reading. Recognizing parody can involve the reader or audience in the unsettling (and comic) process of recognizing how things can be taken otherwise – and how each reader's complicity remains integral to that process."[13]

Exploiting the resources of the audience's education, experience and memory, parody represents and objectifies a literary target (either a particular text or a general style), simultaneously placing its target in the preserve of memory and exposing it to ridicule, mockery or other sorts of ironic recontextualization. Bakhtin's view that parodic forms were a catalyst in the development of the flexible and expressive capabilities of novelistic discourse is a frequent touchstone in recent discussions of epic parody in the *Satyricon*.[14] Viewing epic and biblical texts as authoritarian or "monologic" works, Bakhtin argues that the authority of these texts was destabilized by the "dialogic" texts, such as Socratic dialogue and Menippean satire, which incorporated elements of the "monologic" texts but treated their authority with a critical distance, overturning their harmony and order with a carnivalesque celebration of disorder. Though his own remarks on the *Satyricon* are quite brief, in his discussion of ancient serio-comic genres he says of the *Satyricon* that its "role in the history of the novel is immense and as yet inadequately appreciated by scholarship." He then goes on to describe the effect of such serio-comic works:

It is precisely laughter that destroys the epic, and in general destroys any hierarchical (distancing and valorized) distance... Laughter has the remarkable power of making an object come up close, of drawing it into a zone of crude

---

[12] Rose (1993), 51.
[13] Goldhill (1991), 210.
[14] Bakhtin (1981), 22; Slater (1990), 167–83.

contact where one can finger it familiarly on all sides, turn it upside down, inside out, peer at it from above and below, break open its external shell, look into its center, doubt it, take it apart, dismember it, lay it bare and expose it, examine it freely and experiment with it. Laughter demolishes fear and piety before an object, before a world, making of it an object of familiar contact and thus clearing the ground for an absolutely free investigation of it.[15]

This assertion, like many of Bakhtin's arguments, rings true for the *Satyricon* in a general sense. Petronius does expose epic monuments to laughter. Yet, by relying heavily on fragmentary texts to build up a teleological theory of the development of prose fiction, Bakhtin ends up putting forward a rather monolithic picture of ancient parody, giving the impression that it was uniformly and resolutely rebellious, in effect focusing mainly on the destruction of the monuments than on the particular artifacts produced in this process of parodic refashioning. A better understanding of the *Satyricon* as a parodic artifact requires an investigation of the ways in which Petronius uses and transcends various ancient parodic techniques to fragment epic and refashion it as fiction.

The wrath of Priapus

In one strand of the parodic tradition, the contamination of epic by mixing it with the lower material is a primary goal. Such works are (or their fragments seem) fairly limited in their ambitions: not competing with epic or replacing it, they break it up into amusing pieces. The mixing of trivial subjects with epic vocabulary, meter, and motifs characterizes the earliest Greek parody: poets seize verbal fragments from Homeric lines and refashion them in tales of food, animals or other low subjects.[16] Thus the parodist Matron begins a description of an extravagant meal (Ath. 4.134d):[17]

δεῖπνά μοι ἔννεπε, Μοῦσα, πολύτροφα καὶ μάλα πολλά,
ἃ Ξενοκλῆς ῥήτωρ ἐν Ἀθήναις δείπνισεν ἡμᾶς.

---

[15] Bakhtin (1981), 23.

[16] See Householder (1944), and LeLièvre (1954). In his discussion of types of literary mimesis, Aristotle says that Hegemon of Thasos was the first to compose parodies (*Poet.* 1448a12–13). Athenaeus cites Polemon's account, in which Hipponax the Iambographer is credited with the invention of parody (Ath. 15.698b), while Hegemon is credited with being the first to perform parodies in competitions (Ath. 15.699a). In some ancient contexts, uses of the term parody are not limited to those who composed hexameter verse on trivial themes. According to Polemon, parody is also included in some plays by the poets Epicharmus of Syracuse and Cratinus, and the scholiasts use the term to characterize passages of Aristophanes. See Ath. 15.698c on the dramatists Epicharmus of Syracuse and Cratinus; Householder (1944) usefully categorizes the evidence of the scholia.

[17] Cited from Kaibel's edition of Athenaeus (Leipzig 1887–90).

Muse, sing to me of the dinners, luxurious and very numerous,
which Xenocles the orator hosted for us at Athens.

The reference to the opening of the *Odyssey* is easy to recognize (*Od.*
1.1–2):

ἄνδρα μοι ἔννεπε, Μοῦσα, πολύτροπον, ὃς μάλα πολλά
πλάγχθη, ἐπεὶ Τροίης ἱερὸν πτολίεθρον ἔπερσε·

Sing to me Muse of the man of many turns, who wandered very
    much,
after he destroyed the sacred city of Troy

Hipponax invokes the Muse to sing of the exceptionally large appetite
of a certain son of Eurymedon (Ath. 15.698c):

Μοῦσά μοι Εὐρυμεδοντιάδεα, τὴν παντοχάρυβδιν,
τὴν ἐγγαστριμάχαιραν, ὃς ἐσθίει οὐ κατὰ κόσμον,
ἔννεφ', ὅπως ψηφῖδι ⟨κακὸς⟩ κακὸν οἶτον ὀλεῖται
βουλῇ δημοσίῃ παρὰ θῖν' ἁλὸς ἀτρυγέτοιο.

Muse, sing to me of the son of Eurymedon, that all-devouring
    maelstrom,
who makes havoc with his belly, whose appetite is out of all
    proportion,
how he wretched will perish by a wretched doom, by a vote
at the decree of the people by the shore of the barren sea.

Here the reformulation of the *Odyssey*'s first line is more elaborate: the
Homeric words ἔννεπε and Μοῦσα engulf the gaping maw of Eurymedon's son. Other such parodies would include the *Battle of the
Frogs and the Mice*, along with other lost poems about cranes, spiders,
and starlings (see Suda s.v. Ὅμηρος, 45, 103, and *CHCL* 1, 110).
Sometimes the hexameter remains intact; sometimes it too is fragmented and changed, as it evidently was in the *Margites*, a poem which
told the story of a foolish man in a mixture of hexameter and iambics.[18]
In addition to the mixing of epic hexameters with the trivial tale that
happens within the text itself, another mixing strategy attributes the
low *Margites* to the youthful Homer: in the same way the youthful
Virgil was said to be the author of the *Culex* (cf. Stat. *Silv.* 1. praef.).
The parodic *Culex* tells the story of a gnat whose bite saves the life of a
shepherd by alerting him to the presence of a snake. The gnat is killed
by the shepherd, and comes to him in a dream to complain about its
journey to the underworld. Upon awakening from the dream, the
shepherd builds a memorial to the gnat, rescuing it from oblivion and
honoring its self-sacrifice. Like Greek epic parody, the *Culex* mixes epic

[18] Cf. Arist. *Poet.* 1448b24–1449a1, and West (1972) s.v. "Homerus".

meter, motifs, and vocabulary with low trivial content.[19] The poet even manages to parody the Callimachean values of lightness and delicacy when he compares the poem to a "delicate" spider's web (*ut araneoli tenuem formavimus orsum,* "Like a spider I've made a delicate web," *Cul.* 2) – a perfect device for capturing a gnat. Elsewhere, fragments of epic's traditional stories are reframed in the newer inventions of satire. So in Horace's *Satires* 2.5, Ulysses asks Tiresias how he can restore his fortune from the depredations of the suitors, and Tiresias gives explicit and wholly Roman directions for legacy hunting.[20] Though both Ulysses and Tiresias speak in hexameters, the poem deliberately calls attention to the different hexameter registers available in Latin literary tradition: epic and satire. When Tiresias speaks in the language, style, and topics of satire, Ulysses has trouble understanding and asks for clarification. Horace uses Ulysses' confusion to juxtapose the epic world view (ostensibly held by Ulysses, and itself complicated by his rather un-epic concern to regain the property consumed in the long stay of the suitors) and the satirical world view of Tiresias, who recommends legacy hunting. Menippean satire did similar things; the *Apocolocyntosis* constructs a parodic version of the epic council of the gods which "lowers" both its epic models and the allegedly lofty notion of the deification of Claudius.[21]

Petronius perhaps comes closest to this type of novelty parody in his use of the motif of the wrath of Priapus. In 1889, faced with the problem of bringing order to the fragments, and responding to Rohde's exclusion of the *Satyricon* from his account of the development of the genre of the novel, Klebs argued that the tale was structured around a parody of the epic theme of a hero pursued by the wrath of a god.[22] Drawing together the text's references to Priapus, Klebs maintained that Encolpius' misadventures were the result of the wrath of Priapus, incurred through various offenses, some of which are no longer entirely

---

[19] Ross (1975a) and Most (1987), discuss the parodic strategies of the *Culex.*

[20] The poem evokes Homer's *Odyssey* in a general way and in precise details of language (for example, 2.5.20–21 quotes *Od.* 20.18). Horace self-consciously jokes about his poem's belated status relative to the *Odyssey* from the very beginning, for as the poem opens Ulysses asks to learn from Tiresias more than what has already been told (*praeter narrata, S.* 2.5.1–2).

[21] Epic parody could well have been part of the parodic treatments of myth which were probably some kind of starting point for Menippus' *Necyia* (see the Suda, s.v. φαιός with Relihan [1993], 45, and Relihan [1987], 194 n. 29), and for Varro's satires titled *Armorum iudicium* (*The Contest for Arms,* which would be some kind of reworking of the contest between Ajax and Odysseus for the arms of Achilles), *Oedipothyestes, Prometheus liber* (*Prometheus Unbound*), *Pseudaeneas* (*The False Aeneas*), *Pseudulus Apollo* (*The False Apollo*), and *Sesculixes* (*A Ulysses and a Half*).

[22] Rohde (1914 [first edition 1876]); Klebs (1889).

clear. Early in the fragments we learn that during his wanderings around the Bay of Naples Encolpius interrupted Quartilla at her performance of the rites of Priapus (*Sat.* 16.3 and 17.8) and therefore must make amends. Later, at Croton, he prays in a shrine of Priapus (133.2) and is confronted by the crone Proselenos, who escorts him to the adjoining room of the shrine's priestess Oenothea (134.3). When he defends himself from an aggressive goose on her premises, with fatal results for the goose, he learns that he has again offended Priapus (137.2).[23] Thus, Encolpius' impotence and other difficulties are taken to be the manifestation of the god's wrath.[24] Of course, Priapus is quite clearly different from an epic god. His concerns are not national or cosmic, but private: he stands watch over gardens and threatens thieves with rape. Priapus is to Poseidon (whose wrath persecutes Odysseus) as novel is to epic.[25]

In what survives of the *Satyricon*, the most explicit formulation of this theme of divine wrath is in verse; it is the last poem in the *Satyricon* as we have it. Frustrated by his impotence, Encolpius himself proclaims that he is a heroic victim of Priapus' divine wrath (*Sat.* 139.2):[26]

> non solum me numen et implacabile fatum
> persequitur. prius Inachia Tirynthius ora
> exagitatus onus caeli tulit, ante profanus
> Laomedon gemini satiavit numinis iram,   5
> Iunonem Pelias sensit, tulit ictus Iacchum   4
> Telephus et regnum Neptuni pavit Ulixes.
> me quoque per terras, per cani Nereos aequor
> Hellespontiaci sequitur gravis ira Priapi

> Divine might and implacable fate do not pursue only me.
> Before me, Tirynthian Hercules driven from the Argive shore

---

[23] On the geese and the epithet *sacri* bracketed by Müller at 136.4, see Richardson (1980), arguing against any widespread notion that geese in general were sacred to Priapus.

[24] Heinze (1899), by contrast, played down connections to epic and argued that the *Satyricon* parodied the adventures of separated lovers in Greek novels.

[25] On the figure of Priapus in general, see the detailed study of Herter (1932), and Richlin (1992), 116–27, with her discussion of the *Satyricon*, 190–95, 287. Priapus' separation from the world of epic is comically exploited in *Priapea* 68, in which the statue of Priapus reinterprets the Homeric epics, which he has heard his owner reading in the garden, so that they become simply stories of lust and sexual excess. See Rankin (1966) for a comparison of the mock epic elements of the *Satyricon* and of *Priap.* 68. The novel even brings the Homeric Poseidon and the Petronian Priapus into close conjunction: Lichas says that Priapus appeared to him in a dream and told him that Encolpius was on board his ship (104.1), while Tryphaena answers Lichas' report of his dream of Priapus with her dream that she was told about Encolpius by an image resembling a statue of Neptune in Baiae (104.2).

[26] Cited from Courtney (1991); in line 4, L has *tulit inscius arma* ("unaware he bore arms"), but this does not fit the context; Müller (1995) objects to *tulit* on the grounds that it was mistakenly repeated from the poem's third line.

> bore the weight of the sky, before me
> unholy Laomedon appeased the wrath of two gods,
> Pelias knew the wrath of Juno, smitten Telephus suffered
> at the hands of Bacchus, and Ulysses feared the realm of Neptune.
> Me too the harsh wrath of Priapus of the Hellespont
> pursues over the earth and the sea of white-haired Nereus

The focus on heroic wandering over land and sea places the poem in the tradition of the proems of the *Odyssey* and the *Aeneid*. Ovid too exploits this tradition when he compares his exile to the toils of epic heroes (*Tr.* 1.2.1–12). The adjective *Hellespontiaci* (perhaps signaling an allusion to Virgil's mention of Priapus at *Georgics* 4.111: *Hellespontiaci servet tutela Priapi* ("let the protection of Priapus of the Hellespont preserve ... "),[27] acknowledges Priapus' origins at the Hellespont and his introduction to Rome, construing Priapus' presence in the Roman world as the result of a journey from the Troad. His journey thus parallels Aeneas' heroic westward journey from the Troad to Rome. In one version of the story Priapus makes the journey as an exile, as Servius explains in commenting on *Georgics* 4.111: "indeed, this Priapus was from Lampsacus, a city of the Hellespont from which he was exiled on account of the great size of his *membrum virile*; later when he was welcomed into the number of the gods he won the position of being the protective spirit of gardens."[28] Priapus' exile from the Troad and eventual arrival at Rome could itself be viewed as a vulgar recapitulation of the heroic voyage of Aeneas, just as Encolpius' own adventures are a vulgar recapitulation of epic heroism.

A reference to Petronius by Sidonius Apollinaris in a list of great Latin writers suggests that scenes in the *Satyricon* set at Massilia are closely connected to the theme of the wrath of Priapus (fr. 4 M. = Sid. Apoll. *C.* 23.145–57):

> quid vos eloquii canam Latini,
> Arpinas, Patavine, Mantuane,
> . . .
> et te Massiliensium per hortos
> sacri stipitis, Arbiter, colonum
> Hellespontiaco parem Priapo?

> Why should I sing of you men of Latin eloquence,
> man of Arpinum, of Padua, of Mantua,
> . . .

---

[27] Herter (1932), 40; Collignon (1892), 130.

[28] *hic autem Priapus fuit de Lampsaco, civitate Hellesponti, de qua pulsus est propter virilis membri magnitudinem; post in numerum deorum receptus meruit esse numen hortorum.* Cf. the similarly worded account at Isidore *Orig.* 8.11.25.

and you, Arbiter, who in the gardens of Massilia
are a cultivator of the sacred trunk
equal to Priapus of the Hellespont?

Servius (on *Aen.* 3.57) cites an episode from Petronius in which a plague
at Massilia was expiated by feeding a poor man at public expense for a
year and then driving him out of the city. This may indicate that the
Satyricon began with a plague caused by the wrath of Priapus, just as the
Iliad begins with a plague caused by the wrath of Apollo.[29] The evidence
limits us to speculation, but if Encolpius was a scape-goat figure
somehow driven into exile from Massilia, then perhaps his exile and his
impotence are modelled ironically on the exile of Priapus, himself
exiled from Lampsacus on account of his excessive potency. Encolpius'
exile and wandering unfolds in a pattern which receives heroic form in
the story of Aeneas and vulgar form in the story of Priapus.

Though the complete structure of the novel remains unknown, in
the Priapus motif obscenity is parodically thrust into the epic paradigm
of divine wrath. Priapus' obscenity is juxtaposed with epic in a more
localized and physical way at Trimalchio's table, when the spectacle of
the pastry Priapus is introduced right after the garbled epic performance, encapsulating the *Satyricon*'s whole project of rewriting a heroic
narrative around the obscene Priapus. As in Greek hexameter parody,
here food is made the material of epic performance. To avert an argument between Ascyltos and Hermeros, Trimalchio turns attention to a
performance by a troupe of *Homeristae*, artists who acted out scenes
from epic, rather than reciting the poem as a rhapsode would (59.3). In
a latter-day equivalent of the anger that sets the *Iliad* in motion, the
"real" angry quarrel between Ascyltos and Hermeros is the catalyst for
the epic story. Much has been garbled or misunderstood by the time
that Trimalchio produces his subsequent translation and paraphrase
of the performance of the *Homeristae*, which ends with the statement
that Ajax will wrap up the story right away. A man in the guise of Ajax
carves some boiled veal as if he were the heroic Ajax in an insane
rage.[30] Immediately following this series of garbled "quotations" of
epic, a pastry figure of Priapus, carrying fruits and grapes of all sorts in
his outstretched tunic, is produced (60.4). When the guests reach out
for the fruit and pastries which he carries, they are stained by saffron

---

[29] Sullivan (1968a), 40–42, with further references. It is also possible that other notions
about Massilia were a focus of episodes set there: Plautus, for example, alludes broadly
to notions that Massilia's men were reputed to follow effeminate sexual practices (*Cas.*
963, cf. Athen. 12.523c; contrast the accounts of Massilia's strict moral regulation at
Cic. *Pro Flac.* 63, Val. Max. 2.6.7, 9 and Strabo 4.1.5).

[30] See Starr (1987a), and Jones (1991), 189, on the mock-combats regularly associated
with the *Homeristae*.

which these spew forth when touched. By filling their napkins, the guests become like the Priapus figure, for they too carry cloth bulging with the delicacies; Encolpius envisions his as a gift in Giton's lap. A pastry Priapus is a benign version of the sexual threat figured in the "real" Priapus: pastry presumes that people will eat it, will let it into their mouths willingly, whereas garden Priapus figures are designed to keep thieves away by threatening to penetrate and defile the bodies of violators in various forms of rape.[31] Richlin argues that a self-conscious defilement or "staining" of epic by introducing mock-epic language and situations is one manifestation of the *Satyricon*'s concern with Priapus.[32] Broadly speaking, Richlin is right about the *Satyricon*, but her point becomes interestingly complicated when the motif of "staining" is humorously made explicit in this saffron-spewing pastry carried by Priapus. Saffron does stain, but its scent made it a desirable luxury. It was used as perfume, and mixed with wine it was sprayed in the theater.[33] Trimalchio has it sprayed about his dining room with mica and vermilion for a colorful effect, and this increases the sense that his banquet is an extravagantly staged theatrical spectacle (68.6).[34] Thus the "stain" made by saffron is a sign of luxury, far more pleasant in some ways than Priapus' usual stains. In effect, the figure of the saffron-spewing pastry Priapus is, like the tale of Corinthian bronze, an emblem of the *Satyricon*'s refashioning of its epic models: its threats and transgressions are designed to delight, not to destroy.

The Priapus motifs discussed so far have been broadly thematic, but some of Petronius' "Priapic" attacks on epic also fragment and refashion individual epic lines into new obscene fictions. In the aftermath of apparent erotic failure, Encolpius is driven out of Circe's house, beaten, and spat upon (132.3–4). This seems to be another version of the scapegoat theme which Servius associates with the *Satyricon*'s lost Massilia scenes.[35] Retreating to bed, Encolpius addresses his offending penis in sotadeans (132.8.1–3)

> ter corripui terribilem manu bipennem
> ter languidior coliculi repente thyrso
> ferrum timui, ...

---

[31] For similar pastries see Mart. 14.69 and 9.2.3.
[32] Richlin (1992), 192; cf. her discussion of "staining" in Roman sexual humor, 26–31.
[33] Saffron as perfume: Prop. 4.6.74; in the theater: Lucr. 2.416, Pliny *Nat.* 21.33, Mart. 5.25.7.
[34] On theatricality at Trimalchio's see Rosati (1983), Slater (1990) Ch. 4, Panayotakis (1995), Ch. 3, Bartsch (1994), 197–99.
[35] The forger Nodot (1693), 280, seems to perceive this pattern when he inserts the Servian fragment at the end of his version of the Croton episode.

Three times I snatched up the fearsome axe,
three times, suddenly droopier than a stalk of cabbage,
I feared the blade, ...

The triple attempt at castration mimics heroic triple attempts to embrace the shades of the beloved dead (Virg. *Aen.* 2.791–93; 6.700–
01).[36] With the *ter* in *terribilem*, the *ter* syllable is repeated thrice; the
sound finally softens and dissolves in *thyrso*. The meter, first associated with the third-century poet Sotades, is especially associated with
cinaedi.[37] Moreover, there seems to have been a persistent interest
in rearranging epic hexameters to form sotadean lines: this process of
scrambling hexameter into sotadean is described as arranging or reading
the lines backwards (*retro*, or *retrorsus*).[38] Sotadeans can thus be another form of novelty epic parody, like the parodies of Matron and
others, putting trivial content into a frame that bears the traces of its
epic origins.[39] So, according to Demetrius, the sotadic rearrangement
of *Iliad* 22.133 yields a line which "seems to have changed its shape, like
mythological figures who change from male to female" (*On Style* 189).
The form of the meter is thus intimately related to its content: at a social
level, the *cinaedus* inverts the norms which govern the sexual behavior of
the free man; at the level of literary form, the sotadean meter could
invert the normative structures of the hexameter. This transformation of
the utterances of the heroic past into the sound of the debased present
recasts lines which describe heroic exploits to produce a sexual double
meaning – and that double meaning is hard to erase: for mischievously
sotadic readers, spears in the *Iliad* might never look quite the same. But
because the sotadean meter could be construed as the antithesis of epic
masculinity, the epic past is fragmented and debased both in seizing the
motif of the heroic triple gesture and in the meter itself.

Encolpius' next attack on epic tradition follows hard on the sotadeans. In a reversal of sotadic reformulation of hexameter epic, he
produces three hexameter lines constructed from verbatim quotations

---

[36] Zeitlin (1971a), 71.
[37] For the fragments, see Powell (1925), 238–45. The term *cinaedus*, a Greek word
meaning something like "moving the genitals" is applied to men who fulfill the role
of passively providing sexual pleasure to a man. On the stereotype of the *cinaedus* in
Classical Athens, see Winkler (1990), 45–54; see also Richlin (1993), arguing that the
Roman representations of the *cinaedus* are the traces of a real subculture of passive
homosexuality. In the Quartilla episode, the *cinaedus* sings in sotadeans (23.3); compare
Iolaus lines 14 ff., Stephens and Winkler (1995), 369. Cf. Athen. 14.620e, Strabo
14.648, Martial 2.86.2.
[38] Dion. Hal. *Comp.* 24 (Usener), Quint. 9.4.90, Martial 2.86.2, and cf. Pliny *Ep.* 5.3.2
with Bettini (1982), 66.
[39] Bettini (1982), esp. 68–69 and, on *Sat.* 132.1, 85–86.

from Virgil. The passage has struck readers as the most transgressive of the *Satyricon*'s epic parodies. Even Collignon, otherwise so intent on viewing Petronius as a man of conservative and traditionalist literary tastes, is forced to admit that the Virgilian phrases have been quoted "avec une impudeur singulière" (*Sat.* 132.11):[40]

> haec ut iratus effudi,
> illa solo fixos oculos aversa tenebat,
> nec magis incepto vultum sermone movetur
> quam lentae salices lassove papavera collo.

> When I poured forth my thoughts in anger,
> that one turned aside and gazed fixedly at the ground
> nor is moved by the beginning of the speech any more
> than drooping willows or poppies on their tired necks.

The first two lines of his poetic outburst (in which *illa* refers to an implied "*pars corporis*"; cf. 132.12) are an exact quotation of Virgil's description of Dido's refusal to speak to Aeneas in the Underworld (*Aen.* 6.469–70). As Collignon astutely notes, Virgil's description of Dido emphasizes her stiff and unyielding resolve (*nec magis incepto vultum sermone movetur / quam si dura silex aut stet Marpesia cautes*, "nor is she moved by the beginning of the speech any more than if she were unyielding flint or craggy Mount Marpessa," *Aen.* 6.470–71).[41] Clearly inappropriate to Encolpius' particular predicament, the line about unyielding flint is replaced in the *Satyricon* by different evocations of Virgil. The first part of the last line, *quam lentae salices* seems designed on the model of the pliant willow, *lenta salix*, which yields to the olive tree in *Ecl.* 5.16 (*lenta salix quantum pallenti cedit olivae*. . .). The last half-line, *lassove papavera collo*, quotes Virgil on the death of Euryalus (Virg. *Aen.* 9.436). Virgil describes the death of Euryalus, the boy beloved by Nisus, by incorporating an allusion to Catullus' comparison between the death of love and a flower cut down at the edge of a field (Cat. 11.21–24). Catullus and Virgil are shaping their similes in awareness of *Iliad* 8.306–07, a simile which compares a fallen soldier to a flower, and in itself already juxtaposes the epic world of battle with the "bucolic" image of the flower. Petronius juxtaposes Encolpius' erotic failures with the *Aeneid*'s representations of terrible grief and loss, evoking not just Dido but Nisus and Euryalus too: the valiant self-sacrifice of Virgilian heroes has been parodically debased into Encolpius' histrionic outburst. Slater is clearly right to point out the striking effects of the mixture of models here, but I am less sure that "the result

---

[40] Collignon (1892), 131.   [41] Ibid., 131.

refuses to cohere."[42] In the models carefully chosen by Petronius the loveliness of the "bucolic" world had already been brought into the heart of epic. In its ironic interaction with the Dido context, the replacement of the hard rock by the pliant willow and poppy creates a dynamic interaction between fragmentation and textual integrity: the parodic quotation aggressively fragments and refashions the model text, while at the same time rewarding the reader who knows or can recover the full Virgilian context. Normative and transgressive modes of parody reinforce each other here: the more a reader knows of the contexts in the Virgilian underworld and beyond, the sharper, funnier, and more impudent the quotations become. Like Massa's performance of selections from Virgil with Atellan verses mixed in, and like that of the *Homeristae*, along with Trimalchio's "translation", Encolpius' sotadeans and hexameter quotations refashion individual epic words and lines into new artifacts. In effect, the sotadeans and the epic quotations are programmatic as well as parodic: just as the novel at large does, they emulate and outdo the sotadic strategy of reading epic obscenely backwards.

The Sibyl and the labyrinth

Alongside the sotadic rewriting of epic in the overarching theme of the wrath of Priapus and in the smaller obscene reformulations of memorable moments in Virgil's underworld, in another parodic strategy Petronius fragments one epic model into two (or more) fictional episodes. Petronius uses elements of Aeneas' descent into the labyrinthine underworld in the company of the Sibyl in Encolpius' encounter with Quartilla and at Trimalchio's banquet.

Encolpius' encounter with Quartilla retraces Aeneas' visit to the Sibyl, as Walsh observes: "Her role as priestess of Priapus in the area of Cumae is presumably a comic evocation of the Virgilian Sibyl; the hero's first duty after landing on Italian soil is to visit the Priapic shrine, just as Aeneas repairs to the temple of Apollo."[43] An earlier reader of the *Satyricon* who connected the Virgilian Sibyl with the Quartilla scene was John Barclay, who published *Euphormionis Lusinini Satyricon*, a Latin imitation of the *Satyricon*, in 1605–07.[44] Like Petro-

---

[42] Slater (1990), 179.

[43] Walsh (1970), 89.

[44] Barclay is cited by volume and chapter number from the edition of Fleming (1973). On the publication date see Fleming (1973), xxxiv–v. A number of nearly exact quotations of Petronius seem to operate as quasi-footnotes, authenticating Barclay's reading of his

nius' Encolpius, Barclay's narrator Euphormio travels widely and is often caught up in situations which he cannot control. Barclay's reading of Quartilla as Sibyl emerges in his account of Euphormio's visit to a cave. When a storm threatens Euphormio and his travelling companion Percas, they seek shelter in a cave where they meet an old witch named Hypogaea and two younger women, one of whom Euphormio tries unsuccessfully to sleep with (I.10). The witch's powers and the subsequent sexual scene imitate some features of Petronius' Quartilla episode: the narrator encounters a woman who claims otherworldly powers, sees something he should not have seen, and as a result is caught up in a sudden sexual encounter. At the same time, Barclay introduces echoes of Aeneas in the cave of the Cumaean Sibyl. At one point Euphormio says archly that the old woman was the sort of woman who could have lived in the time of Aeneas.[45] Similarly, Euphormio explicitly compares the approach to the cave to Daedalus' labyrinth: he thus exploits the connections between Underworld and labyrinth which Virgil makes as Aeneas gazes upon Daedalus' carving of the Cretan labyrinth upon the temple doors at Cumae before he begins his descent into the Underworld (*Aen.* 6.27) and when Aeneas learns that the way into the Underworld is easy but the way out is difficult (*Aen.* 6.126–29). Once inside the cave Euphormio reports with a metaliterary wink that the difficulties of the path amused him,[46] and for Euphormio, in a reversal of the *Aeneid*'s easy descent into Avernus (*facilis descensus Averno*, 6.126), it is the entrance into the "underworld" that is a difficult maze. Barclay's allusions to Virgil's Sibyl in his own cave scene footnote the "Sibylline" aspects of Petronius' Quartilla, perhaps most visible when we are told that the door opens spontaneously for Quartilla's serving maid in a way that recalls the spontaneously opening doors in the Sibyl's chambers.[47] Barclay's Hypogaea

source, and they seem to have been drawn from most of the Petronian episodes available to Barclay (before the rediscovery and publication of the manuscript containing most of the *cena*); cf. the remarks of Walsh (1970), 239–40. Collignon (1901) assembles a group of parallel passages; the notes of Fleming (1973) also record the closest parallels. My discussion of this episode of Barclay's novel first appeared in Connors (1995), 64–66.

[45] *erat eiusmodi anus quae etiam Aeneae temporibus vixisse potuisset.*

[46] *repetebam vestigia quae ante triveram, & fallentibus giris reditum meum, non sine proprio risu turbabam*: "I returned to the steps I had taken earlier, and confused my return path in deceptive circles, not without laughter on my part."

[47] Cf. Burman (1743) on *Sat.* 16, suggesting that in saying the doors opened spontaneously to admit Quartilla's serving maid Petronius alludes to Virgil's description of spontaneously opening doors in the chambers presided over by the Sibyl (*respexisse etiam ad illud Vergilii videtur, lib.vi.81, ostia iamque domus patuere ingentia centum/sponte sua*).

bears a name based on the Latin word for underground chamber or tomb, *hypogaeum* (found at Petr. *Sat.* 111.2): this hammers the point home that like the Sibyl, Quartilla presides over an underground chamber, for we are told that Encolpius disturbed Quartilla's *sacrum* which took place *ante cryptam* (*Sat.* 16.3).

The mythical Sibyl of Virgil's epic has been fashioned into the novelistic excess of Quartilla – and then copiously footnoted in her literary descendant Hypogaea. A different transformation of the Sibyl out of her Virgilian guise is mentioned at Trimalchio's, for Trimalchio too followed in Aeneas' footsteps and visited the Sibyl (48.8):

nam Sibyllam quidem Cumis ego ipse oculis meis vidi in ampulla pendere, et cum illi pueri dicerent: Σίβυλλα, τί θέλεις; respondebat illa: ἀποθανεῖν θέλω.

For I myself saw with my own eyes at Cumae the Sibyl hanging in a bottle, and when the boys would say to her "Sibyl, what do you want?" she used to answer "I want to die."

When Trimalchio says that he saw the Cumaean Sibyl hanging in a bottle, the landscape of the present is superimposed on the landscape of the epic past. He too re-enacts in a small way Aeneas' visit to the Sibyl, which was represented both in Virgil's *Aeneid* and in Ovid's *Metamorphoses*. The boys' question to the Sibyl "What do you want?" is embedded in the text in Greek, as is her answer, "I want to die." On one level, Trimalchio uses Greek because the bay of Naples is a Greek milieu. On another level his question in Greek echoes the mythical question put by Apollo to the Sibyl when he asked her what she wished him to give her in return for her favors. Apollo's "original" question to the Sibyl was presumably in Greek since the Sibyl herself is a Greek figure.[48] Like the Sibyl, hanging in the bottle for centuries in suspended animation awaiting death, the Greek words hang unchanged in the narrative of the *Satyricon*, just as they are suspended unchanged at the beginning of Eliot's *The Waste Land*.[49] But in its full context, the latter-day reiteration of Apollo's question in the *Satyricon* seems a schoolboy's taunt, reminding the Sibyl of the flawed answer she once gave, to have as many years of life as there were grains in a nearby pile of sand, forgetting to ask for eternal youth as well.

At Trimalchio's, the evocations of the Sibyl are part of a pattern which associates the episode at his house with an epic descent into a

---

[48] Ovid *Met.* 14.130–53. For the notion that Apollo does not speak Latin, cf. Cic. *de div.* 2.116.

[49] In early editions of *The Waste Land* (e.g. New York 1922), without translation or identification of its source.

labyrinthine underworld.[50] Traditional associations between the labyrinth and the underworld, clearly evident in Virgil, mean that when
Trimalchio's house is compared to a labyrinth it is figured as an underworld. Trimalchio's house is overtly represented as a labyrinth when
Encolpius and his companions have difficulty departing. They encounter a hostile dog, Ascyltos falls into a pool of water, and they are
rescued by an *atriensis* who tells them that they may not leave by this
door: *"erras" inquit "si putas te exire hac posse qua venisti. nemo umquam
convivarum per eandem ianuam emissus est; alia intrant, alia exeunt"*
("You are mistaken," he said, "if you think that you can go out by the
same way that you came in. None of the guests has ever been let out by
the same door: they come in one way, they go out another," 72.10). In
response, Encolpius says that they are trapped in a new sort of labyrinth: *quid faciamus homines miserrimi et novi generis labyrintho inclusi . . . ?*
("What could we men do, wretched and trapped in some new kind of
labyrinth. . . ?" 73.1). And of course, the name of Trimalchio's versatile
chef, Daedalus, also associates the house with a labyrinth (70.1–2).
The Cerberus-like dog pacified by Giton's offer of food reinforces the
connection here as they try to escape. By now, if not before, the
dog depicted at the entrance of Trimalchio's too seems a quasi-
Cerberus (29.1), and Encolpius' examination of Trimalchio's wall-
paintings (29.2–6) re-enacts Aeneas' gaze at the doors of the temple of
Apollo.[51]

These connections between Trimalchio's labyrinthine house and
labyrinthine visions of the underworld make Encolpius' visit into a
mock-epic katabasis, in which, much as in early Greek hexameter
parody, descriptions of food displace epic's heroic and harrowing
visions. Yet the amusements to be found in the parodic labyrinth are
tempered by Trimalchio's obsessions with death, and by a sense that
Trimalchio's house offers a profoundly pessimistic view of the human
condition. The Petronian re-readings of Virgil's Sibyl in the Quartilla
scene and Ovid's Sibyl in Trimalchio's tale function in opposite ways
to show a gap between the debased present and the heroic past: the
Sibyl who greeted Aeneas on Italy's shores has withered away to a voice
in a bottle, and has been novelistically reborn as Quartilla.

---

[50] I have found especially useful and illuminating Bodel (1994), Newton (1982), and Fedeli (1981). On Plato's *Protagoras* 315b–c as a model for envisioning a house as the
Underworld see Courtney (1987).

[51] See Bodel (1994) for a discussion of the contributions of Trimalchio's wall paintings to
the underworld theme.

"... *sic notus Ulixes*?": recognitions of Odysseus

Homer's account of Odysseus in the Cyclops' cave is also fragmented and twice refashioned in the *Satyricon*. When a search is mounted for Giton at the inn where Encolpius is staying, Encolpius tells Giton to hide under the bed and to cling to the ropes which support the mattress just as Odysseus clung to the belly of the ram when he made good his escape from the cave of the Cyclops (*Sat.* 97.4–5):[52]

imperavi Gitoni ut raptim grabatum subiret annecteretque pedes et manus institis, quibus sponda culcitam ferebat, ac sic ut olim Ulixes †pro† arieti adhaesisset, extentus infra grabatum scrutantium eluderet manus. non est moratus Giton imperium momentoque temporis inseruit vinculo manus et Ulixem astu simillimo vicit.

I told Giton to get under the bed right away and wind his hands and feet in the straps by which the bedstead supported the mattress, and as Ulysses once attached himself to the ram ... he should stretch out underneath the bed and escape the hands of the people looking for him. Giton did not hesitate to do what I said, and in a moment he wound his hands in the strap and outdid Ulysses with exactly similar cunning.

Unfortunately, Giton cannot match the guile of his heroic model; he sneezes three times in succession and his hiding place is revealed (*Sat.* 98.4–5).[53] Some might say this destabilizes the case for Odysseus as model for Encolpius, because here it is Giton who imitates Odysseus, rather than Encolpius. But this is precisely why Giton fails, because he is playing the "wrong" role.

Once aboard Lichas' ship, Eumolpus initially mocks the fears of Encolpius and Giton regarding Lichas by playfully calling Lichas a Cyclops (101.5): *hic est Cyclops ille et archipirata, cui vecturam debemus* ("This is the Cyclops, and pirate king, to whom we owe our passage"). Yet when he learns that Lichas is indeed to be feared, Eumolpus says that the danger facing him and his companions is like the danger once faced by Odysseus, and tells his companions to pretend that Lichas' ship is the Cyclops' cave (*Sat.* 101.7):

confusus ille et consilii egens iubet quemque suam sententiam promere et "fingite" inquit "nos antrum Cyclopis intrasse. quaerendum est aliquod effugium, nisi naufragium †ponimus† et omni nos periculo liberamus."

Confused and at a loss for what to do, he told each of us to propose a plan and said, "Pretend we have entered the cave of the Cyclops. We have to find

---

[52] Labate (1990), 187 suggests *sic ut olim Ulixes proditur arieti adhaesisse* ("as it is said that Ulysses once clung to the ram").

[53] This motif is also to be found at Ar. *Wasps* 179–89.

some escape, unless we set up a shipwreck and extricate ourselves from all danger."[54]

Building upon some lines of inquiry laid out by Fedeli, Ferri has made the attractive suggestion that Petronius alludes not only generally to the *Odyssey* but also specifically to Euripides' *Cyclops*, in which Silenus has a conversation with Odysseus about the dangers in the Cyclops' cave. Thus, according to Ferri, Eumolpus plays the role of Silenus here.[55] The Odysseus role, then, is left to Encolpius. To recognize the particular character who plays the Odysseus role can add a certain literary subtlety to what are otherwise broadly comic scenes. And Ferri's proposal of an allusion to the role of the satyr Silenus in Euripides' *Cyclops* is appealing because the *Satyricon* thus acknowledges a model for its own mixing of satyric themes with epic traditions.

Later, the concealment of identity in the Cyclops' cave gives way to a recognition scene which quotes Eurycleia's Homeric recognition of Odysseus: Lichas recognizes Encolpius by feeling his groin (*Sat.* 105.10):[56]

miretur nunc aliquis Ulixis nutricem post vicesimum annum cicatricem invenisse originis indicem, cum homo prudentissimus confusis omnibus corporis indiciorumque lineamentis ad unicum fugitivi argumentum tam docte pervenerit.

Now let someone wonder that Ulysses' nurse found the scar which indicated his origins after twenty years, when a very sensible man so cleverly came to the sole identifying mark of a fugitive whose bodily appearance and distinguishing features were completely disguised.

Fedeli maintains that Petronius' explicit evocations of Odysseus in the Cyclops' cave at the inn and on board Lichas' ship, while casting

---

[54] Panayotakis (1995), 145, following Watt (1986), 181, says *ponimus* should not be obelized and can be taken in the sense of "staging a play," on the analogy of Cic. *Fam.* 10.32.3 and Pers. 5.3.

[55] See Fedeli (1981), 97–99, on the ship of Lichas as a Cyclops' cave; Ferri (1988).

[56] Labate (1990), 187, arguing against the suggestion of Courtney (1970), 67, that *manus* in 105.9 be corrected to *artus*, reads Lichas' gesture as a parody of a handshake. He records in n. 16 the suggestion of Barchiesi that Petronius may allude to ancient debates on the plausibility of Eurycleia's recognition of Odysseus, which have a dramatic counterpart in Electra's skepticism about the usefulness of hair, footprints and clothing as tokens by which Orestes can be recognized (Eur. *Electra* 524–44). Eustathius records that Aristotle objected to the recognition on the grounds that "according to the poet, by this reasoning everyone possessing a scar is Odysseus." See Eustathius, *Commentarii ad Homeri Odysseam*, p. 1873, 29–32, and for discussion of Aristotle's evaluation of how Homer overcomes this "problem" by his skillfully plausible narrative, see Richardson (1983), 230–31.

Encolpius as a mock-epic hero, are also connected to the *Satyricon*'s labyrinthine patterns of action.[57] Like the labyrinth, the Cyclops' cave traps the hero; escape is possible only through guile. The evocations of the Cyclops' cave operate both as parody and within the symbolic pattern of the labyrinth. They also juxtapose present and past with some degree of geographical specificity. The Cyclops scene on Lichas' ship takes place as the ship sails south from the bay of Naples before being wrecked close to Croton.[58] Since Thucydides at least the Cyclops had been firmly associated with Aetna in Sicily; the setting on Aetna is mentioned emphatically in Euripides' *Cyclops* as well.[59] So this imagining of the ship as the Cyclops' cave happens as the ship is on its way past places which were thought of as the "real" haunts of Polyphemus.[60]

Reflections of Circe

The Croton episode also contains a fragmented parody of a Homeric model. In the *Satyricon*'s Croton, after gazing upon the city in a way that recalls Aeneas' shipwrecked arrival at Carthage,[61] Encolpius encounters Circe, and her epic name and seductive behavior are the center of various obvious and less obvious recognitions of the Odyssean past. At some point before his encounter with Circe, Encolpius apparently goes by the name of Polyaenus, which means either "he who tells many tales" or "he who is the subject of many tales," and is borrowed from Homer's Odysseus.[62] Circe mixes belief and disbelief to play along with Encolpius' heroic identity when she carefully distinguishes herself

---

57 Fedeli (1981), esp. 97–99, 111.
58 The received text of 114.3 mentions Sicily and Italy in such a way that the famously stormy straits of Messina seem to be described: †*Siciliam modo ventus dabat†, saepissime [in oram] Italici litoris aquilo possessor convertebat huc illuc obnoxiam ratem...* ("Now the wind was making Sicily accessible, and very often the North wind, possessor of the Italian shore, drove the vulnerable boat this way and that way ..."). Müller obelizes the reference to Sicily, remarking that he would expect a reference to the southern wind Africus to complement the subsequent reference to the northern wind Aquilo. The textual problem and the fact that the straits of Messina are so far from Croton leads Sullivan (1986), 197 n. 30 to argue that the locale of the storm is the gulf of Squillace, or off Cape Rizzuto.
59 Thuc. 6.2.1, Eur. *Cycl.* 20–2; cf. Strabo 1.2.9, Virgil *Aen.* 3.570–691.
60 On the geography of the *Odyssey*, see Romm (1992), 183–96.
61 Courtney (1962), 96, Walsh (1970), 37–38, Zeitlin (1971a), 68–69.
62 πολύαινος appears three times in the *Iliad* (*Il.* 9.673, 10.544, 11.430); each time the epithet is applied to Odysseus. It appears once in the *Odyssey* (12.184), discussed below. On the meaning of the epithet, see the Homeric scholia on *Il.* 11.430 (p. 206 Erbse). The allusion to Homer was recognized by Turnebus (at Burman I, pp. 788–89) and Gonzales de Salas (at Burman II, p. 83). Barchiesi (1984), 171, notes the irony of

from Homer's Circe as she prepares to seduce her own Polyaenus (*Sat.* 127.6–7):

"ita" inquit "non dixit tibi ancilla mea me Circen vocari? non sum quidem Solis progenies, nec mea mater, dum placet, labentis mundi cursum detinuit; habebo tamen quod caelo imputem, si nos fata coniunxerint. immo iam nescio quid tacitis cogitationibus deus agit. nec sine causa Polyaenon Circe amat: semper inter haec nomina magna fax surgit."

"So," she said, "didn't my serving maid tell you that I am called Circe? Of course, I am not the child of the Sun, nor does my mother hold back the movement of the gliding cosmos while it suits her; nevertheless, I will put it down as divine intervention if the fates have brought us together. Yes indeed the god with his silent thoughts is doing something; not without a reason does Circe love Polyaenus; between these names a great flame always springs up."

Circe here uses precisely Homeric terms of reference to distinguish herself from her Homeric model.[63] Her flirtatious mixture of belief and disbelief in the Homeric-ness of the names Polyaenus and Circe replicates the combination of belief and disbelief that readers themselves bring to ancient (and modern) fictions.[64] Encolpius has already exploited his "Homeric" identity a bit by observing that Circe's voice sounds like the song of the Sirens (*Sat.* 127.5). As they sailed down the coast of Italy, the companions would have passed by the places associated with Sirens along the coast of southern Italy. Encolpius playfully "authenticates" his Odyssean identity in the implication that he, like Odysseus, has actually heard the song of the Sirens and lived to speak of it. In this connection, a mention of the Sirens may function as kind of "footnote" to Encolpius' pseudonym Polyaenus, for the epithet πολύαινος ("the man of many stories") was addressed to Odysseus by the Sirens (Hom. *Od.* 12.184), and appears nowhere else in the *Odyssey*.[65] Like the Greek question put to the Sibyl by Trimalchio's mates which echoes Apollo's ancient words, here in the *Satyricon*'s Circe episode the name Polyaenus hangs unchanged in the text, a faint but recognizable echo of the Sirens' song. And after all, Odysseus had learned to master the song of the Sirens from none other than Circe herself (*Od.* 12.39–54).

In the midst of the seduction, Encolpius inserts epic verses com-

---

the pseudonym, pointing out that Polyaenus, when taken in the sense "the man who is the subject of many tales," is a complete reversal of Odysseus' pseudonym Outis, Nobody, the one of whom nothing is known.

[63] See *Od.* 10.136–39, with Fedeli (1988), 18.

[64] See the fine discussion of the interaction of belief and disbelief in the reception of fiction at Feeney (1993).

[65] Barchiesi (1984), 172.

paring the embraces of Encolpius and Circe to the *hieros gamos* of Zeus and Hera on Mount Ida in the *Iliad* (127.9):[66]

> Idaeo qualis fudit de vertice flores
> terra parens, cum se concesso iunxit amori
> Iuppiter et toto concepit pectore flammas:
> emicuere rosae violaeque et molle cyperon,
> albaque de viridi riserunt lilia prato:
> talis humus Venerem molles clamavit in herbas,
> candidiorque dies secreto favit amori.

> Just as mother earth brought forth flowers on Mount Ida
> when Jupiter joined himself to Hera in sanctioned love
> and kindled flames in his whole heart:
> roses sprang up and violets and soft galingale,
> and white lilies smiled from the green meadow:
> such earth beckoned Love to the soft grass,
> and a clearer day benevolently looked down upon the secret love.

In the Homeric model, Hera borrows a powerful enchantment from Aphrodite in order to seduce Zeus and distract him from the events at Troy. Through Hera's use of erotic magic, Zeus is, at least for a while, powerless to affect events at Troy. Though Zeus wishes to sleep with her out in the open on Mount Ida, Hera says that they should adjourn to their bedroom. To meet her objection to sleeping together in the open air, Zeus promises to surround them with a golden cloud which not even Helios will be able to see through (14.343–45). As Zeus and Hera embrace, up spring the lotus, crocus, and hyacinth; and the cloud surrounds them (14.347–51). On one level the Petronian verses are an obvious imitation of the Homeric model, eliciting an easy recognition of the model text and its ironic and incongruous transformation. The recognition of the model suggests a punning sense in *compositi*, describing the lovers as literally "lying down" but also literarily "composed" when the prose narrative resumes after the poem ends (127.10). Upon closer inspection, one might notice first the *candidior dies* which surrounds these latter-day lovers. The notion of brightness may be a response to Homer's description of the cloud and its gleaming drops of moisture (14.350–51):

> τῷ ἔνι λεξάσθην, ἐπὶ δὲ νεφέλην ἔσσαντο
> καλὴν χρυσείην· στιλπναὶ δ' ἀπέπιπτον ἔερσαι.

> There they lay down together and shrouded themselves in a cloud,
> beautiful and bright; a glittering shower of dew fell.

---

[66] See *Il.* 14.346–51. Courtney (1970), 69, and (1991) *ad loc.* suggests *cumulavit* for the manuscripts' *clamavit* in line 6.

But the Homeric cloud shielding the lovers from prying eyes has lifted. Indeed, in Homer the description of the earth's fecundity acts as a substitute in the narrative for any direct narration of the divine sexual encounter, and the cloud shields the lovers from the gaze of the reader. By contrast, in the *Satyricon* the embraces of Encolpius and Circe are narrated directly (at least until the text breaks off). The model is transformed in another small but telling way when different flowers are catalogued: Petronius lists the rose, violet, galingale, and lily, instead of the Homeric lotus, crocus, and hyacinth. Courtney suggests that the galingale, *cyperon*, is a reference to Aphrodite's amorous assignation with Anchises amid oaks and galingale on Mount Ida at Theocritus 1.106, an attractive explanation of this difference from Homer. The roses are introduced, I think, because their absence in Homer was re-marked upon by readers, for the scholia on the Homeric passage record the remark that Homer left out the rose "on account of its thorniness" (Schol b T ad *Il.* 14.347). In the Mount Ida poem, the roses (thorns and all) bring hints of love's discontents into the very heart of a poetic landscape perfect for love.

When Encolpius fails to perform, he has succumbed to what the Homeric Odysseus had escaped: Odysseus is erotically successful with his Circe because he has received a drug named moly from Hermes as protection from her enchantments, and is able to make her promise not to render him "unmanned" ἀνήνωρ (*Od.* 10.301, 341).[67] Later in the *Satyricon* Mercury is instrumental in Encolpius' recovery in another allusion to the Homeric Circe episode (*Sat.* 140.12). At this point, though, Petronius' latter-day Circe draws back and wonders if she is to blame (128.1): her first thought is a catalogue of possible ways her own body may be objectionable. Subsequently Chrysis does not respond to her mistress' rapid-fire questions, again about the possibility of bodily imperfections. Circe seizes her mirror to see for herself (128.4):

rapuit deinde tacenti speculum, et postquam omnes vultus temptavit, quos solet inter amantes risus fingere, excussit vexatam solo vestem raptimque aedem Veneris intravit.

Suddenly she snatched up the mirror from Chrysis who was keeping silent, and after she tried all the expressions which usually raise a smile between lovers, she shook out her clothes, rumpled from lying on the ground, and quickly went into the shrine of Venus.

---

[67] Maass (1925), 449; Barchiesi (1984), 172. Pliny (*Nat.* 25.26) discusses moly at the opening of his account of medicinal plants and remarks that he has been told it can be obtained from Campania.

Circe turns her gaze upon herself to find out why her assignation has turned out badly. Her mirror is a traditional erotic accessory, but when Circe snatches up the mirror, Petronius also makes playfully explicit the fact that his Circe is a doubling repetition of Homer's. Petronius' latter-day Circe recognizes herself in the mirror, angry and puzzled over her impotent, "unmanned," lover while Petronius' readers measure her distance from the erotic successes of her literary ancestor.

Oenothea

One of the reasons Circe is frustrated with Encolpius is that, unlike her Homeric ancestress she has no magic to try on him, as is evident when she says that her mother does not have magical control of the heavens (127.6). Subsequently, Encolpius attempts to remedy his predicament through prayer to Priapus, and at the shrine of Priapus he meets an old woman who takes him to Oenothea, who in turn proclaims that she can cure him (134.10). In Oenothea's claim to magical power, it becomes clear that "Circean" magical powers have been displaced onto her: here again Petronius scatters fragments of Homer across his kaleidoscopic fiction. Yet in the allotment of this "Circean" magic to Oenothea, Petronius is not just practicing fragmentation for the sake of fragmentation; he takes to a logical extreme the literary representations which tend to count "Circean" erotic magic, called *Aeaea carmina* (songs of Aeaea, Circe's home) as the expertise of an old dipsomaniacal procuress (*lena*).[68] And the poem in which Oenothea proclaims her magical powers in universal terms (beginning *quicquid in orbe vides, paret mihi*, "whatever you see on earth obeys me," 134.12.1) is clearly designed to recall the universal magical powers of a *lena*, such as Ovid's Dipsas, who knows the *Aeaea carmina* (*Am.* 1.8.5); the name Dipsas ("thirsty") carries the same connotations of drunkenness as are obvious in the name Oenothea ("wine goddess").[69]

Thus in one fragmentation of epic, Petronius allots "Circean" magic to Oenothea, an old woman modelled on the *lena* figures represented in elegy, who themselves are the inheritors of "Circean" magic. At the same time, this episode also parodies a long tradition of depicting what happens when heroes receive the hospitality of ordinary folk. The earliest treatment of the theme is Odysseus' visit to the shelter of Eumaeus

---

[68] The phrase *Aeaea carmina* can also refer to magic of Medea, Circe's niece: see McKeown (1989), on *Am.* 1.8.5–6. On the possibility that Ovid's description of the old woman performing a bibulous religious rite in honor of Tacita at *Fasti* 2.571–82 is also a model for Oenothea, see Perutelli (1986), 141–43.

[69] See Ov. *Am.* 1.8.5–20, with McKeown (1989) *ad loc.*, cf. 3.7.27–35, 79.

(Hom. *Od.* 14. esp. 48–51); Callimachus and Ovid also describe the visits of epic characters to lowly but virtuous households. In the *Hecale*, which Callimachus was said to have composed as a response to those who criticized him for not writing a big poem,[70] the poet treated the story of Theseus' heroic defeat of the bull at Marathon in an innovative fashion, emphasizing Theseus' meeting with the old peasant woman Hecale. Although most of the poem is lost, it is clear that Theseus, on the way to Marathon to fight the bull, finds shelter from the rain in the house of Hecale, and spends the night there. When he returns victorious from Marathon, he learns of Hecale's death and establishes sacred rites in her honor.[71] Ovid alludes to Callimachus' *Hecale* when he tells the story of how the gods Jupiter and Mercury in the guise of men visit the home of the poor peasants Baucis and Philemon. The virtuous couple are rewarded for their generous hospitality by having their small house transformed into a magnificent temple and themselves turned into a linden and an oak tree (Ov. *Met.* 8.611–724). Aside from other evidence that Ovid's Baucis and Philemon are closely modelled upon Hecale, Callimachus' hero Theseus is also not forgotten in Ovid's reworking of the *Hecale*; he is in the audience and he especially (*Thesea praecipue* Ov. *Met.* 8.726) is moved by the story.[72] The *Hecale* was well known in antiquity,[73] and Petronius would certainly have known Ovid's reworking of Callimachean material in the Baucis and Philemon story.[74] Hecale's humble larder even made a big impression on Pliny.[75] Hecale and Baucis and Philemon exemplify an idealized life of rustic simplicity and virtue in the heroic past. Nevertheless their humble existence is contrasted with the loftier world of the divine and the heroic: the gods must bend their heads to enter the house of Baucis and Philemon (Ov. *Met.* 8.638), and Theseus is undoubtedly somewhat out of his element in the little home of Hecale. Thus, in representing Encolpius as a lower version of the hero enjoying

---

[70] Schol. on Call. *Hymn* 2.106 (= test. 37).

[71] Fragments of the *Hecale* are cited by the numbering of Hollis (1990).

[72] For Ovid's imitation of Callimachus in this passage see Hollis (1970) on Ov. *Met.* 8.611–724, and (1990) on fr. 27–39, and p. 350; Kenney observes the allusive implications of Theseus' presence at Melville (1986), xxviii.

[73] Plutarch tells the story of Theseus and Hecale citing the historian Philochorus (who was probably Callimachus' source as well) as his authority (Plut. *Thes.* 14 = *FGrHist* 328 F 109). Aside from Ovid's allusions to the *Hecale* (most notably at *Met.* 2.531 ff. as well as in the Baucis and Philemon episode), Crinagoras wrote an epigram to accompany a copy of the text (*Anth. Pal.* 9.545), and Hecale is mentioned at *Priap.* 12.3. A brief allusion to the story of Hecale was recognized by Politian at Apul. *Met.* 1.23.

[74] Persius 4.21 mentions Baucis as an example of a poor old woman.

[75] Pliny *Nat.* 22.88; 26.82; cf. Hollis (1990) on fr. 38–89.

epic hospitality, Petronius parodies literary models which had themselves already somewhat reduced the grandeur of epic models.[76]

An explicit allusion to Callimachus' *Hecale* in the Oenothea episode is clear despite some textual problems. Encolpius' hexameter verses in praise of Oenothea's *paupertatis ingenium* make a direct comparison between the two characters: *qualis in Actaea quondam fuit hospita terra/ digna sacris Hecale* (with Pius' *Hecale* for the manuscripts' *Hecates*, "Just as once in the land of Attica Hecale, deserving of sacred rites, welcomed strangers," *Sat.* 135.8.15–16). This combines a free translation of the first line of Callimachus' *Hecale* ('Ακταίη τις ἔναιεν 'Ερεχθέος ἔν ποτε γουνῷ, "Once a certain Attic woman lived in the fruitful land of Erechtheus," fr. 1) with a reference to the probable conclusion of the *Hecale*, Theseus' establishment of rites in Hecale's honor (see Hollis fr. 80, 83). The manuscripts' reading *Bachineas* in line 17 probably conceals some kind of reference to Callimachus as a "son of Battus."[77] While the poem uses quotation of Callimachus to compare Oenothea and Hecale, in his prose account Encolpius contrasts Oenothea's squalor with the idealized rustic simplicity of Hecale and her literary heirs Baucis and Philemon. When Oenothea takes the *camella* (wine cup or bowl) down from the wall and the nail falls out of the wall after it (*Sat.* 135.3), this is only one signal that her house is full of decay. Oenothea's beans in their dirty shells in the ragged sack with the meat (*Sat.* 135.4) are quite different from Baucis' fresh vegetables (*holus*, 647) and the ripe and preserved olives which both Baucis and Hecale carefully set before their guests. Like Philemon (Ov. *Met.* 8.647–50), Oenothea lifts down smoked meat from a rack. The frugal and careful housekeeping suggested by Ovid's description of the smoked meat as *servatoque diu* ("kept for a long time" Ov. *Met.* 8.649) is transformed by Petronius into evidence of neglect and decay; Oenothea's meat is full of cuts and is as old as she is (*coaequale natalium suorum sinciput*, *Sat.* 136.1). Oenothea's hospitality takes the Callimachean and Ovidian rustic ideal to parodic extremes. Her sharp command that Encolpius clean and prepare the beans is followed by her rebuke of his sluggishness and then by her own revolting way of cleaning the beans in her mouth (*Sat.* 135.6). Baucis stirs up a carefully banked fire in order to

---

[76] The relationship of the Oenothea episode of Petronius to the *Hecale* of Callimachus and to Ovid's story of Baucis and Philemon is briefly noted by Pfeiffer (1949) on fragment 264; Hollis (1970) on Ov. *Met.* 8.611–724 and (1990) p. 34 and on his fr. 83; Sullivan (1985), 86–87; and Garrido (1930), 10–11, who focuses especially on echoes of Ovid's Baucis and Philemon in Petronius' story of Encolpius and Oenothea.

[77] See Courtney (1991) *ad loc.* and Müller (1995) *ad loc.* in his apparatus criticus.

heat water for her guests (Ov. *Met.* 8.641–45), and apparently Hecale does the same for her guest (fr. 32, 33).[78] When Oenothea reaches up to put back the meat, she breaks the stool on which she stands, falls to the ground, knocks over the *cucumula* (small cooking pot) and puts out the fire, hurting herself and getting ashes all over her face (*Sat.* 136.1–2). What happens to Oenothea self-reflexively acknowledges the way Petronius has lowered and dirtied the Callimachean and Ovidian models. And Encolpius' response too incorporates a self-reflexive comment on his parodically "elevating" comparison of Oenothea to Hecale – who herself had been "elevated" by Theseus' establishment of rites in her honor and by Callimachus' poem: *anumque non sine risu erexi ...* ("I raised the old woman, not without a laugh," 136.3).

While Oenothea is at a neighbor's getting some embers to kindle the fire and, as suits her name and her literary ancestress Dipsas, having three glasses of wine (*Sat.* 136.3, 11), Encolpius is frightened by three geese which arrive at the door. Encolpius as narrator parodies his reaction to the geese when he says that he took the situation altogether seriously and to arm himself broke a leg off Oenothea's table (*oblitus itaque nugarum pedem mensulae extorsi*, 136.5).[79] Encolpius' choice of weapon is especially funny since Ovid makes much of the way in which Baucis props up the faulty leg of her table with a broken piece of pottery (Ov. *Met.* 8.660–63): what was precariously whole and stable in Ovid is violently broken in its debased Petronian imitation. Encolpius asserts his heroic identity by killing one goose. In the following hexameter verses he parodically compares the goose to the Stymphalian birds and the Harpies (*Sat.* 136.6). Encolpius clearly is claiming the role of the heroes (Hercules, and the sons of Boreas, respectively) who defeat these winged epic monsters, but he himself is more of a Harpy, snatching up various bits of epic texts and making a mess. Of course, Encolpius' epic battle with the goose re-stages Baucis and Philemon's unsuccessful pursuit of their goose when they realize that their guests are divine and decide to serve them something more appropriate to their dignity and importance (Ov. *Met.* 8.684–88). Their comically unsuccessful attempts to catch the goose end in the transformation of their little house into a temple of marble and gold; in Encolpius' assertion that there is no marble floor in Oenothea's house (*Sat.* 135.8.2), Petronius contrasts Oenothea's squalor (and the meaningless

---

[78] See further Hollis (1970) on *Met.* 8.651 and (1990) on *Hecale* fr. 34.

[79] Rosenmeyer (1991) makes a convincing case that Encolpius' battle with the goose is also modelled on the mock-epic battle of Molorchus with the mouse in Book 3 of Callimachus' *Aetia*.

divinity of her name) to the divine transformation of Baucis and Philemon's house into a temple, and the paving of their earthen floor with
marble.[80]

One more shard of epic may have found its way into the Oenothea
mosaic. An anthology poem (fr. 37M = AL475 = 473SB) describes the
tears of an old person with the metaphor of a storm (*imber*, parallel to
17.3, of Quartilla's tears) and an epic-sounding simile of a "shameless
river" (*improbus amnis*) overflowing with spring floods; Dousa suggests that this belongs after 137.3 and describes Oenothea's reaction to
the death of the goose.[81] Since the Hecale model is so overt in the
Oenothea episode, could this poem be a parody specifically targeted
at the *Hecale*? Hecale apparently gives Theseus a sad account of her
poverty and isolation: she used to be wealthy, she met (and possibly
married) a wealthy man, but he and the two boys (perhaps her own)
whom she raised died, one of the boys at the hands of Cercyon (fr.41,
47–49, with Hollis' extensive comments). Her speech probably ended
with tears (fr. 57), and this is probably alluded to by Statius: *nec fudit
vanos anus hospita fletus* ("nor did the hospitable old woman pour forth
tears in vain," *Theb.* 12.582, in Evadne's appeal to Theseus). These
tears may have been the basis for an appeal to Theseus to free the area
from the menace of the Bull of Marathon.[82] If the anthology poem
belongs at 137.3, Hecale's tears may be a specific target of parody in
the mock-epic storm of tears for the goose and Encolpius' promise of
restitution.

The parrot and the swan

Finally, though it does not deal with epic specifically, one of the poems
attributed to Petronius in the Latin Anthology seems also to give a self-
consciously literal account of the *Satyricon*'s imitative and competitive
relations to lofty poetic forms of literary discourse:[83]

> Indica purpureo genuit me litore tellus,
>   candidus accenso qua redit orbe dies.
>   hic ego divinos inter generatus honores
>   mutavi Latio barbara verba sono.

[80] Garrido (1930), 11, argues that both the goose and the non-marble floor are allusions to
Ovid's story of Baucis and Philemon.
[81] Burman (1743), ad 137. Cotrozzi (1979) surveys the poem's use of epic language and
imagery.
[82] So Hollis (1990) on fr. 57, citing for the Statius allusion Hecker, *Commentationes
Callimacheae* (1842), 123.
[83] Fr. 45 M = AL 691.

iam dimitte tuos, Paean o Delphice, cycnos:
dignior haec vox est quae tua templa colat.

The land of India bore me on its purple shore,
    where bright day returns with its fiery orb.
Born into divine honors here I exchanged
    barbarian words for the sound of Latin.
Now, O Delphic Paean, send away your swans:
    My voice is worthier to inhabit your temple.

The speaker is a parrot, identifiable by its origins in India; the text may be a tablet labelling a parrot.[84] The parrot calls for Apollo to dismiss his swans, and will presumably supplant the swan's unique song with his own imitative art. Swans are often associated with Apollo and with the production of uniquely beautiful poetry. Horace famously compared Pindar to a swan (*C.* 4.2.25), and earlier, in closing the second book of the *Odes*, he celebrates his own poetic fame by describing (in something that comes close to a grotesque excess of detail) his metamorphosis into a swan (*C.* 2.20).[85] Since the parrot is positioned as a rival intent on displacing Apollo's swan, rich in its own literary associations, the poem associates the parrot with some type of literary enterprise. Parrots have their own potential as figures for literary works. In Ovid's elegy on the death of Corinna's *imitatrix ales* (*Am.* 2.6), the parrot is an *imitatrix* not only because its voice imitates human speech, but because Ovid's lament for its death imitates Catullus' lament for the death of Lesbia's *passer*.[86] Ovid associates the imitative parrot with the qualities found pleasing in neoteric poetry: smallness of scale and lightness of diction.[87] Ovid's lament ends with a "quotation" of the parrot's epitaph, an elegiac couplet spoken in the first person. Statius too composes a lament for a parrot (*Silv.* 2.4); he has a close eye on Ovid, especially in the address to birds mourning for the departed parrot (cf. Ovid *Am.* 2.6.1–14). In Statius' dirge, the first line begins with *occidit* (24) and the second with *psittacus* (25); this reverses Ovid's poem, whose first line begins *psittacus* and whose second begins *occidit*. Statius' birds are all well-educated (*doctae*, *Silv.* 2.4.16), and in a slight correction or capping of Ovid, who summons good birds in general (*piae volucres*) to the lament (*Am.* 2.6.1–6), Statius summons to the

---

[84] Pliny *Nat.* 10.117.
[85] On the beauty of the dying swan's song, see especially Plato *Phaed.* 84E, discussed at Cicero *Tusc.* 1.73, and for the association of swans with Apollo see Nisbet and Hubbard (1978) on 2.20.10. Keith (1992), 137–46, discusses Ovid's programmatic associations between swans and elegiac poetry.
[86] Hinds (1988), 7.
[87] Boyd (1987); Rauk (1989); Myers (1990).

lament *only* those birds who are well known for their capacity to produce human speech (*Silv.* 2.4.16–23), and then teaches them the
actual words of the dirge (*Silv.* 2.4.24–37). Thus, on the evidence of
Ovid and Statius, parrots, like swans, are available to poets as a device
for signaling their literary tastes and especially their relationships to
their models.[88]

In the Petronian poem, the *Satyricon*'s fashioning of fiction out of
quotation and imitation of epic is embodied in the parrot's imitative
utterance and its ambitions to displace the loftier and more poetic
swan. A metapoetic parrot is would confirm yet again the novel's
playfully self-conscious representations of the processes of its composition. Parrots imitate what they hear, and indeed, Petronius' "parroting" imitations of epic add up to a pre-history of his novelistic
discourse, incorporating his recollections of earlier ways of fracturing
epic's inherited structures to accommodate fictionalizing inventions.
Constructing a fictitious identity around the Odyssean name Polyaenus
recapitulates Odysseus' own lies, one location of the production of
fiction in epic form. The Callimachean version of the epic of the every-
day in the *Hecale* opens epic forms to accommodate narratives about
ordinary people. Even the trivial sotadean rewritings of epic offer a
miniature model of opening up epic to the obscene.

In a sense, it is easy to dismiss the *Satyricon*'s epic parody as a dis-
traction from the novel's real business of inventing fiction. But Petronius is constantly telling the tale of refashioning epic into fiction, and
these metapoetic winks and nods draw the epic structures tightly into
their narrative frame. The stakes of refashioning epic as fiction and of
re-telling belated epics in invented prose are highest in the novel's
parroting of epic versions of Rome's rise to empire. Before we turn
to the poems on the Fall of Troy and the Civil War in chapters 3 and 4,
in chapter 2 I will demonstrate some other ways in which Petronius fits
verse into fiction.

---

[88] Persius *prol.* 8 may mock this.

2   In the frame: context and continuity in the short poems

As everyone will agree, the short poems on moralizing or erotic themes performed by Trimalchio, and Eumolpus, and Encolpius (both as character and as narrator) represent utterly conventional habits of thought. In this they differ from the *Satyricon*'s epic parody, which is aimed quite precisely at fragmenting and reshaping particular models. The short verses pause to reflect on the narrative, rather than carry it forward, and their universalizing assertions about love, luck or money can seem oddly trivial distractions or interruptions, clashing sharply with the messy details of the world inhabited by the characters. The short poems use conventional topics and forms to distill the details of the plot into timeless truths – and over and over Petronius constructs a plot that fights back, resisting the constraints of verse at every turn. Consequently, the poems are most often viewed in a disjunctive way. They are judged eligible for medieval anthologizing, or discussed as opportunistic displays of literary skill for its own sake, incongruous in the mouths of the characters who perform them, as signs that "stylistic disorder mirrors world disorder," or, in Bakhtinian terms, as evidence of a multiplicity of stylistic levels, destabilizing the generic boundaries of established and authoritative literary forms.[1] Yet an exclusive emphasis on the disjunctive qualities can be misleading; a close-up view of these poems "in the frame" will demonstrate some of the pointed and precise connections which Petronius contrives between the performances of his poets and the narrative of the novel.

The short poems are uttered by the characters who perform them as educated (or in the case of Trimalchio, as pseudo-educated) responses to particular situations. The more closely these poems are read within their narrative contexts, the more they show the gaps between the traditional certainties of poetry and the untidy spontaneity of prose fiction. As we shall see in a moment, the poems are often framed in such a way

---

[1] See Sullivan (1968a), 215–16 on literary opportunism, and Zeitlin (1971), 645 on stylistic disorder; Bakhtinian perspectives are thoughtfully considered by Slater (1990), 160–86.

that what is figurative within them is made literal in prose. The novel's punning juxtapositions of the literal with the figurative are in some ways analogous to its juxtaposition of novelistic characters who look and talk rather like "real" people with their literary ancestors from the epic past as formulated by Homer, Virgil, or Ovid – in each case what is ostensibly "familiar" or "ordinary" is brought into conjunction with what has been shaped by the process of literary artifice. Figurative language is sometimes hard to categorize with precision: there is not always a clear demarcation when each word stops being a description and starts being a metaphor.[2] Puns too will always be slippery to discuss and describe: depending on the eye of the beholder they can be either far too obvious or excessively subtle, arid ornaments or richly evocative expressions of ambiguity and paradox.[3] Most of Petronius' puns are so obvious that the least sophisticated character can seem to enjoy constructing them, and one feels slightly foolish pointing them out. But beyond this frivolous surface deeper perspectives open up. Like a hall of mirrors, the *Satyricon* reveals an inexhaustible supply of amusing, and uncannily boundless, perspectives.

Trimalchio's poetic performances

Trimalchio's poetic performances display a punning manipulation of figurative language which transcends their function as demonstrations of his literary pretensions and limitations. His first poetic performance is a trivial moralizing epigram to accompany the display of the silver skeleton near the beginning of the meal (34.10):[4]

> eheu nos miseros, quam totus homuncio nil est!
> sic erimus cuncti, postquam nos auferet Orcus.
>   ergo vivamus, dum licet esse bene.
>
> Ah, wretched us, that a mere man is, in sum, nothing!
> So we shall all be, after Death carries us off.
>   So now let us live, while we can live well.

The moralizing point is banal (Horace's city mouse uses just such reasoning to get the country mouse to venture into town, *Sat.* 2.6.95–97),

---

[2] For probing discussion of the boundaries of figurative language in the context of love elegy see Kennedy (1993), 46–63, who draws on the arguments of Lakoff and Johnson (1980) that metaphor is not a decorative element in descriptions of reality but has a role in structuring perceptions of reality.

[3] Good starting points for the investigation of puns can be found in Culler (1988) and Ahl (1985).

[4] On Trimalchio's epigrams, see Sochatoff (1970) and the reactions of Huxley (1970), Baldwin (1971) and Barnes (1971).

the verse technique unimpressive (instead of the standard pattern of elegiac verse, he places a single pentameter after two hexameters, and the sound of the two monosyllables at the end of the first line is especially unpolished).[5] Moving out from the poem to the prose frame, however, we notice that in the poem death is figured (in the verb *auferet*) as Orcus carrying one away, while in a punning reversal, a new dish (*ferculum*, from the same root as *aufero*) is literally carried in as the poem on being carried off ends (35.1). So the conventional exhortation to live well while one can becomes playfully pointed when read "in the frame." The interchangeability of life/death and food is punningly embedded in the poem itself, for *esse* is the infinitive both of *sum* (to be) and *edo* (to eat).[6] The *ferculum* too is itself a coded figure for mortality because it depicts the zodiac. For astrologers and those who believe them the position of the stars at a person's birth holds the secret of his death because the death of an individual was astrologically determined by the alignment of the zodiac at the moment of birth: so Manilius can say, *nascentes morimur, finisque ab origine pendet* ("being born we die; the end derives from the beginning," Man. *Astr.* 4.16). Thus the zodiac dish which is carried in itself reaffirms the inevitable fact that death carries us all off, as Trimalchio had asserted with his silver skeleton and his poem.[7]

Trimalchio performs a second epigram later in the meal. Here too a web of punning connections links the verses to their prose frame. When the acrobat falls on Trimalchio, he declares the boy free and asserts that the event (*casum*) must be marked by an "inscription." After calling for writing tablets, he recites a three-line poem (55.3, with Heinsius' supplements):

> quod non expectes, ex transverso fit ⟨ubique,
> nostra⟩ et supra nos Fortuna negotia curat.
>   quare da nobis vina Falerna, puer.

> What you don't expect happens unexpectedly ⟨anywhere⟩,
> and above us Fortuna looks after ⟨our⟩ affairs.
>   So, boy, give us Falernian wine.

Again, the literary technique is by no means impressive; the juxtaposition of present convivial pleasures with future uncertainties is banal; what sharpens the humor is the particular relation between the poem's content and its frame. The moralizing sentiment encompasses both the

---

[5] See further Barnes (1971), 255.
[6] For the pun, Huxley (1970), 69.
[7] On Trimalchio's zodiac as a sign of mortality, see further Grondona (1980), 17–23. On the theme of mortality and Trimalchio's *horologium*, see Barchiesi (1981).

trivial and momentary "transformation" of Trimalchio's life by the boy's fall and the significant and permanent (if it is not simply a staged ruse) "transformation" of the boy by his sudden manumission. A conventional metaphor in the word *casus* regularly associates happenstance with the metaphor of falling; this conventional metaphor is made literal and concrete in the acrobat's fall. In effect, the actual "threat" posed by the fall of the acrobat is tamed by being transformed into metaphor, and at the same time, the conventional metaphors of falling are enlivened by the acrobat's mishap. In the group discussion which follows the freeing of the acrobat, the metaphor of falling underlies the formulation that human affairs are *in praecipiti* ("on the brink" 55.1), as it does in Trimalchio's word *casum* (55.2). In his poem, Trimalchio even seems to be thinking of the acrobat who fell on him from above when he imagines Fortuna "above" *supra* (55.3).[8] And already when Encolpius first suspects some kind of trick, he defends his suspicion by saying that the cook who "forgot" to gut the pig had not "fallen away" (*exciderat*, 54.3) i.e. from his memory.

Now the *auferet/ferculum* pun and the vision of Fortuna "above" us construct a rather simple relation between poem and frame: the action in the frame is the literal version of the metaphor in the poem. Other relations between poems and their frames can be more complex, drawing upon implicit features of the narrative frame for their effects. Just after the zodiac course is brought to the table, a song from a mime is performed: *circumferebat Aegyptius puer clibano argenteo panem ... atque ipse etiam taeterrima voce de Laserpiciario mimo canticum extorsit* ("An Egyptian boy was carrying around bread on a silver tray ... and he himself ground out in a very unpleasant voice a song from the Silphium Man mime," 35.6). Naturally, the performance (probably Trimalchio's) of a mimic song adds to the theatrical atmosphere of Trimalchio's banquet.[9] In addition, though the verse performance is suppressed entirely in the report of its unpleasant effects, the title itself gives enough hints about its content that we can see several points of contact with the narrative frame.

The title *Laserpiciarius*, one who deals in *laserpicium*, resembles other extant mime titles which refer to a profession.[10] *Laserpicium* is the name given in Latin both to the plant silphium (Col. 6.17.7, Pliny *Nat.*

---

[8] Cf. Walsh (1970), 39 n. 6.

[9] Bücheler posited a lacuna before *atque*; it seems likely that *ipse* refers to Trimalchio. So Smith (1975) *ad loc.*

[10] Titles referring to a profession include *Augur, Centonarius, Colorator, Fullo, Piscator, Restio, Salinator, Staminariae*; see Bonaria (1965), at lines 21, 36, 40, 60–62, 89, 90–98, 99, 107–08.

16.143), and to a strong-smelling gum produced from this plant (Pliny *Nat.* 20.141).[11] The earliest references to silphium specify that it came from Cyrene.[12] A related plant, now known as *Ferula asa foetida*, was available from other locations, but ancient discussions make it clear that Median, Syrian or Parthian silphium was regarded as less effective than that gathered at Cyrene.[13] The supply of silphium at Cyrene declined because of over-harvesting in the wild and the failure of attempts to grow it under cultivation.[14] This of course increased its rarity and value, and Pliny indicates that it became extinct in his own time.[15] In Plautus' *Rudens*, when Trachalio meets Daemones, the old man who lives by the shore not far from Cyrene, he assumes Daemones is somehow involved in the *laserpicium* trade (Plautus, *Rud.* 629–31),[16] and characters like him could have been expected in a mime about a silphium dealer. The strong odor of silphium could have been part of the humor. A mime called *The Fuller* might have made much of the fact that fullers treated cloth in vats of urine.[17] So too, an audience might expect strong smells to be at issue in a mime about *laserpicium*. Indeed, in a technique which we shall see in many of the prose descriptions of the production of poetry, Petronius describes the poetic performance with language that suits the subject of the poem. So here, the adjective *taeterrima* ("very foul"), describing the voice of the performer, playfully alludes to the strong odors associated with *laserpicium*.[18]

Another sort of connection between poetic performance and frame emerges from the fact that Cyrenaic and other, inferior, types of

[11] On the plant and its nomenclature, see Gemmill (1966).

[12] Ar. *Equ.* 893–94, Hdt. 4.169; cf. Theophr. *H. P.* 6.3.3, Strabo 17.3.22.

[13] So Dioscorides 3.80, Pliny *Nat.* 22.100; cf. the distinction made at Col. 12.59.4–5. References to the great wealth which the silphium trade brought to Cyrene can be found as early as Aristophanes (*Plut.* 925), and the plant was regularly depicted on the city's coins; see Robinson (1927) ccli–cclviii.

[14] Andrews (1941–42), 232–36.

[15] Pliny reports that silphium was sold for its weight in silver *denarii* (*Nat.* 19.38). As a result it seems to have taken on a status like precious metal bullion: in 93 BCE thirty pounds of *laserpicium* was brought to Rome at public expense; in 49 Caesar took out of the public treasury, along with silver and gold, 1500 pounds of *laserpicium* (*Nat.* 19.40). And elsewhere Pliny includes silphium in a list of the most expensive substances on earth (*Nat.* 37.204). Pliny also asserts "the only stalk of silphium found in my own time was sent to Nero the emperor" (*unus omnino caulis nostra memoria repertus Neroni principi missus est*, *Nat.* 19.39); on the representation of Nero in the *Natural History*, see Beagon (1992), 17–18, Baldwin (1995), 73–76. On *Sat.* 35.6 Gonzales de Salas cites Pliny's account of the last stalk of silphium and remarks that Petronius is alluding to Nero; see Burman (1743), II. 149.

[16] On this passage see Gowers (1993), 98.

[17] Cf. Plautus' references to fullers: *As.* 907, *Pseud.* 782.

[18] For *taeter* used of unpleasant smells or tastes, cf. Cic. *Ver.* 3.23; Lucr. *DRN* 6.11, 787 and others cited at *OLD* s.v. *taeter* 1 c.

silphium were used in small quantities as a condiment.[19] In the sentence which follows the performance of the song, Trimalchio exhorts his guests to eat (*Sat.* 35.7): ... *"suadeo" inquit Trimalchio "cenemus: hoc est ius cenae"* ("'I tell you,' he said, 'let's eat: this is the sauce of the meal'"). The pun on *ius* (sauce/law) juxtaposes food with words;[20] the song from the fictional silphium man mime performed at Trimalchio's *cena* effects a similar pun, in which the *canticum* is a musical condiment served along with the food.[21] The same punning impulses which juxtapose the poem on Death carrying us off with a frame narrative of slaves carrying in a new course (itself a coded signal of death) are at work more subtly in the silphium song. As a musical condiment whose flavor is heard, not tasted, the *canticum* from *The Silphium Man* is an ironic comment on Neronian Rome: instead of serving the best Cyrenaic silphium, one can serve only songs about it, and even the song itself, reported but not recorded, is an absence not a presence in the text.

Before proceeding to Trimalchio's other performances, we may note one more feature of the natural and cultural history of silphium which may connect the "content" of this performance with its novelistic frame. Riddle, using the evidence of Soranus and other authorities in combination with modern scientific studies of related plants, has argued that silphium was known in antiquity as an effective anti-fertility drug.[22] In this case, Petronius may introduce this mime performance as part of a larger pattern in the *cena* and the *Satyricon* of images and symbols of thwarted reproduction. The theme of interrupted fertility of course underlies Priapus' vengeance on Encolpius, and it dominates in the spectacle of legacy hunting at Croton, where childlessness is the key to social success. In the *cena*, it is implicit that

---

[19] Ar. *Av.* 534, 1582; Ath. 4.147d, 7.286d; at Ath. 2.64e (=Eubulus fr. 7, on which see Hunter [1983] *ad loc.*), Heracles rejects *silphium* and other ancillary food items in favor of real food, i.e. meat. Cf. Plaut. *Pseud.* 816. On its medicinal uses (both internal and external), see Pliny *Nat.* 22.100–6. See also Dalby (1996), 140–41, with further references.

[20] The younger Pliny uses the same pun at *Ep.* 1.15.1; see Gowers (1993), 77 n. 98 and 128 for other examples of this pun. On the Petronian passage, see Avery (1960).

[21] For recipes for a sauce containing *silphium* or *laser*, see Apicius, *de re coquinaria* 1.30.

[22] Riddle (1992), 26–28, cites Soranus *Gyn.* 1.63 and Dioscorides 3.80. Pliny discusses the efficacy of *silphium* for expelling a dead fetus or promoting menstruation at *Nat.* 22.100, 101; on Pliny's transmission of information about anti-fertility drugs, see Riddle (1992), 82–84. Riddle's analysis of the uses of silphium in the ancient world has prompted Johnston (1993), 328–29, to suggest that the anti-fertility properties of the plant may be alluded to at Catullus 7.4, where Catullus compares the vastness of his love for Lesbia to the number of grains of sand that lie on the *laserpicium*-bearing shores of Cyrene. See now Fisher (1996).

Trimalchio and Fortunata have had no children of their own; readers guess at their infertility during the zodiac course when Encolpius learns about Fortunata and the whole household, with no mention of any children. So the mention of a song from *The Silphium Man* may reflect Trimalchio and Fortunata's rich and childless state.

In the examples discussed so far, Trimalchio himself apparently manipulates the connections between his verse performances and their context. Another mime performance by Trimalchio suggests connections which are less securely under his control. After Trimalchio launches into a discussion of the comparative poetic merits of Cicero and the mime poet Publilius Syrus, he "quotes" moralizing verses on luxury which he attributes to Publilius (they are probably the invention of Petronius).[23] Some kind of discourse on luxury is probably implicit in his earlier mime performance; here it is explicit (*Sat.* 55.6):

> luxuriae rictu Martis marcent moenia.
> tuo palato clausus pavo pascitur
> plumato amictus aureo Babylonico,
> gallina tibi Numidica, tibi gallus spado;
> ciconia etiam, grata peregrina hospita
> pietaticultrix gracilipes crotalistria,
> avis exul hiemis, titulus tepidi temporis,
> nequitiae nidum in caccabo fecit tuae.
> quo margaritam caram tibi, bacam Indicam?
> an ut matrona ornata phaleris pelagiis
> tollat pedes indomita in strato extraneo?
> zmaragdum ad quam rem viridem, pretiosum vitrum?
> quo Carchedonios optas ignes lapideos?
> nisi ut scintillet probitas e carbunculis.
> aequum est induere nuptam ventum textilem,
> palam prostare nudam in nebula linea?

> The walls of Mars grow rotten in the maw of luxury.
> The peacock, garbed in a golden Babylonian tapestry of feathers,
> is imprisoned and fattened up for your palate,
> and the Numidian guinea-hen, and the eunuch capon;
> even the stork, pleasing visitor from afar,
> loyal to its parents, a slim-legged castanet dancer,
> a bird in exile during winter, whose return heralds a
>   milder season,
> has made its nest in the cooking-pot of your decadence.

---

[23] Courtney (1991) *ad loc.*, follows Bendz (1941), 53, arguing that the verses are by Petronius, and suggests that they are introduced to parody Seneca's quotation of Publilius in philosophical discourse. Cf. Sullivan (1968a), 192. Sandy (1976) argues that the verses are by Publilius on the evidence of Seneca the Elder's characterization of Publilius' mimes: Seneca *Contr.* 7.3.[18]. 8–9.

Why do you want a pearl, an Indian berry?
So that an ungovernable matron can lift her legs
on a stranger's couch, bedecked in spoils of the sea?
Why do you covet the green emerald, costly glass?
Why fiery Carthaginian stones?
Unless you want it so that moral rectitude may gleam amid the
     carbuncles.
Is it right that a bride should put on a mere woven breeze,
and walk the streets nude garbed in a linen cloud?

In formal terms, the poem's wordplay based on sound or sense seems to be an extreme version of the sort of thing elsewhere celebrated or deplored in quotations of Publilius. The style is ornate, the expression pointed. Alliteration is used repeatedly: *Martis marcent moenia* (1), *palato ... pavo pascitur* (Scaliger's emendation of *nascitur*)/*plumato* (2–3), *titulus tepidi temporis* (7), *nequitiae nidum* (8), *strato extraneo* (11) *palam prostare* (16), *nudam in nebula* (16). In the poem's indictment of the luxurious eating at Rome, *luxuria* itself is possessed of a mouth (*rictus*, 1). The stork unnaturally makes a nest (*nidum*, 8) in the cooking-pot. The appearance of propriety is assimilated to the sparkling of an improper woman's jewels in the sarcastic phrase *nisi ut scintillet probitas e carbunculis* ("Unless you want it so that moral rectitude may gleam amid the carbuncles," 14).

The conventional argument is made that luxurious sea trade ruins Rome: three birds in the first half of the poem (fattened peacock, guinea-hen, and stork) come to Rome from afar, as do the jewels and sheer clothing (regularly associated with Coan silk) in the second half.[24] Images create analogical connections between the different objects of criticism in the poem. The first luxury, the peacock, is "garbed in a golden Babylonian tapestry of feathers,"[25] while the bride described last is clothed in a woven breeze and a linen cloud. The contrast between the bird's embroidered, gold-decorated tapestry of feathers and the woman's sheer light fabric frames the poem neatly. Another link between the birds at the beginning and the bejewelled

---

24 Transparent clothing was regularly described as Coan silk; see *Nat.* 11.76, Pliny's denunciation of Pamphile, described as the inventor of Coan silk, who reduced clothing for women to nudity. In this connection, cf. Quintilian's report of Caelius' characterization of Clodia, which probably turns on similar associations of Coan silk and sexual availability: *in triclinio coam, in cubiculo nolam,* "a Coan in the dining room, a Nolan in the bedroom" (*Inst.* 8.6.53); *coam* puns on *coire* (have intercourse) and the island of Cos, and *nolam* is a pun on *nolle* (be unwilling) and the city of Nola.

25 The origins of the peacock were in the east, and its plumage is elsewhere compared to elaborate eastern textiles: Ael. *NA* 5.21; cf. Ath. 9.397c. For the "feather-stitched" tapestry suggested by *plumato*, cf. Lucan *Ph.* 10.125.

matrona in the second half is the fact that peacocks' feathers are regularly imagined as encrusted with gems.[26] A similar sort of analogy between women and jewels emerges in Pliny's discussion of amber, a precious item so decadent that only women prize it (*Nat.* 37.30), when he says that in a poem Nero called Poppaea's hair "amber" (*sucinos*), thus giving women a third color (besides fair and dark) to wish their hair to be (*Nat.* 37.50). Another Neronian fragment, quoted by Seneca in a discussion of optics, describes the iridescent gleam of a dove's neck: *colla Cytheriacae splendent agitata columbae* ("the trembling neck of a Cytherian dove gleams ... " *N.Q.* 1.5.6); arguably this alliterative line has something of the flavor of the Petronian poem, though because so few scraps of Nero's poetry survive, it is hard to tell.

The stork's presence requires comment. It is conventional for moralizing writers to deplore the consumption of exotic poultry at Rome, and there are even remarkably detailed accounts of which Roman was first to eat a particular bird.[27] Peacocks became fashionable fare in the time of Cicero, and the fashion was mocked by Horace's spokesman for the simple life, Ofellus: *num vesceris ista/quam laudas pluma?* ("you don't eat the plumage which you praise, do you?" *S.* 2.2.27–28).[28] The guinea-hen was a relatively recent delicacy.[29] Delians were the first to fatten the *gallina* for the table, and Pliny says that people fattened male birds to avoid a provision in the sumptuary laws against eating fattened hens (*Nat.* 10.139). According to Cornelius Nepos, the stork was more popular than the crane in his time (cf. Hor. *S.* 2.2.49 with the comment of Porphyrion), but Pliny reports that by his time the fashion for eating stork had passed (Pliny *Nat.* 10.60), and there are no recipes for stork among the poultry recipes in the collection of Apicius. Why is the stork included in Trimalchio's recitation? Perhaps because the verses are devised as the authentic product of Publilius, and stork was a popular dish in his time, though no longer in Trimalchio's. But it is

---

[26] For peacock feathers described as encrusted with gems, see Phaedrus 3.18, Columella 8.11.8, Pliny *Nat.* 10.43, Martial 13.70, 3.58.13.

[27] Pliny reports that there was a dispute about whether Scipio Metellus or Marcius Seius was the first to eat foie gras, and that Messalinus Cotta was the first to eat grilled goose feet (*Nat.* 10.52). Elsewhere he reports that the tragic actor Clodius Aesop was reputed to have eaten a meal costing 100,000 sesterces: it consisted of a pie made from birds which could imitate the human voice, and Pliny terms it a kind of cannibalism (Pliny *Nat.* 10.141). Cf. Varro *RR* 3.5.8–17 on famous men who built elaborate aviaries.

[28] Hortensius was said to be the first to have a peacock killed for the table; the practice rapidly became increasingly popular: Varro, *RR* 3.6.1, 6; Cicero *ad Fam.* 9.18.3 (191 SB), 9.20.2. (193 SB); Ael. *NA* 5.21.

[29] Varro *RR* 3.9.18; Pliny adds that it was not even very tasty: *Nat.* 10.74.

more likely that the stork's reputation for family loyalty was the real attraction.

The stork is described by the striking line *pietaticultrix gracilipes crotalistria*, ("loyal to its parents, a slim-legged castanet dancer"). The association of the stork with *pietas* derives from the belief that migrating storks returned to the same nest every year, and took care of their elders in old age;[30] the associations of the stork with family loyalty probably also underlie stories attested later than the *Satyricon* which connect the stork to episodes of the punishment of adultery.[31] The term *crotalistria*, "castanet-dancer," refers in the first instance, as Courtney notes, to the clattering sound of storks' beaks.[32] Yet there is an inherent tension or paradox in the connection of a stork with both *pietas* and castanet dancing, for castanets are elsewhere explicitly associated with lascivious dancing by women.[33] The description of the adulterous pearl-wearing *matrona* focuses on her feet (*an ut matrona ornata phaleris pelagiis/tollat pedes indomita in strato extraneo?* "So that an ungovernable matron can lift her legs on a stranger's couch, bedecked in spoils of the sea?") and thus creates a visually precise analogy between the migrating graceful-legged stork, which makes its nest in the cook-pot of the listener's wickedness, and the *matrona*, who betrays her husband by visiting another's bed. The speaker of the poem sets up the stork's *pietas* and loyalty to its nest as an ideal which is unnaturally overturned in the excesses of Roman cuisine. But the word *crotalistria*, used to describe the stork's clattering beak, suggests that the stork itself already partakes in the castanet dancing associated with adulterous (or at least potentially adulterous) women.

The prose narrative frame too makes connections between women and birds and far-flung wealth; these connections are somewhat contradictory to what the poem suggests with its pointed figures. Encolpius' neighbor at the table calls Fortunata a *pica pulvinaris* ("a magpie on the couch") and says that Trimalchio's estates extend as far as kites (*milvi*) can fly (37.7–8). In a more elaborate way, the poem's generalized account of ostentatious jewelry is later made particular in prose when Fortunata and Scintilla show off their jewelry to each other, and

---

[30] Pliny *Nat.* 10.63, perhaps misplaced from 10.62; cf. Cic. *Fin.* 3.63. For storks depicted with *Pietas* on coins see the references collected by Courtney (1991) *ad loc.*

[31] See Ael. *NA* 8.20 and Perry (1952) p. 706, no. 713, *Ciconia infidelis*; the fable of the adulterous stork killed by her mate is also retold by "Petronius Redivivus" in Dublin 602: see Colker (1975) sections 142–46.

[32] See Juv. 1.116, Isidore *Or.* 12.7.16 and compare Pers. 1.58 (of a derisive hand gesture).

[33] P. Scipio at Macr. *Sat.* 2.10; Cic. *Pis.* 9.20.

Trimalchio and Habinnas trade boasts about the cost of their wives' gold and jewelry (67.6–10). Then, Habinnas mischievously raises Fortunata's feet on to the couch and makes her blush (67.12–13):

dumque sic cohaerent, Habinnas furtim consurrexit pedesque Fortunatae correptos super lectum immisit. "au au" illa proclamavit aberrante tunica super genua. composita ergo in gremio Scintillae incensissimam rubore faciem sudario abscondit.

And while they were clinging together like this, Habinnas sneakily got up, seized Fortunata's legs and put them up on the couch. "Oh dear!" she exclaimed, with her tunic rising up over her knees. Pulling herself together in Scintilla's arms she buried her fiery blush in a handkerchief.

The discussion of jewelry, the raised feet, the actual gleaming of Fortunata's blush (in *incensissimam*, the conjecture of Reinesius), and the gleaming implied in Scintilla's name (meaning something like "Sparky"), and what could be described as an appearance of *"improbitas"* all refract in the prose frame what the poem had said about jewelry: why do you want it, *nisi ut scintillet probitas e carbunculis* ("Unless you want it so that moral rectitude may gleam amid the carbuncles"). In the course of this scene, Scintilla shows off her earrings, calling them *crotalia* (67.9). According to Pliny, earrings with multiple pearls are given this name, derived from *crotalum*, "castanet," because women enjoy the rattling sound they make when worn (*Nat.* 9.114). For Pliny, then, who elsewhere deplores the wounds inflicted on the ears for the wearing of jewels (*Nat.* 12.2), these earrings are by their very name associated with the improprieties of castanet dancing which the poem had connected with the stork. Moreover, the *Satyricon* has already made connections between lascivious dancing and *matronae*. Just before his recitation from Publilius, Trimalchio boasts of Fortunata's remarkable talents in the *cordax*, a salacious dance, though she declines to perform. He is about to perform the dance himself before she intervenes to stop him (52.8–11). Only the recitation of the accounts of Trimalchio's immense wealth and the performance of the acrobats, ending in the unfortunate fall, intervene between Fortunata's refusal to dance and Trimalchio's performance of these verses on luxurious food and adulterous women. The poem's condemnation of women's behavior is thus contrasted with Trimalchio's own encouragement of Fortunata's dancing.

In the immediate context of Trimalchio's performance, then, the prose frame subverts a moralizing message, and characterizes Trimalchio as a hypocrite who revels in luxury while he deplores it. Elsewhere, the prose dramatizes what is only implicit in the verse, that the exotic jewels worn by wives display their husbands' status, just as the exotic poultry consumed at Roman tables displays men's status. In their giggling and jewelry display, Fortunata and Scintilla come rather close to the poem's images of lascivious women. But the fit is not exact: Fortunata declines to perform the *cordax* and Scintilla does not wear her castanet-clattering earrings dangling from her ears – she keeps them in a tiny box which she wears hung around her neck (67.9).

Implicitly, the poem denounces sea trade in cloth and jewels and birds. Thus, an additional dimension of Trimalchio's hypocrisy is evident when we learn that he won his fortune in overseas trade (76.3–6). But in his life story the elements of women, jewels, and food are combined in a different way from the typical patterns which are the target of the poem. According to Trimalchio, Fortunata's willingness to sell her jewels was an essential part of his commercial success after initial losses in shipwreck. As in other moralizing historical narratives, a sort of primitive golden age is reconstructed in which Fortunata was without jewels, and all that they imply. In Trimalchio's narrative of this early state of his fortune, Fortunata's renunciation of her jewels is associated with humble, indigenous, non-exotic food, for Trimalchio says that her contribution was the yeast which made his fortune rise: *hoc fuit peculii mei fermentum* ("This was the yeast of my fortune," 76.7).

By representing Trimalchio's epigrams and "quotations" from mime, then, Petronius elaborates his characterization and adds to the overall atmosphere of spectacle and performance at the *cena*. At one level Trimalchio controls the relation between his poetic performances and his life, lived, as everyone's is, in prose. The next course is bound to be carried in soon after he composes the Orcus epigram; he composes the epigram on Fortuna's position above us after the fall of the acrobat (which he may well have planned). His performance transposes the literal function of silphium as a condiment to a musical condiment for the meal. Silphium's associations with over-consumption and sterility may be less on his mind, but they contribute to the themes of luxury and decadence which structure the *cena*. Trimalchio's "Publilius" poem constructs straightforward analogies between women and birds and other signs of decadence. Events in the frame bring his poem's metaphors to life when the gleam of decadent jewelry, and the "gleam" of a woman's *probitas* are restaged in Fortunata and Scintilla's jewelry scene. Still, the validity of what the poem says about women in general is undercut by Trimalchio's revelation that Fortunata's willingness to sell her jewels was the "yeast" of his fortune. Petronius has constructed Trimalchio's poetic performances and their prose frame in such a way that poetry's conventions tell only partial truths.

Eumolpus' minor verse

In addition to his "major" poems on Troy and the Civil War, the poet Eumolpus also performs several shorter poems on moralizing themes: his introductory poem upon meeting Encolpius in the picture gallery, his verses on luxury when he joins Encolpius as a rival for the affections of Giton, and his poetic outburst on baldness while on board Lichas' ship. Like Trimalchio's verses, these poems are generalizing reflections on standard themes of fortune, money and death, often arranged around a moralizing geography which contrasts safe, simple, familiar life on land with dangerous sea trade. And like Trimalchio, but more cleverly, Eumolpus constructs connections between the poems he performs and the frame narrative which he inhabits, though he does not control these connections as much as he might wish to.

In the picture gallery Encolpius gives a detailed record of his first impression of Eumolpus, saying that he was a white-haired old man with a vexed expression (*exercitati vultus*), who seemed to promise something great (*qui videretur nescio quid magnum promittere*, 83.7). This initial impression of "something big" spells out the implications of Eumolpus' name (first appearing in the text at 90.1), "one who sings well," which is borne by several figures associated with poetry.[34]

Eumolpus addresses Encolpius and asserts his poetic identity: *"ego" inquit "poeta sum"* (" 'I am a poet,' he said"). Eumolpus is quite anxious to show Encolpius the correct way to interpret his shabby appearance, and offers his poverty as a guarantee of his poetic skill. Even the structure of Eumolpus' remark may arise from poetic tradition: in conversing with Encolpius, Eumolpus uses the satirist's favored device of imagining the questions of an interlocutor in order to represent his poem as a "real" conversation: *"quare ergo" inquis "tam male vestitus*

---

[34] See the *Homeric Hymn to Demeter*, 154, with the full discussion of Richardson (1974) *ad loc*. In the *Metamorphoses* Ovid says that Eumolpus learned the rites of Bacchus from Orpheus (11.92–93). In flattering Cotys, a Thracian king, Ovid praises the king's poetry by claiming that it befits his descent from Eumolpus: Ov. *ex Pont*. 2.9.1–2, 17–20, on which see the detailed discussion in Williams (1994), 139–42. In a discussion of "speaking names" in Plautus, Seneca, and Petronius, Petrone (1988), 70, (with her own metaliterary ironies) usefully compares the use of names like Eumolpus' to theatrical masks which depict specific character types.

es?" (" 'Then why,' you ask, 'are you so badly dressed?' " 83.9).[35] Eumolpus then repeats his point in six lines of verse (83.10):

> qui pelago credit, magno se faenore tollit;
> qui pugnas et castra petit, praecingitur auro;
> vilis adulator picto iacet ebrius ostro,
> et qui sollicitat nuptas, ad praemia peccat:
> sola pruinosis horret facundia pannis
> atque inopi lingua desertas invocat artes.

> He who trusts the sea exalts himself with great profits:
> he who seeks out battles and military camps girds himself with gold;
> a worthless flatterer lies drunk on richly embroidered purple coverlets,
> and he who propositions brides sins for profit:
> only eloquence shivers in freezing rags
> and calls upon abandoned arts with destitute tongue.

This short hexameter poem plays upon the traditional mode of Roman satire, that is, the *sermo*, or conversation. Eumolpus embraces the conventions of poetic satires and thinks that a poet should "actually" speak in versified *sermones*. A satirist's poetry book comes to life in a conversational frame.

These lines also create another impression of a "living" poetry book. Their list of occupations which are more lucrative but of less integrity than poetry are similar to programmatic lists of various occupations, including poetry, in Horace *Odes* 1.1 and Tibullus 1.1. Eumolpus' verses may be read, like Horace's and Tibullus', as the beginning of a poetic collection.[36] He enters the narrative and begins his acquaintance with Encolpius as if he were being read like a poetry book. Obviously, he knows the difference between himself and a poetry book, but he enjoys collapsing (or pretending to collapse) distinctions between what is metaphorical and what is real. Encolpius as narrator has already been playing the same game of "reading" Eumolpus. He deduces already from Eumolpus' relatively poor appearance that he is in the presence of a literary man: *sed cultu non proinde speciosus, ut facile appareret eum ⟨ex⟩ hac nota litteratorum esse, quos odisse divites solent* ("but insofar as he looked shabby, it was easily apparent from this mark that he was one of the lettered men whom the wealthy tend to hold in contempt," 83.7). In a literal sense, the noun *nota* denotes a written mark, though

---

[35] That the imagined interlocutor is perceived as a characteristic device of satire is clear from Persius' joke *quisquis es, o modo quem ex adverso dicere feci* ... ("whoever you are, whom I just made speak in the opposing role," Pers. 1.44).

[36] See Loporcaro (1984), 255.

metaphorical uses of it, as here, are not uncommon. In this instance, however, it is combined with a pun on two senses of *litteratus*: "learned" and "marked on the forehead (with F for *fugitivus*) as a runaway slave." It thus suggests that Encolpius figuratively "reads" Eumolpus the poet just as he might literally read the text inscribed on the forehead of a runaway slave.[37] The notion of a literary work coming to life spins slightly out of Eumolpus' control as Encolpius "reads" Eumolpus before he can present himself as a book come to life. The slippage between literature and reality is also beyond Eumolpus' control as his poetic account of Greeks attacking unsuspecting Trojans (89.62–end) gives way (there is a break in the text but it seems brief) to a real attack when the people who hear him reciting throw stones (90.1).

After the gallery scene, Eumolpus rejoins Encolpius, who is back at the inn and now reunited with Giton. Eumolpus offers praises of simplicity at their simple meal (93.2):

> ales Phasiacis petita Colchis
> atque Afrae volucres placent palato,
> quod non sunt faciles: at albus anser
> et pictis anas involuta pennis
> plebeium sapit. ultimis ab oris
> attractus scarus atque arata Syrtis
> si quid naufragio dedit, probatur:
> mullus iam gravis est. amica vincit
> uxorem. rosa cinnamum veretur.
> quicquid quaeritur, optimum videtur.

> The bird sought from Phasian Colchis
> and the fowl from Africa please the palate
> because they are not easy to come by; but the white goose
> and the duck clad in colorful feathers[38]
> have a plebeian taste. The parrot-wrasse,
> brought here from far-away shores, and whatever
> furrowed Syrtis yields for the price of a shipwreck, find favor;
> the mullet is not amusing. Mistress wins out
> over wife. The rose is in awe of cinnamon.
> Whatever has to be sought from afar seems best.

Like Trimalchio's recitation of "Publilius," Eumolpus' verses map a familiar moral geography: life on land is safe and simple; the sea is

---

[37] Cf. Pl. *Cas.* 401. For an example of the same pun operating in the opposite direction (papyrus compared to a fugitive), see Laevius fr. 13 in Courtney (1993). On the practice of marking recovered fugitives, see Jones (1987).

[38] Though the text is corrupt, the various suggestions all yield something like this: see Courtney (1991) *ad loc.*

dangerous and decadent. In this geography of luxury, pheasants all the way from Colchis and Numidian guinea-hens are desired only because of their rarity and expense, while indigenous geese and ducks have a plebeian savor,[39] and the rose yields to the imported luxury cinnamon.[40] The analogy between women and luxurious birds which dominates Trimalchio's poem prevails here too, as the poem makes the mistress exactly equivalent to imported luxuries while the wife is the equivalent of the homegrown plain birds. But the dangers that Eumolpus condemns in the poem become a lived reality when the companions are beset by a storm on Lichas' ship. Their fellow passenger is Tryphaena, yet another rival for Giton's affections. Tryphaena, who travels about for the sake of pleasure (*voluptatis causa*, 101.5), sporting a name derived from the Greek τρυφή (luxury), and on the way now to "exile" in the notoriously luxurious city of Tarentum (100.7), thus embodies the soft luxurious women whom moralizing poems rail against.[41] The general moralizing poems connecting such women with the sea trade are made particular in her presence on Lichas' ship.

There is some disagreement among the characters over whether the presence of Encolpius and Giton on Lichas' ship is due to fortune or the vengeance of the gods. Encolpius sees it as chance: *"aliquando" inquam "totum me, Fortuna, vicisti"* ("'Now at last,' I said, 'Fortuna, you have completely conquered me,'" 101.1). Lichas reports a dream in which Priapus told him Encolpius was on board, and Tryphaena reports a similar message from Neptune about Giton (104.1–2). Eumolpus tries to convince Lichas and Tryphaena not to trust in these prophetic dreams, arguing that they are actually wish-fulfillment dreams: *"hinc scies" inquit Eumolpus "Epicurum hominem esse divinum, qui eiusmodi ludibria facetissima ratione condemnat"* ... ("'From this you will realize,' said Eumolpus, 'that Epicurus is a "godlike" man, who condemns this sort of foolishness with very witty reasoning" ..., 104.3).[42] It is plausible that a poem on dreams which survives in the Latin Anthology (fr. 43 M = AL 651) is performed by Eumolpus at this point. The poem asserts that dreams merely reflect one's waking

---

[39] E.g., Pliny *Nat.* 19.52, E.g. Hor. *S.* 2.2.14 ff.

[40] On the wide availability of roses and their popularity, see Pliny *Nat.* 13.9. On the role of cinnamon and the similar spice cassia cf. the discussion in Gowers (1993), 64, regarding Plaut. *Cas.* 217–26 where Lysidamus puns on the associations of Casina, whom he desires to have as a mistress, with the spice cassia.

[41] On Tarentum's luxury, see Strabo 6.3.4, who reports that for a time they had more public festivals than there were days in the year. For other background on the name Tryphaena, see Baldwin (1976).

[42] For further discussion of the dream sequence and its playful and parodic references to Epicurean views of dreams, see Kragelund (1989).

concerns, and emphasizes their "playful" qualities: dreams "mock minds" (*mentes ludunt*) in the first line; in the fourth line we hear that this takes place while the mind "is idle" (*mens . . . ludit*). Conventional examples of soldiers', advocates', misers', hunters', sailors', courtesans', adulterers' and dogs' dreams follow. If the poem on dreams did follow 104.3, its argument does not convince Lichas, who goes right back to Eumolpus' description of Epicurus when he suggests searching the ship anyway: *"quis" inquit "prohibet navigium scrutari, ne videamur divinae mentis opera damnare?"* ("'Who forbids,' he said, 'searching the ship, lest we seem to condemn the workings of the divine mind?'" 104.4). For Lichas the divine mind (*divinae mentis*) is not the mind of the "godlike" (*divinum*) Epicurus, but of whatever god sent the dream: in mentioning the workings of this "divine mind" Lichas sets aside the "divine" Epicurus' mockery of prophetic dreams. The ludic Epicurean account of dreams is itself discounted by Lichas' ludic redirection of Eumolpus' language. If we could be sure the poem is correctly placed here, it would even be possible to speculate that its emphatic statement that dreams are merely reiterations of what one already experiences, and its repetition of *mens* and *ludit*, are curiously reflected in the way that Lichas repeats and reformulates the terms of Eumolpus' introductory assertion about Epicurus and his witty reasoning.

Eumolpus' *elegidarion* on sudden baldness (109.9–10), composed for his companions after they have shaved their heads in a futile attempt to disguise themselves on Lichas' ship, is an amusingly extravagant version of the kinds of moralizing about mortality that we see in Trimalchio's epigrams. Baldness is connected to the "seasons" of life, *vernantesque comas tristis abegit hiemps* ("gloomy winter has driven off blooming locks"), and the word for bald spot (*area*) also evokes the threshing floor (*area*); both are scorched (*adusta*) by the sun.[43] In general baldness is the sign of the body's mortality (5–6):

> o fallax natura deum: quae prima dedisti
> aetati nostrae gaudia, prima rapis.

> O deceiving nature of the gods: the joys which you gave
> first to our youth you snatch away first.

At this point there seems to be a break; the verses resume in hendecasyllabics and address Encolpius in more personal terms. The allusions to nature continue, as Eumolpus says how attractive Encolpius and Giton looked with hair (more lovely than Phoebus and his sister) and how ludicrous they look now (smoother than polished bronze or a

---

[43] See Courtney (1991), on 109.9.4

round truffle). And, he adds, baldness will show how quickly death will come (15–16):

> ut mortem citius venire credas,
> scito iam capitis perisse partem.

> So you'll believe that death comes quicker than you think,
> know that part of your head is already dead.

After the poem, the "misfortune" of suddenly contrived baldness and its intimations of mortality pass away quickly when Encolpius and Giton are restored to curly-haired bliss as Tryphaena's maid provides them with her mistress' wigs.

Initially, Eumolpus' trivializing of death in his verses on baldness seems ridiculous. But like Trimalchio's, Eumolpus' short poetic performances are constructed in such a way as to set what is general and metaphorical in the poems against what is particular and concrete in the prose frame. His first poem makes him enter the text like a poetry book; his second poem on luxury and the dangerous sea voyages which bring it to Rome ironically foreshadows his own involvement in the subsequent sea voyage with Lichas and the luxurious Tryphaena. How are the verses on baldness sharpened by their position in the narrative frame? According to a superstitious view of events, the sudden baldness of Encolpius and Giton did lead directly to the shipwreck and thus to Lichas' death. Hesus, who saw Encolpius and Giton while their heads were being shaved, interpreted their action as a bad omen because at sea only those threatened by shipwreck would cut off their hair and dedicate it to the gods: *execratusque omen, quod imitaretur naufragorum ultimum votum* ("he cursed the omen as being like the final prayer of the shipwrecked," 103.5). Later he adds, *"audio enim non licere cuiquam mortalium in nave neque ungues neque capillos deponere nisi cum pelago ventus irascitur"* ("For I hear that it is not permitted to any mortal on board a ship to cut his nails or hair except while the wind and the sea rage," 104.5). Lichas plans to punish the culprits with forty lashes each to expiate their transgression, but this is interrupted when Giton and Encolpius are recognized, though Lichas later insists on the punishment being carried out and Tryphaena agrees (106.3–4). Eumolpus intervenes verbally and physically to prevent the beating, and eventually a struggle breaks out which is only brought to an end by Tryphaena's peace-making (107–8). Thus, in the superstitious interpretation, by ordering that Encolpius' and Giton's hair be cut Eumolpus himself becomes part of the cause of the shipwreck.[44] When the

---

[44] Lichas also thinks that the fact that clothing and a sistrum belonging to Isis were stolen from the ship causes the ship to be vulnerable (114.5, and see further Ciaffi [1955], 16–17).

ship is overwhelmed by the storm and Lichas dies, Eumolpus' frivolous verses on sudden baldness as a reminder of death take on foreboding undertones.[45]

Encolpius *poeta*

In the surviving fragments, thirteen short poems are clearly or apparently attributable to Encolpius.[46] His status as poetic performer differs from that of the other characters because he controls the narrative framing of his verses in a more complete way than any of them do. From what we can tell, Encolpius composes most of these poems not as a performance for his fellow characters but as a sophisticated self-deprecating commentary on his earlier naïveté.[47] Two appear when he loses Giton to Ascyltus; the others are concentrated in the episodes with Circe and Oenothea at Croton. He does not perform in front of Eumolpus. Five poems which make the most overt use of epic material have been discussed in chapter 1.[48] These verses establish a rhythm in their episodes. Encolpius finds himself in situations where erotic satisfaction seems possible; he celebrates in verse, only to narrate his dashed hopes in prose. Then he apparently rounds off the episode with generalized verses on fortune or disappointment. Vulgar or ridiculous events in the prose frame are repeatedly and indecently rubbing up against idealizing verses on love or the vagaries of fortune. The effect is generally a discordant one, characterized aptly in Dronke's remarks on verse in the Circe episode: "The total story here is simultaneously the demeaning happenings and half-theatricalised emotions in the prose, and the fleeting thoughts and images of erotic perfection in the poetry. It lies in the way these discordant elements act upon each other."[49] Still, just as Trimalchio's and Eumolpus' poetic conventions are sharpened by the connections contrived between the verse and its prose frame, so too the relations of Encolpius' poetry to its prose frame create both an obvious impression of discord and a more subtle – and funny – impression of coherence. He constructs the poems in such a way that the poetic metaphors and images themselves, conventional and un-

---

[45] On the ironies of Lichas' name and the ways in which his swift and terrified disappearance into the sea (*Sat.* 114.4–6) evokes the ancient Lichas who was hurled into the sea by Hercules (Ov. *Met.* 9.211–29) see Barchiesi (1984), 173–75.

[46] *Sat.* 79.8, 80.9, 126.18, 127.9, 128.6, 131.8, 132.8, 132.15, 133.3, 135.8, 136.6, 137.9, 139.2.

[47] This is emphasized by Beck (1973).

[48] 127.9, 132.8, 135.8, 136.6, 139.2.

[49] Dronke (1994), 12.

remarkable enough in their own terms, ironically undercut the erotic idealization they ostensibly project.

First the Giton episode: after recounting the dinner with Trimalchio, Encolpius celebrates the pleasures of love when narrating a night spent with Giton (79.8):

> qualis nox fuit illa, di deaeque,
> quam mollis torus. haesimus calentes
> et transfudimus hinc et hinc labellis
> errantes animas. valete, curae
> mortales. ego sic perire coepi.

> What a night it was, gods and goddesses,
> how soft the bed. Feverishly we clung together
> and in kisses we poured out our wandering souls
> on this side and that side. Farewell mortal cares.
> So I began to die.

Sex is straightforwardly celebrated: souls pass from one mouth into the other in kisses, cares are bid farewell, and sex is figured as "death."[50] Though the motifs are standard ones (indeed, Petronius repeats the soul-mixing at 132.1), the poem's particular language of passion, with its emphasis on wandering, parting, and death, turns out to have been chosen for maximum ironic effect, which Encolpius as narrator signals by dryly resuming in prose with *sine causa gratulor mihi* ("I call myself happy for no reason," 79.9). Ascyltos takes Giton into his bed; upon discovering the treachery, Encolpius wonders whether to make their sleep into death; after a parodically mortal struggle, Ascyltos stipulates that Giton choose which companion he prefers, and Giton departs with Ascyltos (79.9–80.8). In the poem *errantes* clearly refers simply to the souls wandering from mouth to mouth, but when betrayal and departure ensue, the word's other associations with making mistakes and wandering off seem oddly apt too. In other contexts *transfundo* can be used of indiscriminately transferred affections (e.g. Cic. *Phil.* 2.77); with Giton's choice its presence in the poem is ironically prophetic. Even the first word *qualis* displays an ironic openness: the sort of night it first seems in verse is transformed in prose – though by now we know to expect Encolpius' passionate moments to be interrupted. The episode is rounded out with four lines on the fickleness of friends who remain only so long as *fortuna* remains (80.9.1–4), to which the epigram comparing the novel's action to a mime has been

---

[50] See especially Prop. 2.15, "Plato" *AP* 5.78 (with Gell. 19.11.2), and the passages collected by Stubbe (1933), 170. On *perire* see Prop. 1.10.5 and Adams (1982), 159.

attached (80.9.5–8, discussed above at p. 13). The *fortuna* poem, which as we shall see below participates in the novel's treatment of the power of chance, fits oddly into its frame here, for the aggression of Ascyltos has separated Encolpius from Giton, rather than any discernible reversal of fortune.[51] These reflections on *fortuna* seem to mask the "real" reasons for the loss of Giton. A similar mixing of love and luck shapes a poem Encolpius introduces after Circe has left him in disgust: he compares his erotic frustration to waking from a dream of finding buried treasure (128.6).

In the surviving text, Encolpius' most concentrated poetic performances take place in the Circe episode and its aftermath. Here too an ironic network of imagery connects the prose frame with the inserted verses. On beholding Circe, Encolpius lists her physical perfections with an effect that is rather Pygmalionesque: hair, face, eyes, nose, mouth, neck, hands, feet are all elaborately described, with the final summary: *Parium marmor extinxerat* ("She had quenched the glow of [or outshone] Parian marble," 126.14–17). The comparison to Parian marble is a standard one, similar, for example, to Horace's description of Glycera: *urit me Glycerae nitor/splendentis Pario marmore purius* ("The glow of Glycera, shining brighter than Parian marble, burns me" ..., *C.* 1.19.5–6) or the chorus in Seneca's *Phaedra* saying of Hippolytus, *lucebit Pario marmore clarius* ("[this face] will shine more brilliantly than Parian marble," 797). But Petronius slightly changes the terms of the comparison. Where Glycera glowing like marble burns Horace, Circe quenches the glow of the marble itself. The metaphor of putting out a fire in *extinxerat* seems chosen not just for novelty value but also to set up a joke. When Encolpius next measures Circe against beautiful women in myth, he marvels in verse that Jupiter has not come down to rape or seduce her, and again he uses figurative language connected with fire (126.18):

> ... tempta modo tangere corpus,
> iam tua flammifero membra calore fluent

> ... just start to touch her body,
> and your limbs will melt with fiery heat.

Clearly, Encolpius is predicting in the poem that he himself will be "on fire" for Circe, and Beck suggests that he performs this poem for Circe.[52] If so, she flirtatiously seizes on this when she says that a great flame always arises between lovers named Circe and Polyaenus (*semper inter haec nomina magna fax surgit* [with a double entendre in *surgit*]

---

[51] As Slater (1990), 164, notes.   [52] Beck (1973), 50.

127.7). But when they lie down together, Encolpius cannot perform. Circe's power to extinguish has in effect "extinguished" the flames of passion. The fire imagery in the Circe sequence allows the interplay between desire and frustration to be more complex than a simple contrast between prose and verse. In chapter 1 we saw a similar complexity on display in Encolpius' transplant of roses into the Homeric *hieros gamos*. A subsequent poem, also apparently part of the Circe sequence and drawing more on pastoral traditions perhaps, describes a spot for a lovers' assignation as a place fit for love, *dignus amore locus* (131.8):[53]

> mobilis aestivas platanus diffuderat umbras
> et bacis redimita Daphne tremulaeque cupressus
> et circum tonsae trepidanti vertice pinus.
> has inter ludebat aquis errantibus amnis
> spumeus et querulo vexabat rore lapillos.
> dignus amore locus: testis silvestris aedon
> atque urbana Procne, quae circum gramina fusae
> et molles violas cantu †sua rura colebant†

> The mobile plane tree had spread out summertime shade,
> and Daphne adorned with berries, and the trembling cypresses,
> and the shorn pines, with their swaying tops.
> Amid these trees played a bubbling stream with wandering waters;
> it stirred up the pebbled stream bed with its plaintive flow.
> A spot fit for love: of this the nightingale from the woods is a witness,
> and Procne, the swallow from the city; scattered through the
>   meadows
> and the tender violets, they filled their haunts with song.

The idyllic landscape contains the shade of various trees, a stream, and birdsong. But the actual phrases used to designate these traditional features hint at disappointment and frustration. In the choice of the Greek word Daphne instead of the Latin *laurus* for the laurel tree, Apollo's thwarted desire for Daphne is evoked. The adjective *redimita* "adorned with" ironically transfers to the laurel tree the vocabulary appropriate to the wearing of laurel crowns (cf. *Aen.* 3.81, of Anius, a priest of Apollo). The cypress recalls Apollo's disappointment in the death of his beloved Cyparissus.[54] The pine too is associated elsewhere with the failed attempt of Pan to win Pitys.[55] The birds whose song fills the air are the nightingale and the swallow, *silvestris aedon atque urbana Procne*; the aetiological tale of Procne and Philomela is hardly a good

---

[53] Courtney (1991) does not obelize *sua rura colebant* in the last line.
[54] Ov. *Met.* 1.452–567; 10.106–42.
[55] Nonnus *Dion.* 42.258–60, cf. Longus *Daphnis and Chloe* 1.27.

omen for a love affair. The stream too has undercurrents suggesting trouble for these lovers. The metaphor of plaintive complaining used to describe the sound of the stream (*querulo ... rore*), and the generally violent connotations of *vexo* suggest that this ideal lovers' landscape might contain its own shifts between pleasure and discontent. If the plane tree is *mobilis* (following R, with Courtney; other manuscripts have *nobilis*) trembling in a light breeze, then it is probably important that this word can also carry connotations of fickleness and changeability.

Driven away from Circe's house (presumably for sexual failure), Encolpius retreats to bed. Structurally, the scene parallels Encolpius' soliloquy on the beach after his loss of Giton (81). It is hard to say much about the function of the verses on Tantalus at 82.5, but by drawing attention to connections made elsewhere between Tantalus' frustrated desire and the frustration of erotic desire, Di Simone has recently made an attractive argument that the verses on Tantalus could aptly follow the impotence episode described in 132.1.[56] After his sotadeans and his "shocking" quotation of Virgil, Encolpius is ashamed at his shamelessness and blushes though no one can see him (*coepi secreto ... rubore perfundi*, "... I began to be covered with a secret blush," 132.12). Then, overcoming this shame, he braves himself to speak in his own defense, *mox perfricata diutius fronte* ("soon, having rubbed my forehead for quite a while," 132.13), and utters a poem in elegiacs to cap his apology for candor (132.15):[57]

> quid me constricta spectatis fronte Catones
>   damnatisque novae simplicitatis opus?
> sermonis puri non tristis gratia ridet,
>   quodque facit populus, candida lingua refert.
> nam quis concubitus, Veneris quis gaudia nescit?
>   quis vetat in tepido membra calere toro?
> ipse pater veri doctos Epicurus amare
>   iussit et hoc vitam dixit habere τέλος.

> Catos, why do you look at me with furrowed brow
>   and condemn this work of new directness?
> The light-hearted charm of my simple language is delightful,
>   whatever people do, my lucid tongue reports.

---

[56] Di Simone (1993).

[57] Because Tacitus attributes to Petronius the appearance of frankness (*speciem simplicitatis, Ann.* 16.18.2), some have read this poem as a direct address by Petronius to his readers which defends the sexual frankness of the whole *Satyricon*: Sullivan (1968a), 98–102; Collignon (1892), 53. Clearly though it is best to read this poem within the frame of Encolpius' character: Beck (1973), 50–53; cf. Slater (1990), 129, 165–66; Panayotakis (1995), 175–76.

> For who does not know about sleeping together, and the joys of
>   Venus?
> Who forbids warming up the body in a cozy bed?
> Epicurus himself, father of truth, told learned men to love,
>   and said that life had this as its end.

Because it was notoriously difficult to make the younger Cato laugh
(Plut. *Cat. Min.* 1.2), his stern gaze served as a popular image of severe
moral standards.[58] A famous anecdote dramatized the notion: when
Cato was in attendance at the Floralia, the audience was apparently
reluctant to exhort the mime actresses to perform their customary
strip-tease. In effect, Cato becomes arbiter of the spectacle he has
come to watch. Realizing that his presence was inhibiting the spectacle,
Cato departed, and thus withdrew his arresting gaze. The anecdote
of Cato's withdrawn gaze opposes mime and moralizing, specifying
for each an appropriate time and space: the audience, the performers,
and Cato all know the rules.[59] Martial, for his part, snidely asks
whether Cato went to the Floralia in the first place just so he could
make a spectacle of his departure (1. praef.). Encolpius' Cato poem,
like the *Satyricon*'s numerous references to mime, associates the
Satyricon's narrative with mime's festive license.

Part of a pattern of opportunistic references to Epicureanism in the
Satyricon, in a neat correspondence of form and content, the poem
ends with the word for end, τέλος, which "footnotes" the parodic
distortion of the ideas advanced in Epicurus' περὶ τέλους.[60] In fact, in
the framing of the poem too Encolpius takes representations of Epicurus himself as a model. Cicero and Athenaeus both emphasize Epicurus' boldness in putting forward the assertion in this work that
physical enjoyments are central to "the good." According to Athenaeus, Epicurus spoke these things shouting (ὃς καὶ βοῶν ἔλεγεν, Ath.
7.280 a–b). Cicero imagines that Epicurus has to wipe away a blush:
*quid tergiversamur, Epicure, nec fatemur eam nos dicere voluptatem, quam
tu idem, cum os perfricuisti, soles dicere?* ("Why do we hesitate, Epicurus,
and not say that we are talking about the same kind of pleasure which
you yourself talk about once you have rubbed away the blush from your

---

58 Cf. Mart. 10.19.21, 11.2.1; Phaedr. 4.7.21, and for another address to "severe" readers, Ov. *Am.* 2.1.3.
59 For the anecdote see Val. Max. 2.10.8; Sen. *Ep.* 97.8, 10. In an epigram of Martial's
   (9.28) a mime actor proclaims that he is so talented he could make Cato himself stay for
   the show.
60 For recent discussion of Epicurus' understanding of the *telos* of life see Purinton (1993)
   with further bibliography. Epicurean ideas are parodied at *Sat.* 104.3, fr. 28 M (=AL
   466 = 465 SB), fr. 42 M (=AL 650), fr. 43 M (=AL 651), fr. 48 M (=AL 694); see
   Courtney (1991), 11–14, reacting to Raith (1963).

cheek?" *Tusc.* 3.41). In rubbing away his blush, Encolpius recapitulates the gesture imaginatively attributed by Cicero to Epicurus himself: before quoting Epicurus in verse he describes himself in terms which seem to fit the way in which Epicurus is imagined to have moved. Even in the Epicurean tradition there is the notion of the power of the gaze to induce shame. So Seneca quotes Epicurus in a discussion of the inhibiting power of shame: *sic fac, inquit, omnia, tamquam spectet Epicurus* ("Do everything, he [Epicurus] said, as though Epicurus is watching," *Ep.* 25.5). Seneca translates the image to the Roman situation by suggesting that one imagine that Cato (this seems to be the elder Cato) or Scipio, or if a less severe option is desirable, Laelius, is watching everything one does.[61] This notion of the availability of one's every action to the gaze of Epicurus is seriously translated for Romans by Seneca, substituting a Cato for Epicurus, and is parodically exploited by Petronius, contrasting *Catones* with Epicurus, and asserting that "whatever people do, my lucid tongue reports."

When Encolpius placates Oenothea by offering her money as recompense for killing her goose, he celebrates in a poem. The neat moralizing appealed to the person who made the exemplar of the manuscripts of the O class, for he decides to end his *Satyricon* with this poem (thus avoiding the obscenity of the remaining scenes at Oenothea's and elsewhere in Croton). Encolpius begins with the claim that the wealthy can control fortune to suit themselves (137.9, with Courtney's *Danae* for the manuscripts' *Danaen* in line 4):

> quisquis habet nummos, secura navigat aura
>   fortunamque suo temperat arbitrio.
> uxorem ducat Danaen ipsumque licebit
>   Acrisium iubeat credere quod Danae.
> carmina componat, declamet, concrepet omnes
>   et peragat causas sitque Catone prior.
> iurisconsultus "parret, non parret" habeto
>   atque esto quicquid Servius et Labeo.
> multa loquor: quod vis nummis praesentibus opta,
>   et veniet. clausum possidet arca Iovem.

> Whoever has cash sails with a safe wind
>   and directs fortune according to his own wishes.
> He will be able to marry Danae
>   and bid Acrisius himself to believe what Danae believes.

---

[61] Sen. *Ep.* 25.6, and see too the similar precept in Seneca's letter on blushing *Ep.* 11.8–10.

> Let him compose poetry, declaim, he'd snap his fingers at everyone
>   and plead cases and be better than Cato.
> As a lawyer, he shall have "proven, not proven"
>   and be all that Servius and Labeo were.
> I say many things: choose what you will with money at hand,
>   and it will come. The money chest has Jove enclosed in it.

From the general statement that a man with money can direct fortune as he likes, the poem moves to the debased and rationalized version of the myth of Danae in which the visitation of Jove as a shower of gold becomes a lover's illicit bribe. After the list of poetic, declamatory, and legal successes that come with money, the poem's final claim that a money box contains Jove shut up within it (*clausum possidet arca Iovem*, 137.9.10) neatly reverses the myth of Danae shut up in a chest with her son Perseus and put out to sea. The poem is introduced as a celebration of Encolpius' placation of Oenothea by the offer of money. But as in other poems, these rather placid generalizations contain hints of future disappointments. For one thing, the claim that wealth can make the sea safe is plainly implausible. Encolpius collapses a conventional opposition between chance and design, that is between *fortuna* – especially as figured in shipwreck – and *arbitrium*, which we see affirmed, for example, in Horace's figuring the wind Notus as an *arbiter* of the Adriatic (*C.* 1.3.15). Like the mythical chest of Danae, which Acrisius set adrift at sea to protect himself from danger, the poem itself contains the materials of its speaker's undoing. The fatal "shipwreck" obviously intended for Danae and Perseus by Acrisius never takes place. Shutting Danae showered with gold in a chest for safekeeping was no protection for Acrisius, and the constant lesson of Roman moralizing is that a chest full of money is no protection at all against reversals of fortune. There may be a metaliterary irony here too. In a marvellously suggestive essay, Barchiesi has recently argued that the name Arbiter is an especially apt description of the kind of unseen control which Petronius exerts over his narrative.[62] Along these lines, this poem too is open to a self-reflexive reading which lays bare the fiction of chance: in ironically signaling Encolpius' usual inability to subject *fortuna* to his *arbitrium*, it acknowledges that the ultimate control over *fortuna* in the *Satyricon* is of course wielded by Petronius Arbiter. Unbound by the traditional rules of established genres, free of the constraints imposed by legendary characters, he devises a plot to his own design – that is, until *fortuna* and excerptors had their way with the text.

---

[62] Barchiesi (forthcoming).

fortuna, naufragium, arbitrium

The foregoing suggestions about the *Satyricon*'s participation in a discourse which opposes chance and design can be taken further still in interpreting the "real" shipwreck which the characters suffer. In the Lichas episode, Petronius juxtaposes literal and figurative storms while alluding to the moralizing use of shipwreck as a figure for life's unpredictability.[63]

The first such juxtaposition is discernible in a small pun which frames Tryphaena's "epic" rebuke of her companions for fighting. Why fight battles like these, she asks, when the sea itself is full of uncertainty and danger? (*Sat.* 108.14):

> "quis furor" exclamat "pacem convertit in arma?
> quid nostrae meruere manus? non Troius heros
> hac in classe vehit decepti pignus Atridae,
> nec Medea furens fraterno sanguine pugnat.
> sed contemptus amor vires habet. ei mihi, fata
> hos inter fluctus quis raptis evocat armis?
> cui non est mors una satis? ne vincite pontum
> gurgitibusque feris alios immittite fluctus."

> "What madness," she cries, "turns peace to war?
> What blame have our hands incurred? The Trojan hero
> does not carry off cuckolded Menelaus' wife in this ship,
> nor does raging Medea do battle by killing her brother.
> But despised love is powerful. Ah me, who summons death
> by snatching up arms amid waves like these?
> For whom is one death not enough? Do not outdo the sea
> and send new waves upon its fierce swirling waters."

As Slater acutely notes, the presence of *exclamat* ("she exclaims") in the opening line points to a tension between lived reality and literary conventions: "The hearer/reader suddenly wonders: did Aeneas and the other characters of epic really go about speaking to each other in hexameters? What parts of their speeches were effaced by the frame when the narrator inserts *exclamat* or *ait* into a passage of direct discourse?"[64] Other linguistic details of this passage also measure lived reality and literarily figured language against each other. Tryphaena's last line neatly juxtaposes the real "swirling waters" (*gurgitibus*) where the ship sails with the metaphorical "new waves" (*alios ... fluctus*) of the

---

[63] For background on the representation of sea-storms in Latin literature, see Morford (1967), 20–36.

[64] Slater (1990), 173.

quarrelling: like Trimalchio she uses verse opportunistically to create correspondences between figurative language and lived reality. Encolpius as narrator takes this punning a step further by describing Tryphaena's utterance in language which suits the meteorological dangers her poem hints at: *haec ut turbato clamore mulier effudit* ("as the woman poured forth these words with a stormy outburst ..." 109.1). The verb *turbo* can be used of stirring up the sea (*OLD* s.v. 2); *effundo* can be found in connection with pouring rain (*OLD* s.v. 2); and *clamor* can be used in connection with thunder (*OLD* s.v. 5). Though none of these words individually must evoke a storm metaphor for every reader, in combination and in context for a reader attuned to Petronius' practice, the poem cataloguing epic motifs could become a storm of sorts itself, foreshadowing the epic-influenced storm that will destroy the ship (114).[65]

The storm itself begins with another type of pun: *dum haec taliaque iactamus, inhorruit mare* ... ("while we toss off these words and other such things, the sea shuddered ..." *Sat.* 114.1). Because there is a break in the text, we do not know exactly what is referred to by *haec*. Petronius' phrasing *taliaque iactamus* could be read as a borrowing from Virgil's description of Aeneas' speech in the face of the rising storm at the beginning of the *Aeneid*: *talia iactanti* ... ("tossing off such words ..." *Aen.* 1.102). The verb *iacto* can be used in many contexts to denote bold utterances, but Virgil is already setting its various meanings against each other here by describing his "storm-tossed" hero (*iactatus, Aen.* 1.3) with the active form of the participle *iactanti*: Aeneas hurls words out in the face of the rising storm while the storm in turn tosses him about on the sea. It is not really the case that one meaning (the sea tossing a ship) is more or less figurative than another (a person tossing words). Virgil is clearly playing the two senses against each other, and Petronius is glossing Virgil's linguistic move by bringing the tossing of words and the heaving of the sea into the same sentence.

Yet another kind of pun, derived not from epic but from the moralizing tradition, emerges on the day after the shipwreck, when Encolpius discovers a corpse on the shore and launches into a lament for the dead man in highly rhetorical prose. When a wave shifts the body, he realizes it is Lichas, at which point the lament becomes even more rhetorical (115.7–19). Sullivan has argued that Petronius is parodying Senecan moralizing here,[66] and it is clear enough that Petronius is evoking

---

[65] On this storm's evocation of the storm at the opening of the *Aeneid*, see Collignon (1892), 126–28, Walsh (1970), 37, Zeitlin (1971a), 67.

[66] Sullivan (1968a), 196–204 and see 195 n. 1 for references to earlier scholarship.

moralizing conventions (as we see for example in the fact that the florilegia select some of his remarks at 115.16–18). Looking at Seneca's
more straightforward use of these conventions will clarify Petronius'
humorous manipulation of them. Seneca uses the figure of shipwreck
on numerous occasions. In giving philosophical advice, Seneca represents philosophy as a force which can keep one safe from the storms of
fortune.[67] In his consolation texts, he uses the figure of sea-storms and
shipwreck to argue that all of life is unpredictable.[68] It is this notion
that Petronius parodies in Encolpius' outburst. Death comes from all
sorts of causes: war, collapsing buildings, wagon accidents, gluttony,
austerity. Accurate reckoning reveals every area of life to be dangerous;
nowhere offers a guarantee of safety: *si bene calculum ponas, ubique
naufragium est* ("if you reckon well, shipwreck is everywhere," 115.16).
In the *Consolatio ad Marciam* Seneca says that Marcia should be re-
strained in her grief for her son because every stage of life represents a
loss of the ones before – young manhood is the loss of youth, and so
on: *incrementa ipsa, si bene computes, damna sunt* ("those stages of
growth, if you reckon well, are losses," *Dial.* 6.21.7). In the *Consolatio
ad Polybium*, Seneca argues that death is a release from life's uncertainties: *si bene computes, plus illi remissum quam ereptum est* ("If you
reckon well, more was granted to him [in death] than was snatched
away," *Dial.* 11.9.4). In both of these consolatory arguments, Seneca
uses the phrase "if you reckon well" to coerce the grieving reader to
go along with the counter-intuitive arguments that death is not loss
but gain, and life is not gain, but loss. Part of what is funny about
the Petronian scene is thus the utter obviousness of this observation:
there is nothing counter-intuitive about it – in the midst of shipwreck,
of course shipwreck *is* everywhere. Even the vocabulary of reckoning
contributes to the construction of coherence between the figurative and
the literal. One expression of "if you reckon well" would be *si bene
computes*; but standing on a shore, Encolpius uses a description of
reckoning that includes pebbles – already implicit in the shoreline
landscape where he speaks.

In a broader, thematic way, the poems which survive in the Anthology use this moralizing discourse about chance, design and shipwreck
too. Because the poems lack a specific narrative context, we sometimes
cannot tell whether they commented on literal dangers at sea, or used

---

[67] On philosophy as *gubernator* (helmsman) see *Ep.* 16.3, 30.3, and for a counter example
of a bad teacher compared to a sea-sick *gubernator*, *Ep.* 108.37; on a life of philosophical
detachment as a safe harbor see *Dial.* 7.19.1, 10.18.1

[68] *Dial.* 6.6.3, 6.15.4, 11.9.6–7; *Ep.* 99.9.

the dangerous sea as a metaphor for the toils of life. In one, arrival into
a safe harbor is celebrated; a note of ironic foreboding about troubles
yet to come intrudes in this poem's insistence that *fortuna malignior*
cannot take away pleasures which have already been enjoyed.[69] Another
poem argues that poverty brings safe obscurity while wealth makes a
man a target: in a shipwreck, gold falls to the bottom of the sea, while
an oar can save a life.[70] A denunciation of modern decadence decries
sea trade,[71] and shipwreck is mentioned in a series of typical misfor-
tunes.[72] One poem contrasts the dangers of the sea with the safer and
simpler water-related pursuits on shore.[73] A charming poem cautions
against the dangers of the sea by praising the delights of the pebbly
shoreline:[74]

> qui non vult properare mori nec cogere fata
>   mollia praecipiti rumpere fila manu,
> hactenus iratum mare noverit. ecce refuso
>   gurgite securos obluit unda pedes;
> ecce inter virides iactatur mytilus algas
>   et rauco trahitur lubrica concha sono;
> ecce recurrentes qua versat fluctus harenas
>   discolor attrita calculus exit humo.
> haec quisquis calcare potest, in litore tuto
>   ludat et hoc solum iudicet esse mare.

Whoever does not want to hasten toward death, nor to force the fates
   to snap the fine thread with a hasty hand,
let him know only this much of the angry sea. See how the
   wave washes over his feet in safety as the swell of the sea flows back;
see how a mussel is tossed amid green seaweed,
   and the slippery conch is dragged along with a hollow sound;
see, where the wave churns up the sands hastening back into the sea,
   there a many-colored pebble emerges from the sand as it is washed
      away.
Whoever can tread on these things, let him play on a safe shore,
   and let him judge that this alone is the sea.

This catalogue of mussel, seaweed, conch, and pebble sets the delicate
pleasures of the shore in stark contrast with the vast dangers of the
unpredictable sea. Indeed, the poem virtually equates going to sea with

---

[69] Fr. 36 M = AL 474 R = 472 SB.
[70] Fr. 32 M = AL 470 R = 468 SB.
[71] Fr. 34 M = AL 472 R = 470 SB.
[72] Fr. 46 M = AL 692 R. Gagliardi (1980), 115, proposes that this is the epigram composed by Eumolpus in commemoration of the death of Lichas.
[73] Fr. 39 M = AL 477 R = 475 SB.
[74] Fr. 40 M = AL 478 R = 476 SB.

suicide. A comparable sentiment is voiced in Ovid's *Amores* 2.11, in which the poet wishes his beloved would not make a sea journey and then imagines her safe return. Ovid says that the sea is uniform, while the shells and pebbles of the shore have a pleasing variety (*Am.* 2.11.12–14):

> non illic urbes, non tu mirabere silvas:
>   una est iniusti caerula forma maris;
> nec medius tenuis conchas pictosque lapillos
>   pontus habet: bibuli litoris illa mora est.

> You won't marvel at cities or forests there:
>   the blue look of the capricious sea is all the same;
> and the middle of the ocean has no delicate shells or colored pebbles:
>   those are what one lingers over on the thirsty shore.

The poet imagines that the shells and pebbles of the shore would be pleasing to his beloved, and she will miss them if she takes to the ocean. The pebbles thus reflect in miniature the whole erotic enterprise of elegy: the poet and his poems focus on what is pleasing to girls.

The Petronian poem's representation of shoreline delights reflects the *Satyricon*'s overarching treatment of the theme of chance. The characters frequently acknowledge the power of *fortuna* over their lives, and a plot twist is referred to as the game (*lusus*) of *fortuna* when they find the lost cloak and think that it still has the gold sewn into its seams (13.1).[75] Pebbles, or *calculi*, were used for reckoning in games and in accounting, and the *discolor calculus* is mentioned as a game piece in accounts of Roman games.[76] Elsewhere in the *Satyricon* the mutability of fortune is figured as calculations with pebbles, as we have just seen in Encolpius' phrase "if you reckon well," *si bene calculum ponas* (115.16). His poetic response to Giton's departure uses the figure too: *calculus in tabula mobile ducit opus./dum fortuna manet, vultum servatis, amici* ("the calculating pebble does volatile work at the board./ While fortune remains, you friends keep your faces attentive... ," 80.9.2–3). The same words, *calculus* and *tabula* (board), could be used to describe the apparatus of gaming and of accounting. In this poem the calculating pebble seems a device of accounting, but, because accounts keep track of one's monetary *fortuna*, the sense of a token in a game played by *fortuna* is not far off. The overlap between gaming and accounts is dramatized in Trimalchio's entrance into the *triclinium*, playing a game in which he uses gold and silver coins instead of white and black *calculi* (*Sat.* 33.2). This recapitulates the money counting being done by

---

[75] 101.1, 114.8; Callebat (1974), 289.   [76] Mart. 14.17, cf. Ov. *Tr.* 2.477.

the *dispensator* whom Encolpius sees on his way into the dining room (30.9). Against this background of associations between *fortuna* and calculating pebbles, it is possible to imagine that the person who plays (*ludat*) by the shore takes up the *calculi* revealed by the waves, and plays some kind of game of chance with them: the image of safety by the shore includes within itself the kinds of calculations with pebbles that are elsewhere associated with sudden shifts of fortune. Going to sea puts the game wholly in fortuna's hands, staying on shore keeps it closer to being in one's own power.

Moralizing discourse about the capricious power of fortune can be exploited to mask or to unmask the machinations of an emperor who himself becomes the source of capricious destruction. So Seneca can compare the quiet pursuit of philosophy which keeps one safe from arousing the anger of the powerful to the prudent piloting of a ship away from a storm (*Ep.* 14.7–8). The figuring of the mutability of fortune as a game of chance is central to a Senecan anecdote in the *de tranquillitate animi* about a certain Julius Canus' extraordinary peace of mind in the face of the emperor's caprice. Sentenced to death by Caligula, he was playing a game when he was summoned to his execution. He left with a warning to his opponent not to claim that he (the opponent) won, and with an appeal to the centurion to witness the fact that he (Canus) was ahead by one. "Do you think he was playing a game (*lusisse*)?" Seneca asks, "He mocked one (*inlusit*)!" (*Dial.* 9.14.7). Here too the figure of the storm of fortune is used, for Canus' calm in the face of the emperor's will is remarked as, *ecce in media tempestate tranquillitas* ("see the calm amidst the storm," *Dial.* 9.14.9). By creating this "storm" to overwhelm Canus, the emperor, rather than nature, becomes the source of capricious destruction.

Though no one can contrive a calm sea, shipwrecks can be arranged, theatrically or otherwise. In the course of arguing in the *de Ira* that true passions arise with the participation of the mind and are thus susceptible to control by reason, Seneca remarks that the sadness (*tristitia*) "which furrows the brow at the sight of a mimic shipwreck" is not a real passion because it has merely been provoked by the spectacle (*Dial.* 4.2.5). Conceivably, the mimic shipwreck could have been staged on land, like the action of Plautus' *Rudens*. But Seneca's focus on sadness perhaps indicates one of the aquatic spectacles which became increasingly popular in the empire:[77] if the spectacle is to be intense enough to move the audience in this way, it probably has to be

---

[77] See Coleman (1993) on the staging of sea battles and aquatic mythical scenes.

staged with real water; if the action is on land as in the *Rudens*, only survivors speak.

The fiction of chance on display in a "mimic shipwreck" could encourage in its audience a certain amount of moral reflection about the unpredictability of fortune.[78] But in Nero's court such fictions take a sinister turn: *nihil tam capax fortuitorum quam mare* ("nothing is as full of accidents as the sea," *Ann.* 14.3), says Tacitus when recounting the reasoning that led Nero to think in 59 that he could have Agrippina killed by the collapsible boat without arousing suspicion. In the *Octavia*'s account of Nero's contrived shipwreck, the presence of the conventional elements of literary shipwrecks brought about by natural causes serves to highlight the unnaturalness of the collapsible boat[79] – itself based, Dio says (62.12.2), on a boat in a theatrical spectacle of some sort which had broken apart to release wild animals and then come back together again. In Tacitus' account, after the boat collapsed and Agrippina made her way to shore, she realized that her only way to safety was to seize the fiction of chance herself and send a message to Nero that by his good luck (*fortuna eius*) she had escaped death in the shipwreck (Tac. *Ann.* 14.6). But of course Nero's murderous impulse was not deterred, and Tacitus says that in writing to the Senate about her murder, which he justified on the grounds that Agrippina had plotted to kill him, Nero once again seizes the fiction of chance, saying that she had been killed *publica fortuna*, "providentially to the benefit of the state." In this communication Nero also mentioned the shipwreck (implying that the shipwreck showed that it was Agrippina's *fortuna* to die). According to Tacitus, the audience understands his manipulations of the fiction of chance as manipulations. Tacitus asks, "Who could be found so dim-witted as to believe that it [the shipwreck] had been fortuitous?" and remarks that Nero's words, composed by Seneca, were read as a virtual confession of matricide (*Ann.* 14.11).[80]

As novelist, Petronius manipulates the conventional discourse which used the terms *fortuna*, *arbitrium*, and *naufragium* as ways of talking about the uncontrollability of life. In the *Satyricon*'s prose fiction, without the narrower constraints of other literary forms, anything can happen to the characters: Petronius is *fortuna* in devising these fic-

---

[78] See Rawson (1987) on the impact of popular moralizing in a theatrical context: "coherent plotting and consistent characterization may have counted for little, immediate effect been crucial; but the *sententiae* seem to have been almost as important as the singing," p. 80.

[79] So Williams (1994a), 178.

[80] See further Bartsch (1994), 20–22. For other imperial manipulations of the fiction of chance see Pliny *Nat.* 37.19, Suet. *Nero* 23.3.

tions of chance for his literary creations. In the world of the real, the emperor and others mask dangerous designs with fictions of chance, though all it would take would be a discreet nod or wink to unmask the imperial fiction that a death was "accidental." And one of our clearest glimpses of resistance to such imperial fictions of chance occurs in Tacitus' account of the death of Petronius Arbiter, who contrived his forced suicide so that it looked "accidental": "he went in to dine and indulged in dozing off, so that though coerced his death would be similar to an accidental death" (*iniit epulas, somno indulsit, ut quamquam coacta mors fortuitae similis esset, Ann.* 16.19). Here, in one final and fatal fiction of chance, the Arbiter imitated making *fortuna* conform to his design, not Nero's.

3   Troy retaken: repetition and re-enactment in the *Troiae Halosis*

Ancient fictional picture galleries are hothouses of meaning: in their confined, lushly descriptive atmosphere, ecphrasis runs riot, intensifying the themes and obsessions of the novel at large.[1] In Petronius' picture gallery, Encolpius and Eumolpus reveal their preoccupations and concerns when they put art into words.

It is not clear why Encolpius goes to the gallery, whether he has just had a narrow escape, or has wandered in by accident, or deliberately come to look at art – though he is clearly upset at losing Giton. He first marvels at the realistic qualities of works attributed to the ancient masters Zeuxis, Protogenes, and Apelles.[2] Then he considers paintings of the myths of Ganymede carried off by Jupiter, Hylas, and the nymph, and Apollo and Hyacinthus. Encolpius' reaction to these paintings distorts the more usual interpretations of the myths depicted (83.4–5):

ergo amor etiam deos tangit. Iuppiter in caelo suo non invenit quod eligeret, et peccaturus in terris nemini tamen iniuriam fecit. Hylan Nympha praedata imperasset amori suo, si venturum ad interdictum Herculem credidisset. Apollo pueri umbram revocavit in florem, et omnes fabulae quoque habuerunt sine aemulo complexus.

So love touches even the gods. Jupiter in his heaven did not find anything to love and so headed to earth for debauchery, yet he harmed no one. The nymph who caught Hylas would have held her passion in check if she had believed that Hercules would come to contest her claim. Apollo called the shade of the

---

[1] On ecphrasis in general, Fowler (1991) is a useful point of departure. The stories told in both Longus' *Daphnis and Chloe* and Achilles Tatius' *Leucippe and Clitophon* begin with conversations struck up in the presence of a painting. Although these particular texts are both to be dated after the *Satyricon*, the earlier novelistic tradition probably included such scenes; see Schissel von Fleschenberg (1913). For other lively accounts of the beholding of artworks see Herodas 4.56–78 and Theoc. *Id.* 15.78–86. On Longus, see Zeitlin (1990), esp. 430–36; on Achilles Tatius see Bartsch (1989), 40–76.

[2] Elsner (1993), 32, suggests some intriguing puns which may lurk in Encolpius' descriptions of these artworks.

boy back into the flower. And all of these stories had embraces without jealous rivalry.

Encolpius contrasts these stories of embraces without a rival, *sine aemulo complexus*, with his own jealous and disappointed love for Giton. In this way Petronius stages a dialogue of sorts between traditional versions of these myths and what Encolpius asserts about them. Encolpius protests too much when he says that Jupiter did no one any harm in snatching up Ganymede. Virgil's Ganymede ecphrasis (*Aen.* 5.252–57) depicts the plight of the guardians of Ganymede after their charge has been snatched away. And indeed, the rape of Ganymede brings far greater trouble, for it is set out at the beginning of the *Aeneid* and elsewhere as one of the causes of Juno's anger, which brings such grief to all the Trojans. Thus, Encolpius' insistence here that Jove did no one harm is a strategy devised to suppress the themes of jealousy and destruction which emerge in other literary treatments of the myth.[3] In other versions of the myth of Hylas, it is surely Hercules' disappointment that is emphasized, not the nymph's supposed self-control had she known Hercules would come to claim him. Similarly, when Encolpius says that Apollo recalled the shade of the boy to the flower (*pueri umbram revocavit in florem*), he seems to imply euphemistically that Apollo is successful in commemorating his love with the hyacinth, especially since the word *revocavit* is often used of "actually" calling back the soul from death.[4] However, calling the soul of Hyacinth back from the dead was precisely what Apollo could not do, despite his medical skills, which are elsewhere mentioned in this connection.[5] Encolpius' word *revocavit* hints at Apollo's failure and loss. In the opening of the picture gallery scene, Encolpius contrasts painted images from the world of legend and myth with his own present-day all too real erotic failures, and the words with which he constructs his versions of the myths encode the way things "really" turn out in the tradition. Thus, when Encolpius puts these paintings into prose, he creates artifacts which function like his poems: idealizing desire they carry hints of that desire's frustration.

When Eumolpus breaks into the story and meets Encolpius in the

---

[3] Cf. Ovid's account of Juno's objections to Ganymede at *Met.* 10.161, and see Leach (1988), 407, for an analysis of "euphemism" in Encolpius' interpretations of this myth.

[4] *OLD s.v. revoco* 11.

[5] Ov. *Met.* 10.188–89: *nunc animam admotis fugientem sustinet herbis:/nil prosunt artes* ("Now he tries to hold back your fleeing soul by applying medicinal herbs. His arts do no good.")

gallery, he offers (like Encolpius, although at greater length) a narrative response to a painting. Just as Encolpius' obsessions shaped his
interpretations of the stories of Hyacinth, Hylas, and Ganymede, so
too Eumolpus' own obsessions – first on display in his prose tale of his
seduction of the boy at Pergamum (85–87) and in his (misinformed)
denunciation of modern decadence in art (88)[6] – shape his poetic interpretation of the painting of the fall of Troy (89). Evaluations of the
poem's literary form have led Walsh to conclude that "Petronius is
demonstrating how fatally easy it is to write tragedies like Seneca's",[7]
and Sullivan to argue more particularly that Petronius parodies Seneca
as a political attack on Seneca to win Nero's favor.[8] Zeitlin's primary
focus is the poem's content; she argues that Petronius' story of the
Trojan horse subverts the Augustan values on display in the *Aeneid* and
epitomizes the themes of deception and disguise which run throughout
the *Satyricon*.[9] Slater's reading puts the process of interpretation into
the foreground, arguing that the poem's failure to fit the expectations
of ecphrasis which its frame creates is part of a pattern of failures of
interpretation which characterize the rest of the novel as well.[10] My
own approach attempts to draw these threads together by looking at
connections between form and content, frame and poem, and con-
sidering these in the broader context of Neronian Rome. The feverish
display of repetition and similarity in Eumolpus' poem insistently calls
attention to the poem's own status as a belated re-enactment of Virgil's
epic treatment of the subject in the second book of the *Aeneid*. In
this, the poem is an extreme instance of a characteristically Neronian
phenomenon crisply described by Gowers: "Nero and his writers, despite the gulf between them, shared the inherited burden of Augustan
perfection, the responsibilities of early promise and the expected standards of another Golden Age ... Everything to come was fated to be
'late'."[11] Furthermore, an explicit concern with repetition and re-
enactment in the tale of Troy has an especial resonance for Rome,

---

[6] Eumolpus gets his art historical facts completely wrong: see Walsh (1970), 96–97; on
 Petronius' parody of art criticism here see Slater (1987), 171, Elsner (1993). Williams
 (1978), 16, usefully compares Eumolpus' denunciation of decadence to Pliny's denunciation of the decline in learning which accompanied Rome's rise to power and wealth
 (*Nat.* 14.2–6); Pliny's critique of modern learning and his celebration of his own in-
 dustry in overcoming the failings of his sources astringently prefaces his learned and
 lengthy disquisition on the production of wine.
[7] Walsh (1970), 47.
[8] Sullivan (1985), 175.
[9] Zeitlin (1971a), 58–67.
[10] Slater (1987), and (1990), 96–101, 186–90.
[11] Gowers (1994), 133.

where legends trace Roman identity back to the crucible of Trojan conflagration. If Rome was Troy re-born, any time Romans looked at or thought about Troy they were at some level implicated in considerations of their own city's – and eventually their emperors' – relations to the distant epic past.

Troy destroyed

Because of the prominence of the fall of Troy in the *Aeneid*, the central cultural document in ancient Rome, Petronius' readers will have read his poem with Virgil's version of the story constantly in the background. The Trojan past is ineluctably the Virgilian past. Eumolpus re-enacts Aeneas' first hand account of the destruction of Troy. Like Virgil's much longer narrative, the Petronian narrative includes the building of the horse, the deception of the Trojans, the resistance of Laocoon, the arrival of the snakes and their attack on Laocoon and his sons, and the slaughter of the Trojans by the Greeks. Unlike Virgil, Eumolpus minimizes Sinon's role, and does not narrate the passage of the horse into the city. A skeptical critic might object that the resemblance between the two texts is not strong or particularly significant because Eumolpus' poem is composed in iambic trimeter, instead of epic hexameter, and, as an eyewitness account of mythical events, it has the structure of a tragic messenger speech.[12] Yet all Latin literature stands in Virgil's shadow: the meter does not signal independence from Virgil's influence but subordination to it, constructing the poem as a less comprehensive, and secondary, version of Virgil's epic tale of Troy.

By way of an introduction to his poem, Eumolpus announces that he will try to "explain" (*pandere*) the painting of the fall of Troy in verse (89). It will come as no surprise that Eumolpus' announcement, while framed in standard terms (e.g. Lucr. *DRN* 1.55, Virg. *G.* 4.284, *Aen.* 6.723, Stat. *Silv.* 5.3.156), is also peculiarly apt for the poem he embarks on because *pandere* can be used of "opening" in more concrete and physical ways. Indeed, this word is used by Virgil's Aeneas in his story of the doomed opening of the gates of Troy, first to let the Trojans out to see the shores left empty by the Greeks' departure, *panduntur portae* ("the gates are opened," *Aen.* 2.27), and then when the horse is drawn into the city (*moenia pandimus urbis*, "we open the walls of the city," *Aen.* 2.234). Eumolpus' poem, while it does not

---

[12] So Stubbe (1933), 40, emphasizing formal features, and Slater (1990), 188, emphasizing the theatrical aspects of a messenger speech.

recapitulate Virgil's descriptions of the opening of the gates of Troy, will cover the events from the admittance of the horse into the city to the opening of the horse itself. Eumolpus' choice of metaphor to describe his poetic project here ends up creating a close correspondence between the opening up of the meaning of the painting achieved by his words, and the opening of Troy achieved by the fabrications of the Greeks, the deceptive departure, the inscribed horse, and Sinon's lie.

We may expect Eumolpus to offer an ecphrastic description of the painting. However, in its opening, the poem displays no overt signals that it is an ecphrasis of a painting, such as spatial pointers or references to an artist's skill. The opening lines are especially hard to imagine in visual terms because their frame of reference seems more temporal than spatial (89.1–6):

> iam decuma maestos inter ancipites metus
> Phrygas obsidebat messis et vatis fides
> Calchantis atro dubia pendebat metu,
> cum Delio profante [ferro] caesi vertices
> Idae trahuntur scissaque in molem cadunt
> robora, minacem quae figurabunt equum.

> Now the tenth harvest was besieging the Trojans
> troubled amid anxious fears, and the honor of the prophet
> Calchas wavered in dark fear,
> when, once the Delian one utters the prophecy,
> the shorn heights of Ida are dragged down and the cut wood falls in a
>   great heap,
> wood which will shape the menacing horse.

These lines are further distinguished by their rather tortured syntax, which may suggest that Eumolpus' control over literary discourse is imperfect or unsatisfactory. It is of course the Greek army who actually besiege Troy and will fashion the horse, but *messis*, not the Greeks, is the grammatical subject of *obsidebat* and the pronoun *quae* (referring to *robora*), rather than the Greeks, is the subject of *figurabunt*. Indeed, the poet does not name the Greeks until after their hiding place in the horse has been elaborately described (89.7–10):

> aperitur ingens antrum et obducti specus,
> qui castra caperent. huc decenni proelio
> irata virtus abditur, stipant graves
> Danai recessus, in suo voto latent.

> A huge cavern is opened and concealed hollows
> which could contain an army. In here valor inflamed by
>   war in its tenth year

is hidden away. The fierce Greeks crowd
into the inner recesses; they lie in wait in their own votive offering.

Linguistic form here is devised to match literary content: the poet
"conceals" the Greek army until they take their hidden places in the
horse.

Only in line 11 does the poet break decisively with the ecphrastic
fiction (89.11–12):

> o patria, pulsas mille credidimus rates
> solumque bello liberum

> O homeland, we believed that the thousand ships had been put to
>   flight,
> and that the land was freed from war.

The exclamation *o patria* and the first person verb *credidimus* change
the narrative viewpoint from that of a beholder of an artwork to that of
an eyewitness of the events depicted, thus helping to confirm the suspicion that the poem is a messenger speech of sorts. And moreover,
because the phrase *o patria* has a particularly powerful textual history in
the literary accounts of the fall of Troy, it tends to shift the poem away
from an image-centered ecphrastic description towards a more literary
exploration of previous texts. At *Aen.* 2.241–42, Aeneas exclaims: *o
patria, o divum domus Ilium et incluta bello/ moenia Dardanidum!* ("O my
fatherland, O Ilium, home of the gods, and walls of the Trojans, famed
in war"). This exclamation alludes to a line from Ennius' *Andromache*
(= Cic. *Tusc.* 3.44), *O pater o patria o Priami domus* ("O Father, O
fatherland, O home of Priam"), which imitates Euripides' *Andromache*
394, and is parodied by Plautus in the line *o Troia, o patria, o Pergamum,
o Priame periisti senex* ("O Troy, O fatherland, O Pergamum, O ancient
Priam you have perished," *Bac.* 933). So when Eumolpus breaks out of
the constraints of describing a picture, he does so by alluding to the
exclamation most closely associated with literary accounts of the fall
of Troy, *o patria*. The phrase seems almost a requirement in literary
accounts of the fall of Troy; in including it Eumolpus walks a fine
line between mastery of literary tradition and banality.

In the representation of Laocoon, Eumolpus departs significantly
from the Virgilian version, as others have noted. Eumolpus makes his
Laocoon a pale imitation of Virgil's: where Virgil's Laocoon is possessed of *validis ... viribus* (*Aen.* 2.50: "powerful strength"), Eumolpus'
Laocoon has only an *invalidam manum* ("weak hand", 23); at *Aen.*
2.50–53 the spear does pierce the horse, but in Eumolpus' poem the
spear falls from the horse (*ictusque resilit*, 22). Moreover, Eumolpus'
Laocoon tries not once but twice to pierce the side of the horse, first

with a *cuspis* (spear) and then with a *bipennis* (double-edged axe): *iterum tamen confirmat invalidam manum/altaque bipenni latera pertemptat* ("nevertheless, again he steels his weak hand and makes an attempt on the lofty flanks of the horse," 23–24). Even the similar sounds of *uterum* (beginning of line 21, in the first attempt) and *iterum* (beginning of line 23, in the second attempt) seem to emphasize the issue of repetition. Laocoon's repeated action becomes a figure for Eumolpus' own reiteration of Virgil, and Laocoon's choice of a double-edged axe (*bipenni*) as a replacement for the spear in his second attempt is an apt figure for the doubling in Eumolpus' handling of the Virgilian material. Laocoon's weakness and the additional detail of his second attempt to pierce the horse acknowledge Eumolpus' poetic weakness in this "second" attempt to give literary expression to the story given authoritative form by Virgil.

The poem makes its transition from the resistance of Laocoon to the menace of the snakes with the phrase *ecce alia monstra* (89.29–34):[13]

> ecce alia monstra: celsa qua Tenedos mare
> dorso replevit, tumida consurgunt freta
> undaque resultat scissa tranquillo †minor†,
> qualis silenti nocte remorum sonus
> longe refertur, cum premunt classes mare
> pulsumque marmor abiete imposita gemit.

> Then lo, other portents: where lofty Tenedos
> fills the sea with its back, billowing swells rise up
> and the shattered wave springs back †smaller† on a calm sea,
> just as the sound of oars in a quiet night
> is carried far, when ships weigh down the sea
> and the surface of the sea sighs as it splashes against the keel.

The phrase *ecce alia monstra* imitates Virgil's announcement of the arrival of the snakes (*Aen.* 2.203–05):[14]

> ecce autem gemini a Tenedo tranquilla per alta
> (horresco referens) immensis orbibus angues
> incumbunt pelago pariterque ad litora tendunt

> But look, from Tenedos, across the tranquil sea
> (I shudder to recall it), twin snakes with huge circling coils
> press upon the sea and together head toward the shore.

---

[13] Borghini (1991) offers an ingenious defense of *minor*: his remarks on *scissa* would suggest that the sea is worn out by washing up against monstrous Tenedos, much as Laocoon's spear weakly falls away from its assault on the monstrous horse. But see Conte (1987a) for the suggestion that *minor* be emended to *minax*.

[14] Collignon (1892), 138, Stubbe (1933), 43.

On 203, *ecce autem*, Austin compares *Aen.* 2.318, 526, and 673 and
remarks: "the formula in each case marks an unexpected disruption of
action in progress." For Petronius, whose audience will have known
this famous passage of Virgil well, this part of the story is not unexpected. Petronius does what we expect when he moves out of his
Laocoon narrative with *ecce alia monstra* in line 29. Yet, somewhat un-
expectedly at least, he does not specifically mention the snakes until
line 35. Instead, Eumolpus describes Tenedos itself, figuring it as a
sea-monster when he says that it fills the sea with its *dorso* which
can describe a ridge of hills or the back of a living being. He adds a
tediously obvious comparison between the waves striking Tenedos and
waters striking the oars of a ship moving across the sea by night. In the
Aeneid the approach of the snakes from Tenedos foreshadows the noc-
turnal approach of the treacherous Greek ships, also from Tenedos. In
Eumolpus' imitation, the snakes themselves are compared to ships as
soon as they appear (89.35–37):

> respicimus: angues orbibus geminis ferunt
> ad saxa fluctus, tumida quorum pectora
> rates ut altae lateribus spumas agunt.

> We look back: the waves bring twin coiled snakes
> to the rocks, whose swollen breasts
> push forth foam from their sides like high ships.

Virgil makes symbolic connections between snakes and ships and
Tenedos: first the deadly snakes then the deadly ships emerge from
concealment behind Tenedos. Eumolpus notices these symbolic connections and takes them a step further. His simile figures Tenedos,
source of the monstrous snakes and the dangerous Greek ships in
Virgil, as itself a threatening monster and as ships stealthily moving
by night. Thus Tenedos figuratively becomes the "real" snakes and
ships which Virgil had concealed behind it. The snakes which readers
expect to see are themselves at first concealed by Eumolpus' figuring
of Tenedos as a sea-monster. These lines can even be read as a metaliterary joke: Virgil literally concealed the snakes and ships behind
Tenedos; Eumolpus figuratively conceals the snakes "behind" his
description of Tenedos; the verb *respicimus* has a primary sense of
looking toward Tenedos, but it can also hint at Eumolpus' stance of
looking toward his Virgilian model.[15]

The rather banal similes in the description of Tenedos and the snakes
display Eumolpus' fascination with constructing close congruences

---

[15] For *respicio* used of looking back at past events, see the passages cited at *OLD s.v.* 5.

between the metaphorical and the real. The poem's final simile also brings the metaphorical and the real into close alignment (56–60):

> cum inter sepultos Priamidas nocte et mero
> Danai relaxant claustra et effundunt viros.
> temptant in armis se duces, ceu vi solet
> nodo remissus Thessali quadrupes iugi
> cervicem et altas quatere ad excursum iubas.
> 58 ceu vi Lachmann: ceu ubi LO: veluti Krohn: ceu qui Birt: ceu
>   cum Watt

> . . . when the Greeks unfasten the bars and pour forth the men
> amid the sons of Priam, laid out by sleep and wine.
> The leaders test their strength in arms, just as vigorously as
> a horse released from the bonds of a Thessalian chariot is wont
> to shake its neck and its high crest as it charges forth.

The choice of the word *effundunt* (pour forth) to describe the Greeks' emergence from the horse assimilates their action to the pouring of wine that brought the Trojans into oblivion. Then, the simile compares its tenor, the men coming out of the horse, to horses, the vehicle of the simile. Tenor and vehicle in a good simile are usually not quite so close. Why are the men coming out of the Trojan horse compared to real horses? Is it simply funny? Just to show us that Eumolpus is a bad poet with a barren aesthetic sensibility? Perhaps. But like the Trojan horse, the horse in the simile has more to it than initially meets the eye. Similes comparing men readying for or approaching battle with horses running free are familiar in epic. At the end of *Iliad* 6, when Paris returns to battle he is compared to a horse which breaks free from the stable and runs to the river, tossing its mane and exulting in its strength. Ennius closely imitated the Homeric passage, and Virgil in turn combined allusions to both Ennius and Homer when he used the simile to describe Turnus. The Homer, Ennius, and Virgil passages all specify that the horse has broken free of confinement or restraint, and emphasize its powerful strength.[16] The Petronius passage, in which men preparing for battle are compared to an untethered horse tossing its mane, alludes to this epic simile, and defuses and debases its power: the horse in question here has not broken free, but has been released (*remissus*) from the yoke of a Thessalian chariot. Epic models are evoked to be juxtaposed with a weakened re-enactment of their traditional glories.

The foregoing examples of Eumolpus' insistence on bringing the

---

[16] See *Il.* 6.506–11 (the same lines are found at *Il.* 15.263–68 in a description of Hector); Ennius *Ann.* 535–39 Skutsch; Virg. *Aen.* 11.492–97.

metaphorical and the real into close alignment display a fascination with reiteration and likeness in retelling the story of the fall of Troy. There are also a number of cruder instances of repetition in the poem. The Troy poem is often criticized for its repetition of words or sounds: *iam* and forms of *metus* and *iubae* and *iubar* are particularly notable. Also striking is the repetitive sound of the number of verbs compounded from *re-* (itself a prefix which can denote various kinds of doubling, reciprocation, etc.): *replet* (19), *reducta* (20), *resilit* (22), *replevit* (30), *resultat* (31), *refertur* (33), *respicimus* (35). In this regard, it is probably no accident that Eumolpus retells Virgil's line beginning *laxat claustra Sinon* ("Sinon opens the chamber," *Aen.* 2.259) with his own line beginning *Danai relaxant claustra* ("the Greeks open the chamber," 57).

Troy translated

The obsessive display within the *Troiae Halosis* of repetition, likeness, and imperfect re-enactment signifies both Eumolpus' lack of literary control and Petronius' self-conscious acknowledgement of his own, and his age's, literary belatedness. In addition, the poem's own thematic emphasis on repetition is matched in the prose frame: the picture gallery is the site of three stories of capture which keep going over the same ground, Troy. Ganymede was snatched by Zeus, and recompense in the form of horses was made to his father in the vicinity of Troy (83.3). Troy itself fell by the ruse of the wooden horse (89). And at Pergamum, regularly associated by the Romans with Troy, Eumolpus' deceptive vow of a horse wins him the boy in a debased re-enactment of the taking of Troy/Pergamum through the stratagem of a horse (85–87).[17] The *Satyricon*'s narrative of Encolpius' pursuit of love is mirrored in the stories of Zeus and Ganymede, and of Eumolpus and the boy at Pergamum, and of the Greeks' deception of Troy. As Zeitlin neatly sums up: "the twin themes of deception and disguise exemplified by the Wooden Horse form perhaps the most consistent and pervasive pattern throughout the *Satyricon* ... The Wooden Horse is a symbol of the fall of Troy; it is also a metaphor of the *Satyricon*."[18]

In a larger sense, the very city of Rome was built out of the fragmentation and refabrication of the epic past. By staging re-enactments of the same plot (capture of Troy or its analogue through the stratagem of a horse) in paintings, poetry and Eumolpus' own life, Petronius'

[17] See especially Zeitlin (1971a), 63; cf. Selden (1994), 141–42.
[18] Zeitlin (1971a), 63.

picture gallery reacts to Roman cultural and political interests which had construed Rome itself as Troy reborn. Eumolpus' jingle, *ibat iuventus capta, dum Troiam capit* ("The young men went forward as captives [confined in the Trojan horse] while they captured Troy," 89.27) recalls Horace's formulation of the cultural conquest of Rome by the captive Greeks: *Graecia capta ferum victorem cepit et artis/intulit agresti Latio* ("Captive Greece captured her fierce victor and brought arts to rustic Latium," *Epist.* 2.1.156–57). With the allusive repetition of the doubled *capta* . . . *capit* formula the *Troiae Halosis* hints that the Greek defeat of Troy is the original on which the later Greek cultural conquest of Rome is modelled.

The fascination with Trojan origins of Rome, initially a Greek intellectual construct, develops in the third and second centuries. The myth of Trojan origins is seized upon by Romans because it provides a means of claiming origins as ancient and distinguished as the Greeks possess, but permanently and profoundly separate from them.[19] The connection between ancient Trojan origins and the Roman present is staged for the public in the spectacle of the Trojan games, the *lusus Troiae*, an equestrian display (probably of Etruscan origin) in which the sons of senators compete (Plut. *Cato Min.* 3.1). The connection to Troy becomes especially important when Julius Caesar emphasizes the descent of his family from Venus through Aeneas, which he celebrated in his eulogy for his aunt Julia in 69 (Suet. *Jul.* 6.1). In 46, in celebration of his victories, Caesar dedicates the temple of Venus Genetrix ("Ancestress" App. *b.c.* 2.15.102). He claims her not just as the ancestress of the Romans as a community (as Lucr. *DRN* 1.1 does), but as the originator of his family. Further Trojan genealogies for leading families are produced by Varro and Hyginus; Dionysius of Halicarnassus states that fifty families of Trojan descent were in evidence in his own time (1.85).[20] Once Augustus emerges as Julius Caesar's imperial successor, discourse about Troy is, in addition to an assertion of general aristocratic Roman connections to the distant past, also at least potentially a discourse about the legitimacy of the imperial authority of his dynasty. So the *Aeneid* represents an Augustus who is the heir of Aeneas, destined to take up the burden of empire. In the forum of Augustus, statues of Aeneas and other ancestors of the Julian house are on display (Ov. *F.* 5.563–64). Livy's account of the sack of Rome by the Gauls is constructed to suggest that this is a second sack of Troy,

[19] On Rome's various expressions of interest in the myth of Trojan heritage during the Republic see Gruen (1990), 1–33.
[20] See further Wiseman (1974).

resulting in a refoundation of Rome.[21] The legendary origins of the Trojan games are prominent in the *Aeneid* (*Aen.* 5.596–602), and according to Suetonius, Augustus had the games staged frequently, praising them as a fine traditional way for the sons of noble families to make their entry on to the public scene, before discontinuing them in the wake of some serious injuries (Suet. *Aug.* 43.2). Tiberius is said to have led the band of older boys at the Trojan games in the celebration of Augustus' triumph after Actium, an occasion at which he and Marcellus seem to have been positioned as Augustus' possible heirs (Suet. *Tib.* 6.4). Caligula stages Trojan games in the intervals between races (Suet. *Cal.* 18.3). The connection of Trojan origins to the legitimacy of the Julio-Claudian emperors becomes an explicit concern as the games become an occasion on which possible imperial successors were displayed to the Roman public. Nero performed in them successfully at a young age (Suet. *Nero* 7.1); Tacitus adds the report that popular opinion favored Nero over Britannicus, his rival (*Ann.* 11.11).

Nero's own fascination with Troy, which should be viewed not just as an academic or literary interest, but as part of his claim to imperial authority, was evident early on.[22] Tacitus reports that Nero gave a speech in 53 in support of the view that the people of Ilium, as ancestors of Rome, should be freed from taxation (Tac. *Ann.* 12.58, cf. Cal. Sic. 1.44–45).[23] Nero also confronted the literary past by composing his own poem on the theme of Troy, which he performed at a public festival (Dio 62.29.1), and in which he made Paris stronger than all, even Hector (Servius on *Aen.* 5.370). Troy and Rome are juxtaposed with hostility to Nero when rumors circulate that he sang his Fall of Troy as Rome burned (Tac. *Ann.* 15.39; Dio 62.18.1), as if the fire at Rome re-enacted the conflagration at Troy. And the stories that Nero was somehow involved in causing the fire (Suet. *Nero* 38.1) collapse the distinction between the Trojan victims and the Greek victors: Nero gets to play both roles. An epigram, quoted by Suetonius as evidence of the sort of thing Nero would tolerate, insolently compares Nero to Aeneas (Suet. *Nero* 39.2):

> Quis negat Aeneae magna de stirpe Neronem?
>   sustulit hic matrem, sustulit ille patrem.

---

[21] On evocation of the Trojan paradigm in these contexts see Kraus (1994).

[22] Néraudau (1985) explores the ways that Nero uses representations of the Trojan past to define his role as princeps.

[23] For republican precedents for this kind of favorable treatment of Ilium see Livy 38.39.10 (in 188), and other examples discussed by Gruen (1990), 14–15.

Who denies Nero is descended from the great line of Aeneas?
Nero carried off his mother, Aeneas his father.

Lucan mockingly represents Julius Caesar's exploitation of the Trojan past by sending him to the ruined overgrown site of Troy during his pursuit of Pompey from Pharsalus to Egypt (*Ph.* 9.950–99). Caesar, tourist at Troy, gapes at the sites made famous in myth, where the natural rocks associated with Hesione, Ganymede, and the judgment of Paris seem more visible and recognizable than the walls and altars built by the Trojans and destroyed by the Greeks. Lucan celebrates his ability to make Caesar famous in poetry, as Homer made Achilles famous (983–86), and (with an allusion to the rumor that Caesar planned to move the center of government to Troy or Alexandria [Suet. *Div. Jul.* 79.4]) awards to Caesar the chance to make a false promise of future splendor for Troy: *grata vice moenia reddent/Ausonidae Phrygibus, Romanaque Pergama surgent* ("in gratitude the Ausonians shall restore walls to the Phrygians, and Roman Pergamum will rise," *Ph.* 9.998–99). Caesar's guided tour of Troy, where past is palimpsest, reshapes Aeneas' tour, guided by Evander, of the landscape where Rome's future is written.[24] Lucan overturns Virgil's integrative vision of Rome-that-is-to-be displayed in Aeneas' visit to Pallanteum with a landscape of fragmentation, forgetfulness, and false promises.

Proving that Petronius' poem parodies treatments of the Trojan theme by Seneca (in the *Agamemnon* and the *Troades*), or by Lucan (in the *Iliacon*, which seems to have treated the end of the *Iliad*, and does not seem to have included the eventual sack of Troy, Stat. *Silv.* 2.7.55–6), or by Nero himself, will remain difficult. To my mind, it is more important to recognize that Lucan and Petronius end up at the same place in their representations of Troy: Lucan's Caesar at Troy in the *Pharsalia* and Petronius' Eumolpus at Pergamum both tell the same story of false promises in the landscape of the ruined Trojan past. We do not know whether Petronius' Troy poem was written before or after the fire at Rome in 64 BCE, or before or after Lucan's account of Caesar at Troy. But Nero seems throughout his life to have been quite interested in narrowing the gap that separated ancient Troy from his Rome, while Petronius' picture gallery, and Lucan's scene at Troy, with their emphasis on imperfect repetitions and re-enactments of the legendary past, seem just as interested in asserting the futility or absurdity of such

---

[24] On Lucan's responses to Virgil in this scene see especially Johnson (1987), 118–21, and Martindale (1993), 48–51.

attempts. Evander gives Aeneas a tour of a landscape where glorious Rome is immanent, Caesar takes a tour of the ruined Trojan past, while Eumolpus is a step removed, giving Encolpius a "tour" of several belated representations of Troy.

The dynamics of difference in the discourse of Roman returns to the Trojan past are constantly being negotiated. Even Nero himself was not always fully in control of his ambitions to re-enact the Trojan past. At the end of his life, Nero is reported to have made a vow that if he survived the threats to his reign posed by revolts in the provincial armies he would perform at games in honor of the victory, giving water-organ, flute, and bagpipe performances, and on the last day he would dance Virgil's Turnus (*saltaturumque Vergili Turnum*, Suet. *Nero* 54). The reference is probably to a pantomime because the verb *salto* "dance" is regularly associated with pantomime performance, and pantomime was the format in which "serious" mythological themes were staged.[25] Nero's lust for the stage is a hallmark of accounts of his reign. His own public performances, first at Naples in 64, and then at Rome in the Neronia of 65 and on frequent occasions thereafter included the roles of Canace giving birth, Orestes as matricide, Oedipus blinded, and Hercules gone mad; by wearing masks in the form of his own appearance or that of whatever woman he was in love with at the time Nero aggressively undermined the theatrical illusion, making it impossible for audiences not to know that the emperor was on stage (Suet. *Nero* 21.3). Of course, identifying oneself with tragic characters could be vulnerable to attack, and graffiti compared Nero, Alcmeon, and Orestes, all matricides (Suet. *Nero* 39.2, Dio 62.16.2). But Nero was known to tolerate lampoons of this sort. He perhaps tries to manipulate the correspondences between his roles on stage and as emperor in a more positive way when in his last public performance, after reports of the revolts led by Vindex and Galba, he plays Oedipus in exile (Suet. *Nero* 46.3) in a performance which ended with the line "father, mother, wife, compel me to die" (Dio has Nero think of a version of this line "off-stage," as he hides in the reed-bed after fleeing for his life, 63.28.5).[26] One might almost believe that in preparing a speech (never delivered, but discovered after his death) in which he planned to ask the Roman people for forgiveness and hoped to be sent

---

[25] On pantomime, see Nicoll (1931), 131, Dupont (1985), 389–98, Jory (1996). On evidence for theatrical performances of poetry, including Virgil's Dido (Macr. *Sat.* 5.17.5) and his sixth eclogue (Servius on *Ec.* 6.11) see also Wiseman (1985), 128 with n. 121.

[26] For discussion of the various dynamics of this tragic quotation in the accounts of the historians see Bartsch (1994), 43–46.

as prefect to Egypt (Suet. *Nero* 47.2), he was hoping to find a way to his own "Colonus."[27]

In one sense, then, this final vow to dance the *Turnus* is just another anecdote of the egregious actor-emperor, and because the vow went unfulfilled, it has little to tell us about Nero as performer. Yet the logic of the vow itself is worth pondering. Why *Turnus*? Dancing a pantomime of Virgil's *Turnus* would presumably involve the duel between Aeneas and Turnus that leaves Turnus dead and readers breathless at the end of the *Aeneid*. In political and mythical terms, a *Turnus* pantomime would aptly celebrate Nero's hoped-for recovery from the imminent threat to his reign: Turnus' death is the violence which founds the Roman state, one ending for the series of events which the Trojan conflagration sets in motion. Caught in his final crisis, Nero imagines the possibility of a Roman state refounded with his identity as emperor intact. A *pantomimus* was a solo performer who danced mute to the accompaniment of musicians and singers, playing multiple roles.[28] Thus in a *Turnus* pantomime Nero would have the chance to represent both Turnus and Aeneas.[29] As Turnus he would fall in death and rise triumphantly from the staged crisis to resume his reborn imperial power; playing the victorious Aeneas he would found Rome over the body of a dead enemy. In fact such doubling would suit a *Turnus* peculiarly well: Virgil himself represents a Turnus who is the "double" of Aeneas, whose trembling limbs are represented with the same half-line which had described Aeneas' entrance into the poem: *solvuntur frigore membra* (*Aen.* 1.92 = 12.951). Turnus' death is an ambivalent spectacle: it can simultaneously be a story of the making of peace out of discord, or of the strife which remains beneath the surface, and "retains its potential to repeat itself in fresh outbursts of chaotic anger (the dreary catalogue of vengeance-killings of Roman civil war)."[30] In real life, Nero played the losing role – though even there experience could be inflected according to the mythical paradigm of Aeneas' defeat of Turnus: according to Suetonius, when Nero heard news of revolt among his armies, and tried to persuade some of the praetorian guard to accompany him into exile, some hesitated, and one answered

---

[27] For an overview of the evidence for Nero's public theatrical performances see Griffin (1985), 160–63. Nero's artistic and political manipulation of the conventions of performance has been the focus of increased attention in recent years: see Dupont (1985), 422–37, Edwards (1993), 134–36, (1994), Bartsch (1994), chapters 1 and 2, and Gowing (forthcoming). None of these discussions addresses Nero's intention of performing the *Turnus*.

[28] On multiple roles in pantomime performances see Lucian *de Salt.* 63–64.

[29] So Néraudau (1985), 2044–45.

[30] So Hardie (1993), 21, and see too Quint (1993), 79.

with an impudent question: *usque adeone mori miserum est?* ("Is it so terrible a thing to die?" Suet. *Nero* 47.2). Turnus puts this question to his sister Juturna as he steels himself for single combat with Aeneas at last (12.646). Everyone can participate in the game of bringing the Trojan past to life to destroy it again. The emperor who would be Turnus on stage now must play the role in truth and the taunting quotation frames his cringing flight as a debased reversal of Turnus' doomed courage. The quotation replicates Nero's own actions upon hearing the news of the imminent crisis – upsetting his dinner table he smashed his prized drinking cups which depicted Homeric scenes (Suet. *Nero* 47.1).

In the end, though the faint and flickering light from Troy casts a long shadow in the literary and cultural traditions of Rome, it is simply not bright or clear enough for us to decide whether Petronius' poem would have been viewed by its audience as an obvious parody of Senecan tragedy, a clear reference to Nero's Trojan follies, or a more general parody of the long Roman fascination with recapitulations of Troy, along the lines of Lucan's parodic ruins of Troy. But surely Petronius did not write this poem on Troy to allow us to date the composition of his novel. The poem's meanings are produced by its relationships to its novelistic frame, in which the story of the Pergamene boy belatedly retells the story of the Trojan horse, and its cultural frame, in which memories of the Trojan past, particularly the Virgilian and therefore Augustan versions of that past, can be manipulated to mask or to unmask Nero's belatedness, the new ending to the story of Rome begun so long ago at Troy.

4   The *Bellum Civile*

Outside a python, a dead rat is nothing special to look at. Inside, though, it exerts a horrifying fascination. Likewise, the *Satyricon*'s *Bellum Civile*, 295 lines on the war between Caesar and Pompey, would be nothing much if it survived only in an anthology, but in the *Satyricon* it seems quite odd; this bulky poem is a big chunk of undigested epic stuck implausibly in the belly of a narrative that has so far been consuming epic in bite-size pieces.

The temptation to treat the *Bellum Civile* as a literary conundrum, a cipher of Petronius' intentions, a mystery to be solved by careful detection, has been hard to resist.[1] Is the poem designed to demonstrate that Eumolpus is an incompetent and hypocritical poetaster, unable to master conventional topoi in an artistically satisfying way? But Eumolpus is already an incompetent and hypocritical poetaster, so why introduce such a long poem to make the same point? Perhaps the practice of imitation is an end in itself, a demonstration of Petronius' literary expertise, the kind of thing boys learned to do in school and men tossed off at dinner? The poem treats the same subject as Lucan's *Pharsalia*; Lucan's poem was remarkable for its exclusion of the traditional epic gods, and Eumolpus' poem includes traditional epic gods. Does Petro-

---

[1] The bibliography is large; for a survey see Soverini (1985), 1754–59. Critics who emphasize the poem's contribution to the characterization of Eumolpus include: Thomas (1902), 93; Ernout (1923), 135; Arrowsmith (1959), 185; Walsh (1968), 210; Beck (1979); cf. Slater (1990), 121, 190–99. Those who view the poem as an exercise in imitation tend to assemble collections of verbal parallels between the *BC* and Virgil and Lucan: so primarily Collignon (1892), 150–69; see also Stubbe (1933), 104–50; Guido (1976), 79–243. Those who see moral critique as the primary aim include Sochatoff (1962), and, in a different vein, Zeitlin (1971a). Eumolpus' declaration of how he thinks poems should be written has sometimes been taken as a simple statement of Petronius' own literary manifesto: cf. Paratore (1933), 381–82; Collignon (1892), 64, 68; Baldwin (1911), 5; Sage (1915), 48; Sochatoff (1962), 455; Rose (1966a), 295, 298. Luck (1972) reads the *BC* as a literary critical response to Lucan and a "specimen to indicate his own way of handling this material," p. 133. For the view that parody is being directed at critics of Lucan, see Sanford (1931), 255; Häussler (1978), 145–46; cf. Walsh (1970), 48–50.

nius polemically demonstrate literary principles to criticize Lucan? Could this critique be political as well as literary? Lucan, after precocious poetic success, joined those who plotted to assassinate Nero and install Calpurnius Piso in power. The conspiracy was uncovered in 65, and Lucan was condemned to death and committed suicide on 30 April 65 at the age of twenty-six.[2] It is not unlikely that artistic jealousy on the part of Nero had led to friction between the emperor and the young poet which culminated in his joining the conspiracy.[3] Does Petronius present an emphatically pro-Caesarian view of the conflict to entertain Nero by criticizing Lucan?[4] I am not convinced that Petronius' representations of the gods are a conservative reaction to Lucan's overturning of epic conventions, or that Fortuna, Dis and Discordia impute moral superiority to the winning side, but I do believe that Eumolpus' poem responds to Lucan's. Petronius died in the spring of 66, about a year after the death of Lucan.[5]

At the outset, though, it needs to be said that many readings of Petronius' poem as a response to Lucan implicitly or explicitly advance the opinion that Lucan's epic was deeply flawed. Recent work on Lucan and other "silver" Latin epic poets has been energized by the impulse to discover in these poets creative responses to the monumental achievements of the epic tradition. Once you read Lucan with Ahl, with Conte, with Johnson, with Masters, with Henderson or Feeney or Fantham or Hardie or Quint, there is no going back to the easy assumption that Petronius mocks Lucan, and Lucan deserves it, because of his failure to achieve a Virgilian ideal. Indeed, Eumolpus' fragmentation and reinterpretation of Virgilian epic has more in common with Lucan's

---

[2] Tacitus *Ann.* 15.49, 56–57, 70. Sources for the life of Lucan include a Suetonian Life, an account by Vacca (probably fifth century, cf. Ahl [1976], 333–34), and a Life included in the tenth-century second Voss codex of Lucan; these are cited by page and line number from Hosius' (1913) edition of Lucan. Nero is said to have banned Lucan from public performances of poetry (Tac. *Ann.* 15.49, Vacca 335.27–336.5). Dio too mentions the ban (62.29.4), placing it out of chronological order at the end of his narrative of 65, in a discussion of Nero's other artistic rivalries. On the quarrel, see Gresseth (1957); Rose (1966), 384–87; Griffin (1985), 157–60. Ahl (1976), 333–53, argues that Lucan's poem on the fire at Rome may have precipitated Nero's ban. It is probable that Lucan was still working on the *Pharsalia* at his death (a matter to be discussed at greater length later in this chapter): the poem ends abruptly with the surrounding of Caesar at Alexandria, and Statius, who seems to list Lucan's works in chronological order, mentions the *Pharsalia* last and says that Lucan died while singing of battles (Stat. *Silv.* 2.7.64–66, 102–04).

[3] Tac. *Ann.* 15.49, Suetonian Life 332.12–13, Vaccan Life 335.19–26, Voss Codex 337.2–5.

[4] The thesis that the *Bellum Civile* is a pro-Caesarian response to the *Pharsalia* was first put forward by Kindt (1892), 355–60. Sullivan develops Kindt's argument at (1985), 162–72; see also his remarks at (1968), 459–61. For a more skeptical view see Griffin (1985), 156.

[5] See Rose (1971), 59.

reshaping of Virgilian norms than has been generally recognized. This is not to say that Eumolpus produces a good poem. Virgil, Lucan or Statius can brilliantly rework inherited motifs: so far as I can tell Eumolpus' poem offers dim, overly studied transformations of tradition. Still, seeking in this poem documentary evidence of a relationship between Petronius and Lucan is to impose excessively narrow limitations on an inquiry which can and should be much broader. By framing the *Bellum Civile* within the *Satyricon*, Petronius negotiates thresholds of representation that divide prose from verse, fiction from history, novel from epic, present from past, and individual from empire, and I wish to explore these processes of negotiation.

Eumolpus' poem (*Sat.* 119–24.1) begins with a description of decadence at Rome (1–60), then introduces the gods Dis and Fortuna, who incite the conflict (67–121); after a display of omens (122–40), Caesar crosses the Alps and advances toward Rome (144–208), and Pompey flees from Rome (209–44); a narrative of the gods' roles in the war closes with a speech by Discordia (245–95). Eumolpus prefaces his performance with the remark that the poem is unfinished (118.6), and indeed it tells only the initial stages of the conflict, breaking off abruptly with the line *factum est in terris, quicquid Discordia iussit* ("whatever Discordia commanded took place on earth," 295). My discussion of Eumolpus' poetic performance will concentrate upon shifts between and correspondences across three levels of narrative: the epic and historical plot of the poem, the poetic programme explicitly stated by Eumolpus before his performance, and the framing plot of Encolpius' novelistic narrative.

Epic and novel

One of the deepest differences between epic and novelistic narrative is their different kinds of telos, or ending. We read novels to see how their characters end; the end of an epic is the beginning of the world order. Bakhtin analyzes epic's characteristic features this way: the "national epic past" serves as its subject matter; its sources are in "national tradition (not the personal experience and the free thought which grows out of it)"; and "an absolute epic distance separates the epic world from contemporary reality, that is, from the time in which the singer (the author and his audience) lives." By contrast, Bakhtin continues, the novel is implicated in experience (not national tradition), knowledge (as opposed to memory) and the existence of a zone of proximity encompassing a novel's subject, author, and audience. These differences have significant implications for the construction of endings: "The *Iliad* is a random excerpt from the Trojan cycle. Its ending (the burial of Hector) could not possibly be the ending from a novelistic point of view. But epic completedness suffers not the slightest as a result. The specific 'impulse to end' – How does the war end? Who wins? What will happen to Achilles? and so forth – is absolutely excluded from the epic by both internal and external motifs (the plotline of the tradition was already known to everyone). This specific 'impulse to continue' (what will happen next?) and the 'impulse to end' (how will it end?) are characteristic only for the novel and are possible only in a zone where there is proximity and contact; in a zone of distanced images they are impossible."[6] One need not go along with Bakhtin's characterization of the *Iliad* as a "random excerpt from the Trojan cycle" to agree with him about the different dynamics of plot in epic and in novels. When Eumolpus performs his Civil War poem, the novel's impulses of continuation and conclusion swallow up the teleological inevitabilities of epic. The jaws have to open wide: even Encolpius thinks the length of the poem is excessive, and he closes off Eumolpus' narrative and resumes his own with these words, *cum haec Eumolpos ingenti volubilitate verborum effudisset, tandem Crotona intravimus* ("When Eumolpus had poured forth this poem with a huge flow of words, finally we entered Croton," 124.2).

What kind of python is this? Whereas the telos of epic is national and imperial, the telos of a novel is individual and personal. In his study of the dynamics of plot in nineteenth- and twentieth-century novels Brooks observes that "the very possibility of meaning plotted through sequence and through time depends on the anticipated structuring force of the ending: the interminable would be the meaningless, and the lack of ending would jeopardize the beginning."[7] Now the *Satyricon* is not a modern novel, and its episodic nature and physical fragmentation makes certainty about its plot elusive. But though it is terribly frustrating that we have no idea how the *Satyricon* began or ended, or how the narrating voice of Encolpius was framed, one thing we do know is that whatever happened to him, Encolpius survived his adventures long enough to tell his tale. The interplay between Encolpius' earlier naive reactions and his older and wiser perceptions, which Beck documents so clearly, keep reminding us that the telos of Encolpius' story is "Encolpius tells the story."[8] The novel even dramatizes an individual desire for narrative telos in the last words we hear from

---

[6] Bakhtin (1981), 32.

[7] Brooks (1984), 93.

[8] For details on the interplay between Encolpius as narrator and Encolpius as actor, see Beck (1973); see too Schmeling (1994/5), on the novel's parodic similarity to a confession; this essay is a useful companion piece to his analysis of the surprising endings and punch-lines constructed for individual episodes (Schmeling [1991]).

Trimalchio: *"fingite me" inquit "mortuum esse. dicite aliquid belli,"*
" 'Pretend I am dead,' he said. 'Say something nice,' " (*Sat.* 78.5). So
Trimalchio speaks to his guests just before Encolpius and his friends
seize the chance to escape. Not satisfied with merely planning his tomb
and epitaph, Trimalchio wants to hear what people will say when he is
gone. Just as Trimalchio tries to seize control of the narrative of his life
by reaching out beyond its boundaries, the fire brigade rushes in,
thinking that the sound of horns which they heard was a fire alarm.
Encolpius seizes back the narrative from Trimalchio, the stager of
spectacles, by fleeing as if from a real fire, and the story goes with him:
we, like Trimalchio, never get to hear how Trimalchio's story ends. In
a sense, Trimalchio's desire to hear what would amount to versions of
his own obituary epitomizes our relation to all plots: we want to get to
the end to see how the whole thing makes sense. So for Brooks, "all
narrative may be in a sense obituary in that ... the retrospective
knowledge that it seeks, the knowledge that comes after, stands on the
far side of the end, in human terms on the far side of death."[9]

Of course, the "knowledge that comes after" any poem on the Civil
War (and, arguably, any epic written in the principate) is the principate. Bakhtin's absolute separation between "epic distance" and the
"zone of proximity" with the present where novels unfold is less useful
when the epic story told is not much more than a century old, and
keeps being replayed in the relations between the emperor and the
senate. Quint brings Brooks' structures and ways of looking at closure
back into discussion of epic, and within the development of the epic
tradition identifies differing constructions of closure: this explicitly
ideological reading of epic yields an understanding of epic's claims to
completeness and distance which is more complex than Bakhtin's
analysis admits.[10] In one branch of the tradition, with Virgil at its head,
the story of the winners imposing order and closure affirms the imperial world order. In the contrasting tradition, with Lucan at its head,
Quint argues, closure is indefinitely deferred in favor of a more open-
ended narrative of a continuing disorder which functions as a gesture
of resistance to the imperial world order.[11] It is important in this connection to emphasize the temporal as well as ideological distance between Virgil and Lucan. The story of Aeneas (as precursor of Augustus) imposing order could only be written in that Virgilian way during

---

[9] Brooks (1984), 95.
[10] Bakhtin (1981), 15, did to a degree acknowledge the ideological path leading between
   the present and the epic past: "the epic absolute past is the single source and beginning
   of everything good for all later times as well."
[11] Quint (1993), especially chapters 2 and 3; his discussion of Brooks is at 51–52.

Augustus' reign: the telos of the strife that ended the republic changes as the principate unfolds. When Virgil tells the story of Aeneas, he is telling a story whose "end" is Augustus. For Lucan, and for Petronius, the story is different: to tell the story of Julius Caesar is to tell a story whose "end" is Augustus – and Tiberius, Caligula, Claudius, and Nero. Even if initial assertions by Nero that he would rule "according to what was laid down by Augustus" (*ex Augusti praescripto*, Suet. *Nero* 10.1) were intended truthfully and were interpreted as a return to an Augustan golden age, promises of ordered stability Nero might offer are undercut by what his audience remembers of his predecessors, and of his own path to power. Petronius could have tossed off an epic treatment of any theme. Why then does the *Satyricon* swallow this particular rat? One context for an answer may be that Petronius had a point to make about Lucan, but another context may be this: the *Satyricon*'s narrative of Encolpius reproduces the world inhabited by Petronius and his audience in an idiom of proximity, while the civil war narrative reproduces that same world in an idiom of epic distance.

Global perspectives

The *Bellum Civile* lacks an invocation of a Muse, and a proem announcing the subject, and its generalized indictment of degeneracy has prompted this reaction from Slater: "Though the meter is hexameter, the genre could just as easily be satire as epic. The subject of the next forty-two lines is the moral decay of Rome, couched in terms so general that we still have no firm signal from the poetry itself that the time is that of the civil war."[12] While it is certainly true that the absence of Muse and proem is striking, and the poem's resonances with satire are important, I want to complicate this impression of generality. Though temporally vague, the narrative is more spatially specific in Roman terms than it may seem in a modern frame of reference: its subject is the world, as the poem's first word, *orbem*, signals. Romans like to represent the world and the empire as coextensive, so a global narrative of luxury is not so much general or vague as it is specifically imperial.

Eumolpus' opening lines (*BC* 1–2)

> orbem iam totum victor Romanus habebat,
> qua mare, qua terrae, qua sidus currit utrumque.

> Now the victorious Roman held sway over the whole world,
> where the sea is, and the land, and where the sun rises and sets.

[12] Slater (1990), 196.

have been judged one of the *Bellum Civile*'s closest parallels to Lucan's text (*Ph.* 1.109–11):[13]

> dividitur ferro regnum, populique potentis,
> quae mare, quae terras, quae totum possidet orbem,
> non cepit fortuna duos.

> The kingdom was divided by the sword, and the fortune of a
>   powerful nation,
> which held sway over sea and land and the whole world,
> was not enough for two men.

Both Lucan's and Eumolpus' universalizing accounts of Roman *imperium* recall a prior vision of Rome's boundless *imperium* expressed with a similar cadence: Venus' question to Jove about the destiny of the Romans (*Aen.* 1.234–37):

> certe hinc Romanos olim volventibus annis,
> hinc fore ductores, revocato a sanguine Teucri,
> qui mare, qui terras omnis dicione tenerent,
> pollicitus –

> Surely you promised that someday as the years moved in their circles,
> the Romans would spring from this source, that from the stock of
>   Teucer returned
> to Italy would come leaders who would hold the sea and all the
>   lands under their sway – ...

Once Augustus defines his establishment of the institutions of empire as an establishment of peace and order throughout the world, civil war is defined as a cosmic conflict. If cosmic order is Augustus' solution, then cosmic discord must have been the problem, and civil war stories are laid out on a global or cosmic map. Virgil places victory at Actium on the cosmic icon of Aeneas' shield (*Aen.* 8.675–713).[14] Lucan compares the outbreak of discord to cosmic conflagration (*Ph.* 1.70–80).[15] It does make a kind of generic sense, then, that Eumolpus begins the Civil War with a global map of luxury and its consequences at Rome.

Eumolpus uses conventional structures when he locates the source of discord in Rome's global *imperium* and the luxuries it brings to Rome. As in his short poem on luxury (93.2) the key terms are

---

[13] Baldwin (1911), ad *BC* 2. Zeitlin (1971a), 75, sees an allusion to Lucan but assigns it to "the simplest and most literal level of Eumolpus' discourse." Slater (1990), 195, finds the parallel "ultimately not persuasive" like George (1974), 123. On the meaning of *sidus utrumque* see Baldwin (1911) *ad loc.* and compare Getty (1951).

[14] For further discussion of these issues see Hardie (1986), 362–69.

[15] On cosmic imagery in Lucan see Lapidge (1979).

searching (forms of *quaero*) and dissatisfaction (negated forms of *satio* and *placeo*). But in the short poem on luxury, the effects of luxury "here" in Rome (or more generally Italy) were in the foreground, while in the *Bellum Civile* the effects of the luxury trade "there" at the edges of empire are also emphasized in a catalogue which maps Roman consumption all over the world: Corinth yields Corinthian bronze,[16] the depths of the earth gems,[17] Numidia marble columns, China silk, Arabia spices, Africa the tiger for bloodthirsty spectacles in the amphitheater, and Persia eunuchs. Rome's decadence changes the landscape in the far reaches of Arabia, Africa, and the Black Sea. The Arabians despoil their land of spices (12), the luxurious citron table is "dug up" (*eruta*, 27) from African soil, and the extent of Rome's power is whispered by the breezes on Phasis' empty shore (36–38):

> iam Phasidos unda
> orbata est avibus, mutoque in litore tantum
> solae desertis adspirant frondibus aurae.

> Now the waters of Phasis
> are bereft of their birds, and on the silent shore
> only breezes whisper amid the empty leaves.

After describing decadence at Rome, the poem offers a second global "map" marked by the sites of the deaths of Crassus, Pompey, and Caesar (*BC* 63–66):

> Crassum Parthus habet, Libyco iacet aequore Magnus,
> Iulius ingratam perfudit sanguine Romam,
> et quasi non posset tellus tot ferre sepulcra,
> divisit cineres. hos gloria reddit honores.

> The Parthian possesses Crassus, Magnus lies on the Libyan shore,
> Julius stained ungrateful Rome with blood,
> and as if the earth could not bear so many graves,
> she has separated the ashes. Fame brings these rewards.

---

[16] A mention of Corinthian bronze seems to underly the corruption in line 9 (*aes Ephyre †cum† laudabat miles*). Heinsius offered the emendation *Ephyreiacum*, but, as Müller points out, there is no other instance of an adjective of this form, so this has not been widely accepted. In beginning his catalogue of luxuries at Rome with Corinthian bronze Eumolpus takes advantage of a temporal ordering of the ways in which military conquest brought luxury to Rome and luxury in turn brought civil discord to Rome: see Pliny *Nat.* 33.150 on the conquest of Corinth in 146 and the defeat of Carthage in the same year as a source of Roman decadence; cf. Sall. *Jug.* 41.1, *Cat.* 10; Vell. Pat. 2.1.1; Flor. 1.47.2–3; and August. *Civ. Dei* 1.30. See further Earl (1961) chapter 1. On Trimalchio's Corinthian bronze, see above, chapter 1 (pp. 20–21).

[17] So Baldwin (1911) on *BC* 10, following Anton (1781) *ad loc.*; *certaverat ostro* signifies that these riches of the earth rival the riches of the sea, Tyrian purple dye.

These lines setting the deaths of the triumvirs in a global framework
are often compared to various poetic treatments which set the death
of Pompey in a global framework: Pompey's meager tomb can be
contrasted with his global conquests;[18] or epigrams suggest a global
perspective by listing the subsequent deaths of Pompey's son Gnaeus
in Europe[19] and Sextus in Asia[20] as well as that of Pompey himself
in Libya.[21] The topos of graves all over the world, which is associated
by other poets only with Pompey and his sons, is made even more
"global" when Eumolpus uses it to encompass the entire course of
the war by listing the deaths of Crassus, whose death hastened the
outbreak of hostilities, Pompey, who lost, and Caesar, who won. The
conceit that the earth needed the weight of the graves to be evenly
distributed exploits Stoic conceptions of the ordered universe and its
vulnerability to cosmic dissolution.[22]

A final universalizing view of discord in the poem belongs to Discordia. After finding a place on the Apennines from which she can see
the whole world, Discordia gives a speech (*BC* 283–94). Beneath her
gaze extends a world in discord: *unde omnes terras atque omnia litora
posset / aspicere ac toto fluitantes orbe catervas* ("from which she could
look upon all the earth and its shores and troops flowing over the whole
world," *BC* 280–81). The universal unbounded scope of her gaze
corresponds to the unbounded reach of her commands: "whatever
Discordia commanded took place on earth" (295).

These views of the world in discord recapitulate on a grand epic
scale perspectives which are part of the poem's novelistic frame: after
their shipwreck, Eumolpus and his companions climb a steep path to
a spot from which they can behold a city (116.1).[23] A local informant
tells them that they behold Croton, which he describes as a site of discord. He reports that Croton is dominated by inheritance seekers and
speaks in terms of civil strife: *scitote in duas partes esse divisos. nam aut
captantur aut captant* ("Know that they are divided into two classes.
For they are either prey for legacy hunters or they are legacy hunters

---

[18] Luc. *Ph.* 8.789–822, *AL* 404 R, 438 R (400, 436 SB).
[19] Gnaeus was killed in 46, just after the battle of Munda, see App. *b.c.* 2.105.
[20] Sextus was killed in 35 in Asia; the actual location is not entirely clear: see App. *b.c.*
5.144; Dio 49.18.4–5; Livy *Per.* 131.
[21] Mart. 5.74; *AL* 400–03, 454–56 R (396–9, 452–54 SB); cf. Luc. *Ph.* 6.817–18.
[22] On Stoic views of cosmic dissolution, see Lapidge (1979). The word *honores* suggests a
pun between *onus* and *honos*: cf. Varro *L.L.* 5.73.
[23] Their viewpoint might be recognized as the promontory of Lacinium, famed for its
temple of Juno; see Livy 24.3.

themselves," 116.6).[24] Just after the companions look upon a decadent and discordant society, epic views of a discordant world are brought before their eyes in verse.

Consuming the world

Eumolpus' picture of decadence at Rome runs parallel to Lucan's account of the conditions under which civil strife arose; Lucan lists wealth in general, decadent architecture, clothing and food, vast agricultural estates, crime, electoral bribery, and a debt crisis (*Ph.* 1.158–82). While covering basically the same material, Eumolpus uses a more overt and extended imagery of eating which collapses empire's cosmic order into the culinary sphere.[25] At Rome itself, the shining surface of a citron table reflects the decadent banquet. Because citron tables were circular, the *orbis* of the table (signalled by *circum*) is the symbolic equivalent of the *orbis* of the world: each is filled with the spoils of the Roman empire (*BC* 27–32):[26]

> ecce Afris eruta terris
> citrea mensa greges servorum ostrumque renidens
> ponitur ac maculis imitatur vilius aurum,
> quae sensum trahat. hoc sterile ac male nobile lignum
> turba sepulta mero circum venit, omniaque orbis
> praemia correptis miles vagus esurit armis.[27]

> There, the citron table dug up from Africa
> is set up, reflecting troupes of slaves and purple trim on togas,
> and with its mottled surface imitates gold to beguile the senses.
> A crowd laid out with wine encircles this unfruitful and foolishly
>   celebrated wood
> and the wandering soldier with arms at hand hungers for all the prizes
>   of the world.

[24] So noted by Zeitlin (1971a), 69. Bodel (1992) has pointed out that this picture of legacy hunting (*captatio*) at Croton has more to do with rhetorical treatments of the subject than with real social practices.

[25] Lucan's use of eating imagery is limited to a brief mention of decadent meals (163–64) and to calling interest *vorax* ("ravenous" 181).

[26] On the round shape of the tables see Lucan, *Ph.* 10.144–46. Pliny (*Nat.* 13.91–103) discusses the fabulous prices paid by Cicero, among others, for tables made of citrus wood. *Eruta*, which Baldwin (1911) *ad loc.* deems a metaphor for the difficulty of bringing the wood out of African forests, is also precise evidence that this citrus-wood table is particularly valuable, because the wood with the most prized markings was part of the roots of the tree (Pliny *Nat.* 13.95).

[27] Gronovius' *vilius* in line 29 is to be preferred to the MSS *vilibus* because one of the features for which a citron table was prized was its pattern of spots, so it would not make

The hunger metaphor in *esurit* connects the soldier's worldwide quest for luxurious booty with the theme of decadent consumption at Rome: when the soldier hungers for all the prizes of the *orbis*, the poet super-imposes the *orbis* of the table on the *orbis* of the world.[28]

The imagery of consumption continues as Roma personified becomes a banqueter suffering the after-effects of overindulgence (*BC* 58–60):

> hoc mersam caeno Romam somnoque iacentem
> quae poterant artes sana ratione movere,
> ni furor et bellum ferroque excita libido?

> When Rome lay submerged in filth and laid out in sleep
> what remedies could rouse her with healing skill
> except madness and war and passion incited by the sword?

Both this personification and the image of the *turba sepulta mero* (*BC* 31), the drunken crowd gathered around the citron table, correspond to Eumolpus' earlier account of the drunken sleep of the Trojans, worn out from celebrating what they thought was the end of the war.[29] Eumolpus, like Virgil, says that Troy fell to the Greeks because the Trojans were sleeping off their celebrations (*Sat.* 89.56).[30] A comparison between the drunken Romans and the drunken Trojans mischievously reinterprets Rome's decadence as a legacy of the legendary past: the Republic, like Troy, was destroyed because those who should have watched over it drank themselves into oblivion. Lucan too had made the body politic an important emblem of civil strife. In the proem of the *Pharsalia*, Rome is the body which has turned against itself (*Ph.* 1.2–3), and the emphasis on dismemberment (e.g. 2.141–42), especially Pompey's beheading (1.685, 8.671–73), makes the point another way.[31] Eumolpus chooses neither the suicidal body nor the dismem-

---

sense for *maculis* to be modified by *vilibus* (see Pliny *Nat.* 13.96). Shackleton Bailey (1987), 463, citing Heinsius' remark that it seems odd for a fruit-bearing tree to be described as *sterile*, suggests that lines 30–32 may be an interpolation because they "seem extraneous, the product of some twaddler." However, in defending the lines as Petronian Kershaw (1991) points out that Pliny, at the end of his discussion of tables made from the citron tree (*Nat.* 13.103), distinguishes between two different kinds of citron trees: one from which tables are made, and another bearing fruit.

[28] So Kershaw (1991).

[29] So Zeitlin (1971a), 64–65.

[30] Cf. Virg. *Aen.* 2.265 *urbem somno vinoque sepultam*; so Collignon (1892), 166; Baldwin (1911), on *BC* 31; cf. Grimal (1977), 83–84. A similar image is also found in a denunciation of decadence in one of the Anthology poems, fr. 34 M = AL 472 R = 470 SB.

[31] On what Most calls the "rhetoric of dismemberment" see further Most (1992), and Quint (1993), 140–47. The *imago patriae* which Caesar sees when about to cross the Rubicon (1.186) gives a body of a different sort to Rome.

bered body as his image of Rome's body politic, but the banqueting body.[32]

Eumolpus' account of an eclipse in his catalogue of portents on the outbreak of the war also uses the figure of eating. Eumolpus, like Lucan (*Ph.* 1.522–83), bases his account of the portents which presaged civil strife at Rome upon a set of portents more usually associated with Caesar's death.[33] Eumolpus' list of portents begins, as Virgil's does, with the eclipse of the sun (*BC* 127–29):

> namque ore cruento
> deformis Titan vultum caligine texit:
> civiles acies iam tum spectare putares.

> For hideous Titan with his bloody face
> covered his countenance with darkness:
> you would think that even then he was beholding civil war.

Virgil clearly states that the sun hid its face because it mourned the death of Julius Caesar (Virg. *G.* 1.466–68):

> ille etiam exstincto miseratus Caesare Romam,
> cum caput obscura nitidum ferrugine texit
> impiaque aeternam timuerunt saecula noctem.

> He [the sun] also pitied Rome at the death of Caesar
> when he covered his shining head with rust-colored darkness
> and the unholy ages feared unending night.

---

[32] In another body-state analogy, Rome in the throes of decadence is compared to a body suffering from disease (*BC* 53–55). The disease analogy is already introduced in the prose frame when the bailiff remarks that at Croton the search for inheritances is like a plague: *"adibitis" inquit "oppidum tamquam in pestilentia campos, in quibus nihil aliud est nisi cadavera quae lacerantur aut corvi qui lacerant"* ("You will come to a town, he said, like a plague-stricken plain, in which there is nothing but bodies being devoured or the crows that devour them," 116.9). Livy uses the analogy between plague and civil strife to describe antagonism between plebs and optimates during the siege of Croton in the second Punic war (Livy 24.2.8). Both in Livy's historical account and in the *Satyricon*, mention of plague in connection with Croton is especially striking because the city was once reputed to be an exceptionally healthy place, and famed for the number of its Olympic victors. In a collection of marvels Pliny says that Croton has never had a plague (*Nat.* 2.211); cf. Cic. *de Inv.* 2.1.2; Strabo 6.1.12. On the high reputation of Croton's doctors see Herod. 3.131.

[33] The source of Eumolpus' and Lucan's catalogues of portents, particularly the eclipse, the eruption of Aetna and the comet, is the Virgilian catalogue of portents upon Caesar's death (*G.* 1.464–88, imitated by Ovid, *Met.* 15.783–98; cf. Livy, preserved by Obsequens 68 and Servius on *G.*1.472), rather than historical accounts of portents before the outbreak of war in 49 (as seen in Appian *b.c.* 2.36, Dio 41.14).The portents at Virgil's Rome lament Caesar's murder, but those at Lucan's and Eumolpus' Rome lament his approach: so Martindale (1976), 52, emphasizing the polemical nature of Lucan's use of Virgil; cf. Fantham (1992), 25.

Unlike Virgil's sun, which is bright and beautiful, *nitidum*, behind its cover of gloom, Eumolpus' sun has been stained by the ugliness of the forthcoming Civil War, and is itself *deformis* and looking as if it has drunk blood, *ore cruento* (*BC* 127). While *os* can be used regularly of the "face" of the sun or moon (*OLD* s.v. *os* 6 b), Virgilian parallels for the phrase *ore cruento* pull the image closer to an "actual" mouth: Virg. *Aen.* 1.296 (of *Furor impius*), 9.341 (of a lion to which Euryalus is compared as he slaughters his enemies in their sleep), 10.489 (of Pallas dying) and 12.8 (of the Punic lion to which Turnus is compared).

On a divine level too, the imagery of cosmic eating prevails, for Eumolpus' gods are just as obsessed with eating as the Romans who loll around the *orbis* of the citron table. Dis asks Fortuna for war because it has been a long time since he and Tisiphone have drenched their mouths with blood (*iam pridem nullo perfundimus ora cruore*, *BC* 96), and Fortuna promises that Tisiphone can have her fill of war's luxuriant death (*BC* 119–21):

> tuque ingenti satiare ruina,
> pallida Tisiphone, concisaque vulnera mande:
> ad Stygios manes laceratus ducitur orbis.

> And you, pale Tisiphone,
> sate yourself on the great disaster, chew on the open wounds:
> the ravaged world is led down to the Stygian shades.

The *orbis* that furnishes the food which weighs down the citron table at Rome is now to be Tisiphone's banquet: for the gods, as for the Romans themselves, the cosmic *orbis* becomes the culinary *orbis*.

Thus Eumolpus' representations of the consumption of empire stuff food into a structure that defines the world order, much as epic parody, or indeed satire, mockingly stuffs food into the structures (meter, vocabulary, style) which epic uses in its construction of a coherent world order. In prose, the novel stages the same process in reverse: Trimalchio stuffs empire and cosmos into his food in his zodiac dish (35.1–6).[34] Trimalchio explains the symbolism of the zodiac dish and announces that he was born under the sign of Cancer (*Sat.* 39.8):

in cancro ego natus sum. ideo multis pedibus sto, et in mari et in terra multa possideo; nam cancer et hoc et illoc quadrat. et ideo iam dudum nihil supra illum posui, ne genesim meam premerem.

---

[34] The conceit of an edible zodiac does not seem especially original, and indeed, this is part of the humor in Encolpius' wonder at the novelty of the dish; see Smith (1975), ad 35.1. The fourth-century comic poet Alexis had described such a dish (Alexis fr. 2.392 Kock, Ath. 2.59 f–60 a); it is an appetizer, like Trimalchio's. For representations of the Zodiac, see D.–S. s.v. *zodiacus*.

I was born in the sign of Cancer. I stand on many feet, and on sea and land I possess many things; for the crab fits right in both on land and sea. And so just now I put nothing above the sign of Cancer so that I wouldn't weigh down my natal star.

Like the Crab, the merchant Trimalchio is at home on land and on sea. Conventional accounts characterize those born under the sign of Cancer as merchants whose business interests stretch over land and sea; the moralizing condemnation of commercial greed is clear in Manilius' version of the identification (*Astron.* 4.165–75). By describing his business interests as possessions on sea and land, Trimalchio does what he can to make their scope seem imperial, drawing on the idea that Roman *imperium* stretched over sea and land, *terra marique*.[35] In addition, Barton argues that Trimalchio's announcement that "there is nothing above the sign of Cancer" is rather imperial: "as emperors were careful to conceal their ascendants in their portrayal of their horoscopes, so he left his own birth sign out of the culinary representations of the zodiac out of superstitious fear."[36] Trimalchio does not limit himself to an imperial role: he portrays himself as a divine creator of cosmic order too. Stoics argued that the orderly movement of constellations in the sky proves that the universe was created by a god according to rational principles; the Stoic *sapiens* can mentally grasp the structure of the cosmos, as Scipio does in Cicero's *Somnium Scipionis* (*Rep.* 6).[37] Trimalchio's assertion that the dish has been designed according to his rational plan (*nihil sine ratione facio*, 39.14) parodically casts him as the world's creator. The opening reference to the *structor* of the dish seems to hint at this sort of parody too (35.2). Though *structor* refers to a person who arranged food for the table, the mere mention of the one who produces a dish which represents the zodiac parodies the notion of a divine creator.[38] In closing his explanation of the zodiac appetizer, Trimalchio introduces another vision of the world: *sic orbis vertitur tamquam mola* ("So the world turns like a

---

[35] See Nicolet (1991), 29–39.

[36] Barton (1994), 193 n. 79.

[37] So, for example, in Cicero's *de Natura Deorum*, the Stoic Balbus says that beholding the heavens is like entering a house or a gymnasium or a forum: the principles of rational order behind its creation are immediately apparent (*N.D.* 2.12–15). Likewise, Balbus argues that if we see rationality in elaborate astronomical models of the heavens, then we must agree that the heavens too are the work of a rational creator (*N.D.* 2.88; cf. Man. *Astron.* 2.60–86). At 2.765–87 Manilius compares the ordering of an explanation of the heavens to the planning that a city founder (*conditor*) must do for the city to be built correctly.

[38] *structor* is originally used to denote a builder: Cic. *Att.* 14.3.1; subsequently it is used for an arranger of food: Mart. 10.48.15; *CIL* 6.33470.

mill," 39.13). This vision of the universe parodies the Stoic notion of a cosmic *machina*, a mechanical apparatus set in motion by a divine being. Poetic and philosophical descriptions of the celestial *machina* do not really elaborate on its precise mechanisms.[39] Trimalchio sees the world in more mundane terms, and the fact that the verb *molo* could also be used obscenely also explains his choice of simile.[40]

Cosmos becomes dinner too for emperors themselves: in his reign after the death of Nero, Vitellius was said to have eaten an extravagant "Shield of Minerva," a huge casserole of rarities brought from all over the empire; the dish itself was so large that it had to be made of earthenware instead of silver, and an entirely new kiln had to be built out in the country for it to be fired.[41] Such dishes as this one, or the huge turbot presented to Domitian in Juvenal's fourth satire, "summed up and trivialized supreme power."[42] In a more permanent, less overtly gustatory, form Nero too elides cosmos with dinner when he replicates the celestial *machina* in his Golden House by building a ceiling for his main dining room which moved to mimic the movement of the heavens.[43] The elision of cosmos with dinner described in the poem as a condition under which civil war arose is still in effect; in the experience of empire, the story of civil war has not yet reached its end.

Weighty problems

In his poetic programme, Eumolpus asserts that poems are too much like history if the gods and other divine phenomena are not represented (118.6):

ecce belli civilis ingens opus quisquis attigerit nisi plenus litteris, sub onere labetur. non enim res gestae versibus comprehendendae sunt, quod longe melius historici faciunt, sed per ambages deorumque ministeria et fabulosum †sententiarum tormentum† praecipitandus est liber spiritus, ut potius furentis

---

[39] Vitruvius, being more mechanically minded, compares part of the movement of the heavens to a lathe and part to a potter's wheel (*de arch.* 9.1.2, 15). Elsewhere, Vitruvius says that all machines were developed through observation and imitation of the great *machina* of nature itself (*de arch.* 10.1.4). Lucan compares the world at war to a *discors machina*, and thus draws on a tradition of imagining a collapse of the world order as a mechanical failure: *Ph.* 1.70–81. For other descriptions of cosmic mechanical failure, see Lucr. *DRN* 5.95–96, Manil. 2.68, 807.

[40] Lucil. 278 (Marx); Pomponius *Com.* 100; Petr. *Sat.* 23.5.

[41] Suet. *Vit.* 13.2, Pliny *Nat.* 35.163–64, Dio 64.3.3.

[42] See the excellent discussion by Gowers (1993) 47, on the *Moretum*; 204–11, on Juvenal 4; 21, on Vitellius' "Shield of Minerva." The quotation is from p. 207.

[43] Suet. *Nero* 31.2, and see Dupont (1977), 144–47, comparing the constructions of world order in the Domus Aurea and Trimalchio's feast.

animi vaticinatio appareat quam religiosae orationis sub testibus fides: tamquam, si placet, hic impetus, etiam si nondum recepit ultimam manum.

Look, if anyone undertakes the huge task of composing poetry on civil war
without being full of literature, he will falter under the burden. For history
should not be recorded in verses – historians do that far better; instead, the free
spirit must rush along through indirect utterances, the works of the gods, and
mythical inventions[44] so that it appears the inspired utterance of a mind out of
control rather than sworn testimony before witnesses: for an example, if you
like, here's my attempt on the subject, even if it has not yet received the final
touches.

Here Eumolpus addresses an issue which is central, and as far as we
know unique, to Lucan's poem on the Civil War: Eumolpus criticizes
poets who are too much like historians (and not poetic enough), and he
insists that the actions of the gods should be represented in an historical epic poem. Feeney has usefully drawn attention to ancient analyses
of the differences between poetic and historical narratives of events:
historical narratives include what is plausible and realistic, while poetic
narratives include what is fabulous, implausible, and most especially
the realm of the divine. In the Roman tradition, Naevius and Ennius
use divine characters in their narratives of Roman history. As Feeney
observes, the representation of the role of the gods in historical epic
can display differing shades of poetic implausibility: divine councils,
gods interacting with humans, gods conversing among themselves, and
iconic representations of the gods such as those on the shield of Aeneas
are all possibilities.[45] Much Greek and Roman historical epic has been
lost, of course, but of the Roman historical poets for whom we have
evidence, Lucan is the only one to have excluded the traditional divine
machinery of epic from his poem, and the only one to have been ac-
cused of not being sufficiently "poetic." Martial composes an epigram
on whether Lucan should be called a poet; Quintilian says that Lucan
is more suitable for imitation by orators than by poets; and Servius
remarks that Lucan should not be numbered among the poets at all.[46]
Lucan's exclusion of the gods evidently struck readers as remarkable,
and Eumolpus' contrast between a poet who narrates history without

---

[44] Though the text seems corrupt it is clear that Eumolpus is contrasting historical narrative with mythical narrative (*fabula*); cf. Feeney (1991), 263 n. 52. Courtney (1970),
68, offers as an "outline of an emendation" *fabulosum argumentum velut* (or *tamquam*)
tormento.

[45] Feeney (1991), 250–69.

[46] Mart. 14.194; Quintilian 10.1.90; Servius on *Aen.* 1.382. On negative criticism of
Lucan in antiquity and the Middle Ages see Sanford (1931), 233–57.

the gods and one who includes the gods in a *fabula* about historical events would strike most readers as a reference to Lucan's bold innovations.[47] Yet Eumolpus' gods are more like Statius' allegorical figures than they are like Virgil's Olympians: Statius can even be described as Eumolpus' "dream come true."[48] Sullivan argues: "Petronius' return to Virgilian practice with perhaps the addition of more abstract deities such as Pietas, Fides, and so on, a growing Silver age tendency, seems a purely conservative reaction; there is no new spirit or deeper treatment than Virgil offered."[49]

The image that a poet who is not "full of literature" (*plenus litteris*) "will collapse under the weight" of civil war narrative (*sub onere labetur*, 118.6), is a peculiarly apt one, reflecting the common figuration of civil strife as cosmic dissolution of a world out of balance. Lucan explicitly compares the Civil War with cosmic dissolution, summing up with the phrase *in se magna ruunt* ("great things collapse upon themselves," *Ph.*1.81). In Eumolpus' poem we have already seen that the graves of Crassus, Pompey, and Caesar are figured as a weight which has to be spread evenly over the earth, lest they become a force for dissolution (65–66). The god Dis, concerned for the integrity of his underground realm, has his own more literal understanding of Rome's weightiness,

---

[47] Eumolpus' remarks are read as a comment on Lucan's exclusion of the gods from epic by e.g., Erhard cited in Burman (1743), vol. I, 708; Heitland in his introductory remarks at Haskins (1887) xxxvi–xxxvii, Sanford (1931), 234; Morford (1967), 85; Ahl (1976), 68; Johnson (1987), 3; Bramble in *CHCL* 2, 533; Häussler (1978), 106. Some readers remain skeptical of the claim that Petronius is commenting on Lucan and deem resemblances between the two texts purely coincidental: George (1974), 132, is followed by Smith (1975), 214–17; cf. Slater (1990), 198–99. The argument of Grimal (1977) that the resemblances result from Lucanian imitation of Petronius is unconvincing; see the review by Walsh (1980), 174.

There is also the question of meter: is Petronius' hexameter style a parody or a critique of Lucan's? It seems to be more similar to Virgil's than to Lucan's: Trampe (1884), 78; Stubbe (1933), 103; Sullivan (1968a), 179. Duckworth (1967), 101–03, 142, characterizes Petronius' hexameter in the *Bellum Civile* as more spondaic than Lucan's, and thus closer to Virgil's, and displaying greater variety than Lucan's, but without Virgil's subtle techniques of variation, especially in the handling of the fourth foot. But in Duckworth's studies the most significant division in hexameter style emerges between the more spondaic "Virgilian norm" and the more dactylic "Ovidian" style, and Lucan is closer to Virgil than to Ovid: see Duckworth (1967), 77–79, 88–91, 147.

[48] Henderson (1991), 31 (contesting this description).

[49] So Sullivan (1968a), 183–84. Some critics defend Lucan's epic strategies from what they perceive as Eumolpus' critique by arguing that since Virgil used the gods to participate (however complicated and equivocal that participation might be) in the view that Rome's history was a fulfillment of a divine plan, Lucan had to exclude the gods because he wished to present Caesar and Caesar's cause as morally inferior to those who opposed him. See Bramble in *CHCL* 2, 533, Johnson (1987), 3–4, and compare Ahl (1976), 68–69.

and asks if Fortuna has been so overpowered by Rome's weight that she is no longer able to elevate it to a height from which it must topple and fall (82–85):

> ecquid Romano sentis te pondere victam,
> nec posse ulterius perituram extollere molem?
> ipsa suas vires odit Romana iuventus
> et quas struxit opes, male sustinet.

> is it that you feel overwhelmed by the Roman burden
> and are not able to raise its mass further to a ruinous height?
> The Roman youth holds its own strength in contempt
> and can scarcely uphold what it has built.

Eumolpus subsequently introduces the gods' participation in the battle with a vocabulary of shifting weight and cosmic dissolution (*BC* 264–66):

> sentit terra deos mutataque sidera pondus
> quaesivere suum; namque omnis regia caeli
> in partes diducta ruit.

> The earth felt the presence of the gods, the stars shifted and
> tried to regain their equilibrium; for the whole heavenly realm
> divided and rushed to take sides.

As we have seen elsewhere in Petronius' verse, the figures deployed in poetry are here too made concretely real in the surrounding narrative. According to Eumolpus' poetic programme, a poet's capacity to represent the works (*ministeria*) of the gods alleviates the metaphorical burden (*onus*) of civil war poetry. Within the poem, he alludes to figures which represent civil strife as cosmic dissolution in the form of a great weight collapsing on itself. Meanwhile, the hired laborer (*mercennarius*) Corax, described as a "shirker of his work" (*detractator ministerii*) has just objected to carrying the baggage, putting it down frequently and saying that he will either throw it away or run away "with the burden" (*cum onere*, 117.11). Eumolpus' capacity to carry this epic narrative, which he figuratively makes as weighty as possible, finds its counterpart in Corax's capacity to carry the luggage. As a treatment of civil war, the poem itself is "unbalanced," for all of its narrative is taken up with various beginnings, breaking off before conflict is joined.

Divine machinery

Dis' condemnation of Roman decadence differs from the poem's first human geography of decadence in that it is constructed around the tripartite division of the world into heaven, earth and underworld and around notions of divine rivalry and strife. Dis explains that Roman buildings make an assault on the heavenly realm while Roman engineering works upset the order of the earth and challenge his own realms (*BC* 87–93):

> aedificant auro sedesque ad sidera mittunt,
> expelluntur aquae saxis, mare nascitur arvis,
> et permutata rerum statione rebellant.
> en etiam mea regna petunt. perfossa dehiscit
> molibus insanis tellus, iam montibus haustis
> antra gemunt, et dum vanos lapis invenit usus,
> inferni manes caelum sperare fatentur.

> They build with gold, and make their houses rise to the stars,
> water is driven back by their stone piers, sea is born in the fields,
> and they rebel by overturning the order of nature.
> They seek my realm too! Earth has been dug up for insane
>   structures
> and gapes open, in mined mountains
> caves moan, and while a precious stone finds useless uses,
> my infernal shades say they hope to see the sky.

The Roman architectural assault on the heavens is parallel to the mythical aggression of the giants against Olympus, and the Roman mining assaults on the realm of Dis are a kind of anti-gigantomachy. The notion of the inhabitants of the underworld perceiving a threat to its structural integrity has a long history. In the *Iliad* as the battle rages among men, Homer describes how the gods join in battle themselves. When men fight, their cries resound in the heavens, but when the gods fight they make so much noise that Hades fears for the safety of his realm (*Il.* 20.61–66). In a simile which describes Hercules' struggle with Cacus, Virgil seems to "correct" the Homeric scene: he represents the shades, not the god, fearing for the safety of the underworld (*Aen.* 8.243–46).[50] In Ovid's *Metamorphoses*, Hades fears the commotion of Typhoeus' struggles to escape imprisonment under Aetna after his defeat by Jove (Ov. *Met.* 5.356–58). Thus, while Dis' complaints in Eumolpus' poem about interference with the underworld are traditional, the source of that interference is untraditional: Eumolpus re-

---

[50] Innes (1979), 169 n. 2. Hades' fears are read allegorically by Theagenes, quoted at Schol. b on *Il.* 20.67 (Diels Kranz 8 fr. 2) and "Longinus" *de sublimitate* 9.7; see Russell (1964) *ad loc.* They were also the subject of discussions of the properties of poetic fictions: *Il.* 20.56–57 T scholia; Plut. *Mor.* 16 d–e.

places traditional divine rivalries and strife with a human assault on the divine order of the world. At the same time, amusingly, Dis himself has an unsettling effect on the world, for when he reaches out to shake Fortuna's hand he causes a breach in the ground where they stand: *rupto tellurem solvit hiatu* ("he made the earth open in a gaping chasm," *BC* 101). At a trivial level, the divine machinery of Dis' gesture re-creates the rupturing of the earth by Romans which Dis has just described (90–93).

At the end of the encounter between Dis and Fortuna, the traditional theme of divine rivalry becomes explicit. After Fortuna foretells civil strife for Rome and a time of plenty for Dis and Tisiphone, lightning flashes (*BC* 122–23). The scene ends awkwardly: Fortuna and Dis do not bid each other farewell; and she is apparently left standing alone in the barren landscape as he, frightened, abruptly retreats to his underground home (*BC* 124–25):

> subsedit pater umbrarum, gremioque reducto
> telluris pavitans fraternos palluit ictus.

> The father of the shades withdrew, and with the bosom of the earth
>   restored
> he grew pale, terrified at his brother's thunderbolts.

Instead of responding to the portent with pleased anticipation at the prospect of war among the Romans and abundance in the underworld, trembling Dis grows pale with fright at the weapons of his brother Jove. Dis' fear of the lightning brings fraternal rivalry between Dis and Jupiter into focus. In Dis' mind at least, the ancient discord between Jove and the giants could be replayed at any time, with Dis himself as a potential victim.

One of the civil war portents also evokes gigantomachic strife. In the earlier accounts of Virgil and Livy, the death of Caesar was marked by a peculiar eruption of Aetna. Like Lucan, Eumolpus shifts the portent to the outbreak of war. With the phrase *ignibus insolitis*, Eumolpus specifies that the eruption was unusual (*BC* 135–36):

> iamque Aetna voratur
> ignibus insolitis

> and now Aetna is engulfed
> by strange flames

Of course, the flames of volcanic eruptions are never ordinary, but Lucan, in his account of the portents which announced the beginning

of the Civil War, speaks in more detail about the strangeness of the
eruption (*Ph.*1.545–47):

> ora ferox Siculae laxavit Mulciber Aetnae,
> nec tulit in caelum flammas sed vertice prono
> ignis in Hesperium cecidit latus.

> In Sicily fierce Vulcan opened the mouths of Aetna;
> he did not raise flames into the sky, but the fire turned its crest
>   sideways
> and fell on the Hesperian shore.

Livy's description of an eruption of Aetna at the time of Caesar's death
is quoted by Servius in his comment on Virg. *G.* 1.472:

et, ut dicit Livius, tanta flamma ante mortem Caesaris ex Aetna monte defluxit
ut non tantum vicinae urbes sed etiam Regina civitas adflaretur.

and, as Livy says, such a great flame flowed out of Mount Aetna before the
death of Caesar that not only the nearby cities but even Regium felt its heat.

Petronius and Lucan both use the detail of the strange nature of this
eruption. Yet, if the peculiar quality of this eruption, as recorded by
Livy and Lucan, is that the flames went sideways toward Italy, why
does Eumolpus go on to say that Aetna did send bursts of light into
the sky, *et in aethera fulmina mittit* (136) when Lucan had specifically
denied this (*nec tulit in caelum flammas* 546)? This can be interpreted
either as poetic incompetence (Eumolpus doesn't know that the flames
went toward the Italian coast), or clever reshaping of a model (Eumolpus has a good reason for denying that the flames went toward the
Italian coast). The choice of the word *fulmina* to describe the flashing
fire of the eruption is significant, because Jupiter's lightning bolts,
fulmina, were forged by the Cyclopes in Aetna after Jove imprisoned
them there in defeat.[51] Indeed, Virgil's description of the eruption
emphasizes that Aetna was the location of the forge of the Cyclopes
(Virg. *G.* 1.471–73). When in Eumolpus' account of the eruption of
Aetna the flames go toward the sky, the effect is to emphasize that
Jove's own weapons are turned against him in a resurgence of gigantic
aggression.[52]

---

[51] See Virg. *Aen.* 8.424–28; Ov. *Met.* 5.346–57; Hor. *C.* 3.4.75–76; Man. 2.877–80.
Cicero ridicules this belief at *Div.* 2.19.43, while the author of the *Aetna* rejects the
mythical accounts of Aetna's volcanic acitivity because they portray violence inappropriate to the true nature of the gods (*Aetna* 37–74).

[52] Other poets too had seen the eruptions of Aetna as a sign of the giants' persistent
defiance of Jove: cf. the remarks of Hardie (1986), 264, on the flames of Aetna
as "a recurrent gesture of defiance" at *Aen.* 3.572–74, as well as his interpretation of

Now the Homeric motif of rivalry among Zeus, Poseidon, and Hades found its way into Plutarch's account of the conflict between Caesar and Pompey. The vast power of Rome over the whole world could not satisfy the two men, Plutarch says, even though they had read in Homer about the arrangement made by Zeus, Poseidon, and Hades to avoid conflict. Plutarch quotes the *Iliad* (15.189) when he makes an explicit comparison between the way in which Zeus, Poseidon, and Hades resolved the problem of fraternal strife by drawing lots, and the way in which Caesar and Pompey rejected all compromise.[53] Plutarch's version of the conflict between Caesar and Pompey constructs a strong contrast between the world of the gods (where conflict is averted) and the world of men (where the Civil War breaks out). Lucan's version of the conflict (*non cepit fortuna duos, Ph.* 1.111) edits out the divine contrast. Eumolpus, as often, makes the figurative and the real closely congruent and constructs a picture of gods who correspond closely to men in their conflicts, rivalries, and potential for fraternal strife.

Phlegraean stories

Dis and Fortuna have their talk in the Campi Phlegraei near Lake Avernus in Campania (*BC* 67–75). Though the name is not mentioned, it does not need to be: the Campanian volcanic landscape described in the ecphrasis is unambiguously the Phlegraean fields. This spot is a logical place for the meeting to take place because it is near an entrance to the underworld. It also allows Eumolpus' narrative to be measured against several other Phlegraean stories.

Eumolpus engages in a small gesture of literary rivalry when he describes the Phlegraean fields. By asserting that there is no birdsong in this place, Eumolpus alludes to the notion that the gases emanating from Lake Avernus would poison birds. Lucretius and Virgil

---

Lucretius' description of lightning from Aetna at *DRN* 1.722–25 as "an attack on heaven with its own weapons" (211).

[53] Plut. *Pomp.* 53.7: οὕτως ἡ τύχη μικρόν ἐστι πρὸς τὴν φύσιν· οὐ γὰρ ἀποπίμπλησιν αὐτῆς τὴν ἐπιθυμίαν, ὅπου τοσοῦτον βάθος ἡγεμονίας καὶ μέγεθος εὐρυχωρίας δυοῖν ἀνδροῖν οὐκ ἐπέσχεν, ἀλλ' ἀκούοντες καὶ ἀναγινώσκοντες, ὅτι 'τριχθὰ δὲ πάντα δέδασται' τοῖς θεοῖς, 'ἕκαστος δ' ἔμμορε τιμῆς' ἑαυτοῖς οὐκ ἐνόμιζον ἀρκεῖν δυσὶν οὖσι τὴν Ῥωμαίων ἀρχήν. So insignificant is fortune in respect to human nature; for fortune does not satisfy human nature's desire, since all that extent of power and magnitude of far-reaching domain was not sufficient for two men. Though they had heard and read that "the universe was divided into three parts" by the gods and "each got his own domain," they did not believe that the dominion of the Romans was enough for themselves, though there were only two of them.

yield evidence for two etymological explanations for the name of Lake
Avernus in terms of "birdlessness": one from the Latin *avis* (bird) and
one from the Greek ἄορνος (birdless).[54] In responding to these ety-
mologies, Eumolpus leaves his own mark on the etymological tradition
surrounding Avernus in his description of the unheard birdsong (*BC*
72–73):

> non verno persona cantu
> mollia discordi strepitu virgulta loquuntur

> nor do tender branches
> resounding with a spring song murmur with a discordant noise.

Though *non* negates *loquuntur* in the following line, the juxtaposition of
non and *verno* momentarily re-etymologizes the name of Lake Avernus.
Non verno, with the Latin *non* replaced by the Greek alpha privative
from ἀ-ορνος, is *A-verno*, Avernian birdsong, that is, no song at all.[55]

The name "Phlegraean," "enflamed," was derived from hot springs
and gaseous emanations which were explained as the lingering results
of the cosmic discord stirred up by the giants and suppressed by Jove
with the aid of Hercules. The name is bestowed on this area of Cam-

---

[54] For the word ἄορνος /*aornos* compare Pliny *Nat.* 4.1.2. Lucretius discusses Lake
Avernus at length (Lucr. 6.740–46), and even refers to a whole category of such
places as *loca Averna* (*DRN* 6.738, 740, 818). Though the etymology from ἄορνος underlies Lucretius' analysis of the name Avernus, with the phrase *avibus contraria*
(harmful to birds) in 6.741 he also seems to etymologize Avernus from the Latin word
avis. So Snyder (1980), 105. When Virgil maps the geography of Aeneas' entrance to
the underworld under the guidance of the Sibyl of Cumae, he does not name Avernus
directly, but designates it unmistakeably by saying that it is a lake which has no birds
(Virgil *Aen.* 6.237–42). Mynors (1969) records that line 242 (*unde locum Grai dixerunt
nomine Aornum*) is an interpolation which appears in only one of the four capital
manuscripts at this point, R, and in two of the ninth-century codices, b and g; in g it
appears before line 241.

[55] Although the etymology of Avernus was susceptible of analysis in both Latin (from *avis*)
and Greek (from ἄορνος), it may seem bold to suspect an etymological pun which
combines both Greek and Latin elements. An example of an etymology from the Augustan period which combines both Greek and Latin elements is found at Isid. 14.8.33,
citing Verrius Flaccus as an authority for an alternative etymology of the word *amoenus*
from *a* + *munus*, that is, "without a product."
   A similarly forced etymological pun is contrived in the description of the comet listed
among the portents signalling the outbreak of war. Like Lucan (*Ph.* 1.529), Eumolpus
incorporates the comet into his catalogue of portents at the beginning of the war: *fax
stellis comitata novis incendia ducit* ("a blazing light accompanied by new stars brings on
conflagrations," *BC* 139). Lucan alludes to the etymology of the word *cometes* from the
word *coma* (and in Greek, κομήτης from κόμη) by mentioning the "hair" of the comet
(*crinemque timendi/sideris*, *Ph.* 1.528–9, cf. Ov. *Met.* 15.849). Against the background of
other poetic treatments of the comet, especially Lucan's, Eumolpus devises an alternative etymology for *cometes* from the verb *comitor* ("accompany") with a pun on the
participle *comitata*.

pania (see Pliny *Nat.* 3.61) by analogy with the volcanic landscape of Phlegra in Greece.[56] By their analogy to gigantomachy, civil war stories are Phlegraean stories, whether the Phlegraean fields are thought of as Greek or Campanian. As part of an imaginative strategy to suggest that during the years which saw the end of the Republic the forces of good and order defeated the forces of evil and chaos, Augustus' victories over Antony and others are described as or assimilated to gigantomachies by Augustan poets, especially in the poetic gesture of *recusatio*.[57] Roman civil discord is figuratively associated with Phlegraean gigantomachy in Statius' references to the battle between the Vitellians and the Flavians on the Capitoline in 69 as a gigantomachy, *Phlegraea ... proelia* ("Phlegraean battles," *Silv.* 5.3.195–97, cf. *Theb.* 1.22, Mart. 9.101.14). Although it is not easy to tell how "serious" or "sincere" Lucan is being in his construction of Nero as a force for order in the Roman world, his proem places his story of Julius Caesar's war squarely within this tradition. Just as the strife of the gigantomachy was all worthwhile because it had established a world order ruled by Jove, he says, the strife of the Civil War was all worthwhile if it was the only way to bring Nero to power (*Ph.* 1.33–38).[58] Lucan suggests that the battles of Caesar and Pompey's Civil War are fought on the site of the gigantomachy by saying that Emathia, the land which fate designated for the Civil War, is bounded by Pelion and Ossa, and that the plain of Pharsalus rose out of the sea when the gods defeated the giants and Ossa was pushed down from the top of Olympus (*Ph.* 6.332–49). In Eumolpus' poem, Caesar's descent into Italy explicitly replays the Olympian suppression of gigantomachy (*BC* 206–08):

> aut torvo Iuppiter ore,
> cum se verticibus magni demisit Olympi
> et periturorum disiecit tela Gigantum.

> or like Jupiter looking fierce,
> when he hurled himself down from the Olympian heights
> and scattered the weapons of the doomed giants.

---

[56] Lucan compares the preparations for war at Pharsalus to preparations for the gigantomachy at Phlegra (*Ph.* 7.144–50). For versions set in Campania, see Prop. 1.20.9, Strabo 5.4.4, 5.4.6, 6.3.5; Diod. 4.21.5, 5.71.4. On Lucan's evocations of gigantomachy see Masters (1992), 39–40, 154–55.

[57] Augustus' victories are likened to the gigantomachy or Jove's victory against the Titans at Hor. *C.* 3.4, Prop. 2.1.17–42, Ov. *Tr.* 2.61–76, with 33–36, and compare Tib. 2.5.5–10 with Smith (1913) *ad loc.* For detailed discussion see Hardie (1986), 85–89.

[58] Hinds (1988), 26–29, with the comments of Feeney (1991), 297–301, on the one hand and Dewar (1994) on the other represent the range of approaches to the rhetoric of Lucan's praises of Nero in his proem.

Later, there is a hint that Pompey may have gigantic qualities when Pompey's triumphs are said to have disturbed Jove (*modo quem ter ovantem / Iuppiter horruerat*, BC 240–41). The suggestion that Jove feared Pompey triumphing three times figuratively associates Pompey's triumphs with the giants' triple assault on the heavens (cf. Virg. *G.* 1.281–83) – and gives a mythical dimension to his name *magnus*.

In addition to the mythical paradigm of gigantomachy which makes a civil war a Phlegraean story, there is also a particular historical "Phlegraean" event which was eventually viewed as significant in the outbreak of Julius Caesar's Civil War. Pompey was gravely ill in Campania in 50, and later it was widely thought that it would have been better if he had died there. According to the historical accounts of Plutarch and Appian, the rejoicing that followed Pompey's recovery was said to have done more than anything else to bring about the war because it made Pompey overconfident of his own power and contemptuous of Caesar's.[59] In the *Tusculan Disputations*, Cicero treats the episode in detail in order to argue that while one usually views an escape from death as good fortune, in some situations, like Pompey's, an escape from death is a great misfortune (*Cic. Tusc. Disp.* 1.86):[60]

Pompeio, nostro familiari, cum graviter aegrotaret Neapoli, melius est factum. coronati Neapolitani fuerunt, nimirum etiam Puteolani; volgo ex oppidis publice gratulabantur: ineptum sane negotium et Graeculum, sed tamen fortunatum. utrum igitur, si tum esset extinctus, a bonis rebus an a malis discessisset? certe a miseris. non enim cum socero bellum gessisset, non inparatus arma sumpsisset, non domum reliquisset, non ex Italia fugisset, non exercitu amisso nudus in servorum ferrum et manus incidisset, †non liberi defleti, non fortunae omnes a victoribus possiderentur. qui, si mortem tum obisset, in amplissimis fortunis occidisset, is propagatione vitae quot, quantas, quam incredibilis hausit calamitates!

There was a recovery for our friend Pompey when he was seriously ill at Naples. The people of Naples were decked out with garlands, and of course the Puteolans too; there were public celebrations from the towns all over. Certainly the whole business was foolish and Greekish, but it was a sign of good fortune. So would he have left good circumstances or bad behind if he had died then? Surely he would have avoided wretchedness. For he would not have gone to war with his father-in-law, nor taken up arms unprepared, nor left his home, nor fled from Italy, nor would he have lost his army and have fallen prey unarmed to a band of armed slaves, †nor would his children have been lamented nor all his fortune be in the possession of the victors. If he had died then, he

---

[59] Plut. *Pomp.* 57; cf. Cic. *Att.* 8.16.1 (166 SB) , 9.5.4 (171 SB); App. *b.c.* 2.28; Vell. 2.48.2; Seager (1979), 157.

[60] Cited from the Teubner edition of Pohlenz (1965).

would have died at the pinnacle of good fortune. By the extension of his life, how many, how great, how inconceivable the catastrophes he suffered!

Cicero explicitly makes Pompey's recovery the catalyst of all the events of the Civil War and implies that Pompey would have been more truly favored by *fortuna* if he had died of his illness. Propertius too says that it would have been better if Pompey had died, and locates the scene of Pompey's illness specifically in the Phlegraean fields (Prop. 3.11.37):

> issent Phlegraeo melius tibi funera campo

> Better for you had the Phlegraean plain witnessed your funeral
>   procession

For Juvenal too, Pompey's recovery led only to trouble (*Sat.* 10.283–86):

> provida Pompeio dederat Campania febres
> optandas, sed multae urbes et publica vota
> vicerunt; igitur Fortuna ipsius et Urbis
> servatum victo caput abstulit.

> Providential Campania had bestowed fevers on Pompey
> which he should have welcomed, but many cities and public prayers
> prevailed; then, once Fortune – his and Rome's – saved his head,
> she snatched it away from him in defeat.

Thus, the poetic invention of the council of war between Fortuna and Dis in the Phlegraean fields, a standard piece of divine machinery, also reaches out to embrace Pompey's "ill-fated" deliverance from death in Campania in 50, which was widely viewed as an instance of the power of *fortuna* and as a cause of war.

Itineraries

In the *Bellum Civile* and its frame, representations of paths and roads cross and recross the thresholds between prose and verse, past and present, individual and empire. While Eumolpus travels toward Croton, he uses the traditional metaphor of the path to describe the correct practice of poetry, and then performs a poem whose characters do little more than travel or talk.

   To introduce Caesar and his role in the war, Eumolpus describes him crossing the Alps and advancing towards Rome. Lucan too gives Caesar a starting point in the Alps, but gets him over them in a single line, *iam gelidas Caesar cursu superaverat Alpes* ("Now Caesar had quickly crossed the frozen Alps," *Ph.* 1.183), to stage the crossing of the Rubicon at length (185–227).[61] In crossing the Alps Caesar is following in the legendary footsteps of Hercules, who was said to have crossed the Alps and descended into Italy on his way home to Greece after obtaining the cattle of Geryon. When Cacus stole the cattle, Hercules killed him, and his destruction of Cacus and establishment of peace in the landscape that would become Rome was commemorated in the establishment of the Ara Maxima.[62] Eumolpus uses a geographical ecphrasis to emphasize that Caesar follows precisely in the footsteps of Hercules (*BC* 144–51):

> Alpibus aeriis, ubi Graio numine pulsae
> descendunt rupes et se patiuntur adiri,
> est locus Herculeis aris sacer. hunc nive dura
> claudit hiemps canoque ad sidera vertice tollit:
> caelum illinc cecidisse putes. non solis adulti
> mansuescit radiis, non verni temporis aura,
> sed glacie concreta rigent hiemisque pruinis:
> totum ferre potest umeris minitantibus orbem.

> In the high Alps, where the crags trodden by the Greek deity
> slope down and allow themselves to be approached,
> there is a place sacred to the altars of Hercules: winter
> shuts it in with unyielding snow, and raises it to the sky on its snowy
>   height.
> You would think that the sky had fallen away from there:
> it is not warmed by the rays of the full sun, nor by the springtime
>   breeze,
> but its frozen land is rigid with ice and winter frost:
> it can bear the whole world on its menacing shoulders.

This place in the Alps once trodden by a Greek divinity, Hercules, and sacred to his altars is Monoecus (Monaco).[63] Virgil too had located the beginning of Caesar's advance in the Alps at Monoecus, when

---

[61] Caesar, in his *Bellum Civile*, maintains that only after repeated attempts at a settlement while he was in Ravenna (*Civ.* 1.1), and after the tribunes M. Antonius and Q. Cassius fled from the violence threatened against them at Rome (*Civ.* 1.6), did he turn from negotiation to arms and seize Ariminum (*Civ.* 1.8.1). In order to represent himself as a man who attempted negotiation as long as possible (cf. *Civ.* 1.5.5), Caesar suppresses any mention of crossing the Rubicon, which marked the boundary between his legal and illegal command of an army.

[62] Livy 1.7.4–15; Virg. *Aen.* 8.193–275; Prop. 4.9; Ov. *F.* 1.543–86. Diodorus Siculus recounts the legend of Hercules and Cacus (1.39), and then presents a rationalizing version of the tale, arguing that Hercules marched over the Alps into Italy with an army and liberated the people from the oppressive rule of tyrants (1.41–42). Elsewhere Diodorus remarks that Hercules' journey over the Alps itself had a lasting effect on the landscape, making the way, which had been impassable, now passable for armies (18.19.3). Nepos too says that Hercules was the first to cross the Alps with an army (*Han.* 3.4).

[63] Pliny *Nat.* 3.47.

Anchises shows Aeneas the future of Rome, and laments the coming of the Civil War (Virg. *Aen.* 6. 828–31):

> heu quantum inter se bellum, si lumina vitae
> attigerint, quantas acies stragemque ciebunt,
> aggeribus socer Alpinis atque arce Monoeci
> descendens, gener adversis instructus Eois!

> Alas, if they reach life's light, what a war,
> what battle lines and slaughter they will create,
> father-in-law making his way down from the Alps and the heights of
>   Monoecus,
> son-in-law arrrayed against him with Eastern enemies!

Eumolpus, typically, devises an excessively close correspondence between Hercules and Monoecus: the place itself is Herculean because it "can bear the whole world on its menacing shoulders" (*totum ferre potest umeris minitantibus orbem, BC* 151), and Eumolpus matches form to content by balancing *totum* at the beginning and *orbem* at the end around *umeris* in the center of the line.[64]

As he makes his way down from the Alps in the poem, Caesar himself is explicitly compared to Hercules descending the Caucasus, where he releases Prometheus from bondage (*BC* 205–06):

> qualis Caucasea decurrens arduus arce
> Amphitryoniades ...

> like the lofty son of Amphitryon, rushing
> down from the heights of the Caucasus

In a reversal of the conceit which bestowed Herculean attibutes on Monoecus, Eumolpus here says that Hercules himself is *arduus*, a word more commonly used of steep or lofty terrain.[65] The Monoecus passage alludes to Hercules' ascent of the Alps; to capture the image of Caesar descending the Alps, the ever deliberate Eumolpus turns to the story of Hercules' descent from the Caucasus after killing the eagle who tormented Prometheus.[66]

---

[64] It was Atlas' task to uphold the world, cf. Virg. *Aen.* 4.481–82. In some versions of the labor of the Apples of the Hesperides, Hercules takes the burden of the world while Atlas obtains the apples (Pher. *FGrHist* 3 F 17; cf. Eur. *Her.* 403–07, where Hercules obtains the apples himself and then takes the world on his shoulders). A rationalizing version of the story appears at Diod. 4.27.2.

[65] Cf. Virgil's description of the Cyclops: *ipse arduus, altaque pulsat sidera* (*Aen.* 3.619–20). See too Hardie (1989), 16, on Silius' assimilation of Hannibal himself to a mountain as he descends from the Alps (*Pun.* 4.751–53).

[66] It is clear from Strabo and Dionysius that Hercules' descent of the Caucasus was the beginning of his journey westward; they cite Prometheus' prophetic account of Hercules' travels in pursuit of the Apples of the Hesperides and the Cattle of Geryon. Thus

Associating Caesar's entry into Italy with Hercules can assimilate Caesar's move toward Rome to Hercules' civilizing progress through Italy. But because Hannibal's march into Italy had already long been figured as a recapitulation of Hercules' crossing of the Alps,[67] the Herculean paradigm is in some ways an ambivalent one, and its negative and dangerous aspects are brought to the surface when Caesar stops at the summit and looks out over the plains of Italy (*BC* 152–54):[68]

> haec ubi calcavit Caesar iuga milite laeto
> optavitque locum, summo de vertice montis
> Hesperiae campos late prospexit . . .

> When Caesar trod on these heights with his high-spirited soldiers
> and chose a spot, from the top of the mountain
> he looked far over the plains of Italy . . .

Here Eumolpus models his account of Caesar's speech to his troops on a scene in Livy in which Hannibal, to encourage his weary troops for the descent from the Alps, shows them the plains of northern Italy and says that they are scaling the walls not only of Italy but of Rome itself. (Lucan had dramatized Caesar gazing upon Rome from the heights of Anxur at a later stage in his journey, *Ph.* 3.88.) Still, there are obvious differences between Eumolpus' Caesar and Livy's Hannibal. For one thing, Caesar's soldiers do not need encouragement; they are *laeti*. And Caesar's speech proves to be an essay in self-justification, not an appeal to the determination of his men. Livy painstakingly counts the days spent in Hannibal's crossing of the Alps,[69] but Eumolpus' Caesar apparently accomplishes the trip swiftly. Yet when Livy describes Hannibal's dangerous descent from the heights of the Alps he says that

Caesar's ascent and descent of the Alps here reverses the Herculean paradigm, in which descent of the Caucasus precedes ascent of the Alps. See Strabo 4.1.7 and Dion. Hal. 1.41.3, citing Aeschylus' *Prometheus Unbound* (Nauck fr. 199) for an aetiological account of the round stones in the Ligurian plain, and cf. Hyginus *Poet. Astr.* 2.6. A section of this play was translated by Cicero (*Tusc. Disp.* 2.23–25), and the story in some form was the background for Varro's Menippean satire *Prometheus Liber.*

[67] Polybius rebukes historians who provide a *deus ex machina* to aid Hannibal in his journey over the Alps (3.47.8–9, 48.8), and this *deus* was probably Hercules: Hannibal probably promoted the resemblance himself by marking his departure from Gades (the beginning of Hercules' journey toward Rome) with vows to Hercules. On the "Road of Hercules" see further DeWitt (1941).

[68] Livy 21.35.7–9. The parallel between Caesar and Hannibal is frequently observed: cf. Gonzales de Salas at Burman (1743) vol.2, 242; Mössler (1870), on 153; Collignon (1892), 173; Baldwin (1911) on 154; Stubbe (1933) on 153 f.; Luck (1972), 138; Grimal (1977), 45.

[69] Livy 21.38.1 says that Hannibal spent fifteen days crossing the Alps, but see the calculations of Walbank (1957) on Polyb. 3.56.3–4.

the snow melted because of the passage of so many men and beasts, and that the way became so slippery that it was almost impassable, and Eumolpus places Caesar in similar difficulties (*BC* 187–92):[70]

> sed postquam turmae nimbos fregere ligatos
> et pavidus quadrupes undarum vincula rupit,
> incaluere nives. mox flumina montibus altis
> undabant modo nata, sed haec quoque – iussa putares –
> stabant, et vincta fluctus stupuere ruina,
> et paulo ante lues iam concidenda iacebat.

> But after the troops broke through the frozen mist
> and the frightened horses burst through the bonds that held the water
>   together,
> the snows melted. Soon just-born rivers rolled down
> from the high mountains, but these too – you'd think they had been
>   commanded –
> stood still, and with the rushing flood reined in the waves were
>   paralyzed,
> and what just moments before was flowing now lay frozen solid and
>   had to be cut through.

In the midst of the disaster, the way freezes again, bringing further troubles. Always reluctant to pass up an opportunity to match literary form to content, Eumolpus halts his own description of the halted rush of the streams with the interjection *iussa putares*.

We know that Hannibal's crossing of the Alps was a favorite rhetorical set-piece.[71] It is possible that Eumolpus is simply under the sway of such rhetorical displays when he sends his Caesar over the Alps in Hannibal's footsteps. But Eumolpus is not the first to perceive Caesar as a second Hannibal. In a letter dated to 21 January 49, Cicero writes to Atticus of Caesar's approach: *utrum de imperatore populi Romani an de Hannibale loquimur?* ("Are we speaking of the commander of the Roman people or of Hannibal?" Cic. *Ad Att.* 7.11.1 = Shackleton Bailey 134). Lucan explicitly compares Caesar to Hannibal several times, and first does so implicitly in the simile comparing Caesar to a Libyan lion as he crosses the Rubicon at *Ph.* 1.205–12.[72] Eumolpus transfers Caesar's attack on Italy from the banks of the Rubicon to the

---

[70] See Livy 21.35.7–36.8; cf. Polyb. 3.55. So Collignon (1892), 173–74; Baldwin (1911) on *BC* 187 ff., and p. 38; Ernout (1923) on *BC* 186.

[71] Cf. Juv. 10.166–67.

[72] Caesar compares himself to Hannibal at *Ph.* 1.303–05; Caesar's presence at Massilia is implicitly compared to Hannibal's siege of Saguntum at 3.349–54; Caesar is much worse than Hannibal at 7.794–803. On Lucan's use of the comparison between Caesar and Hannibal, see Ahl (1976), 105–12.

Alps in order to compare Caesar with Hannibal; Lucan takes the opposite approach to "Hannibalizing" his representation of Caesar when
he invokes the memory of Hannibal's invasion by comparing Caesar to
a Libyan lion on the banks of the Rubicon.

As Beck observes, "Eumolpus descending on Croton at the head of
his band of rogues is himself a burlesque of the very figure that he sets
at the heart of his own epic, Caesar crossing the Alps." For Beck, the
effect of parallels between Caesar in the Alps and Eumolpus on the
road to Croton "is to compromise the seriousness of the verse and to
expose its spurious grandeur."[73] This is clearly right, but we can go
further still along this road. In Eumolpus' poem, history is a series of
re-enactments: Caesar walked over the Alps in Hannibal's footsteps;
Hannibal walked in Hercules', undoing his civilizing progress with war
and destruction. There is one more thing that Hercules and Hannibal
have in common: they each depart from Italy at Croton. Hercules
leaves behind a bright promise of a fine city in return for the hospitality
of a man named Croton;[74] Hannibal's departure leaves Croton in obscurity for good.[75] If the epic character Caesar follows in their footsteps in crossing the Alps, then so too does the novelistic Encolpius in
arriving at Croton. Indeed, Encolpius' whole journey (that is, what we
know of it) has a similar sweep, for he apparently travels to Italy from
the northwest (at Massilia, west of Monoecus), making his way to
luxury in Campania, and eventually, like Hercules and like Hannibal,
to Croton. In journeying toward Croton, the characters re-enact, in
their own spuriously grand way, the "ends" of Hercules' and Hannibal's Italian itineraries, whose beginnings Caesar re-enacts in the Alps.
Eumolpus' plan to "take" Croton in the guise of an African business-
man recapitulates Hannibal's attack on Croton which led to its current
decayed state.[76] Of course there are obvious differences – and no in-
dication that Encolpius crossed the Alps. Hercules comes to Croton
by sea, from Sicily, Hannibal comes to Croton by land, and Encolpius
by sea from the Bay of Naples. Even so, the novelistic journey does
in some sense retrace Hercules' and Hannibal's progress through Italy,
and at the decayed city of Croton Encolpius comes face to face with the

---

[73] Beck (1979), 248.
[74] Ov. *Met.* 15.12–18; Diod. 4.24.7 says that Hercules killed Croton by accident; this is
not mentioned by Ovid.
[75] Livy 30.19.12–20.7.
[76] And, Conte (1987), 532, following Ciaffi (1955), 126–27, suggests that Eumolpus'
stipulation that his heirs consume his body is a reversal of the vegetarianism taught by
Pythagoras at Croton (see Ov. *Met.* 15.75–478).

lasting effects of their journeys through the landscape.[77] Though Encolpius and his companions wander without a particular plan or destination,[78] for the audience their journey may have a kind of geographical inevitability. The connections I am suggesting here are more covert and untidy than the *Satyricon*'s obvious re-enactments of the Odyssean paradigm, and one would not want to insist too much on a Hercules/Hannibal/Caesar/Encolpius analogy. Still, just as a geographical idiom available to author and audience can create a "zone of proximity" which encompasses both the Odyssean or Aenean epic past and the novelistic present, in Eumolpus' *Bellum Civile* a geographical idiom can suggest that Encolpius, whether he knows it or not, follows in ancient footsteps.

As was the case for the imagery of weight and balance, here too Petronius moves the motif of the journey across the registers of Eumolpus' poem, his lived experience and his poetic programme. Eumolpus begins his "poetics" by mocking poets who lay claim to inspiration in the dream landscape of Helicon: (*Sat.* 118.1):

"multos," inquit Eumolpus "o iuvenes, carmen decepit. nam ut quisque versum pedibus instruxit sensumque teneriore verborum ambitu intexit, putavit se continuo in Heliconem venisse."

"Young men," said Eumolpus, "poetry has deceived many people. For as soon as a man has put a line together in meter, and worked in a meaning with a rather delicate arrangement of words, he right away thinks he has come to Helicon."

Eumolpus phrases his disdain for bad poets as mockery of their illusory journeys to the mountain of inspiration. Then, in recommending that poetic discourse be far removed from ordinary speech, he describes the correct practice of poetry as a path which bad poets either do not see or are afraid to tread (118.4–5):

refugiendum est ab omni verborum, ut ita dicam, vilitate et sumendae voces a plebe semotae, ut fiat "odi profanum vulgus et arceo." praeterea curandum est

---

[77] The bailiff's account of Croton places the city at the end of a descent into obscurity (*urbem antiquissimam et aliquando Italiae primam*, "very ancient and once the leading city of Italy," 116.2), and thus is a pointed reversal of Ovid's narrative of the story told to Numa of its early history and rise to prominence: *Met.* 15. 1–59; cf. Cic. *N.D.* 2.6 (and see other references gathered by Pease [1958] *ad loc.*); *de Inv.* 2.1.1; Livy 23.30.6. On multiple patterns of inversion in the Croton episode, see Fedeli (1987).

[78] Frueh (1988), 134–38, concludes, "due to the absence of temporal markers and sequential transition, the various scenes of the *Satyricon* could be arranged virtually at random without changing the essential nature of the work and without significantly altering the outcome – either for the protagonist or for the audience."

ne sententiae emineant extra corpus orationis expressae, sed intexto vestibus colore niteant. Homerus testis et lyrici Romanusque Virgilius et Horatii curiosa felicitas. ceteri enim aut non viderunt viam qua iretur ad carmen, aut visam timuerunt calcare.

All language that is, so to speak, cheap must be avoided, and words far from plebeian must be chosen, so that "I hate the profane crowd and I keep them away" may be put into practice. Moreover, care must be taken that pointed turns of phrase do not leap out from the body of the narrative, but instead shine with brilliance woven into the texture of the piece. Homer bears witness to this, and the lyric poets, and Roman Virgil and the careful felicity of Horace. For others either have not seen the path which leads to poetry, or if they have seen it they have been afraid to tread upon it.

We saw above that Eumolpus' remarks on the role of the gods in historical epic seem to react to Lucan's exclusion of divine machinery from the *Pharsalia*. His manipulations of the conventional imagery of the poetic path are directed not against Lucan, but against other poets who embrace a set of stylistic features which had come to be associated with Callimachean aesthetics in the Neronian period (we can surmise, mostly on the evidence of texts which mock neo-Callimacheanism, that neo-Callimachean aesthetics include a taste for Greek words and metrical patterns, and an interest in esoteric literary *doctrina*). In his programmatic introduction to the *Aetia*, Callimachus says that Apollo told him not to tread the road that wagons go on (πατέουσιν), nor to follow anyone else's track, but to go his own way. Lucretius says that he makes his way through "pathless places" (*avia ... loca*) to assert the novelty of his poetic project. Propertius asserts that he travels an "untouched path" and a "new path" and Ovid describes his poetic path as "soft"; these are strategies of associating their poetry with lightness, delicacy, and freshness of approach as opposed to a handling of martial or otherwise serious themes in heavily traditional style.[79] Neo-Callimachean poets like the ones Persius mocks in his prologue and first satire probably made much of the "untouched" paths of Callimachean programme. The scanty evidence for Nero's own poetry (collected in Courtney [1993]) indicates that he probably took up Callimacheanism

---

[79] Call. *Aet.* 1, fr. 1.22–28 Pf. Callimachus' use of the word πατέουσιν of wagons here is unusual; elsewhere it is attested only for humans or animals. Hopkinson (1988), 96, suggests that Callimachus may have chosen this word "because in its metaphorical senses it represents what is trite (*tritum < tero*), ground which has been 'gone over' many times." Latin examples of the path of poetry: Lucr. 4.1–2 (=1.926–927) *avia Pieridum peragro loca nullius ante/trita solo*; Prop. 3.1.18 *intacta ... via*, 3.3.18, 26 *nova ... semita*; Ov. *Pont.* 4.16.32 *molle ... iter*.

when it suited him; Persius' satire, then, might include Nero himself
among his targets.[80]

The Latin *calcare* is the regular translation for πατέω, the verb Callimachus uses to describe the wagons which travel on the path a good
poet should avoid, and thus by selecting the verb *calco* for his poetic
programme Eumolpus follows the very path Apollo had warned Callimachus away from.[81] Indeed the "progress" metaphor which underlies
the phrase describing "the arrangement of words into a sentence,"
ambitus verborum (and the Greek term περίοδος which it regularly
translates), itself figuratively associates progress through a sentence
with progress along a path. Thus while the *tener ambitus verborum* which
characterizes the bad poets' works refers in the first instance to the
"delicate arrangement of words," perhaps it also can evoke the delicacy and freshness of the paths which neo-Callimacheans could lay
claim to. The verb *calcare* ("tread") regularly carries connotations of
violence and destruction; when this verb describes someone treading
on a surface, or a snake, or an enemy, his feet leave a lasting mark;
when this verb describes travel, it is usually the case that the terrain is
damaged by being trodden on or that it is all but impassable or otherwise "off limits".[82] In fact, Eumolpus's description of a poet's progress
matches Caesar's progress over the Alps: *calcavit* is the verb used to
describe Caesar's journey (*BC* 152), and in the poem it emphasizes the
outrageousness of crossing the Alps and advancing toward Rome.[83] In
a figurative extension of a common conceit which attributes to the poet
the actions which he describes in the poem, Eumolpus makes the

---

[80] On Callimachean style in the Neronian period see Sullivan (1985), 79–108.

[81] *TLL* 3.135 lines 20–25, 56, 81 and 136 line 45 cite examples where *calco* translates
πατέω. Note also Pliny's account of *patetae* (Gr. πατηταί), a kind of date which bursts
open while still on the tree and looks as if it has been trampled (*calcatis similis*, Pliny
Nat. 13.45).

[82] Treading grapes to make wine (Cato, *R.R.* 112.3; Varro *R.R.* 1.54.2; Ov. *Met.* 2.29;
Fast. 4.897), traveling difficult terrain (Ov. *Her.* 2.121; Sen. *Contr.* 1. praef. 22; Sen.
Phaed. 23; 234), provoking a snake by treading on it (Ov. *Met.* 10.23; 13.804; Luc. *Ph.*
9.738; 837; Sil. 1.286), and trampling on a defeated enemy (Ov. *Am.* 3.11.5; *Met.* 5.88;
12.391; *Tr.* 5.8.10; *Pont.* 4.7.47; *Ib.* 29; Luc. *Ph.* 7.293; 7.332; 9.1044; 10.546). Even
when *calcare* does seem to mean simply "go" or "walk," it usually describes walking in
a place where most people never go (on a body of water which is frozen, Ov. *Tr.*
3.10.39; Sen. *Herc. F.* 535; in the desert at the outer limits of human habitation, Luc.
Ph. 9.606), or where one should not walk (on a grave, Prop. 2.8.20; Luc. *Ph.* 8.805;
9.977), or on something which is marked by being trodden upon (snow, Ov. *Met.*
2.853; *Pont.* 2.5.38; fields of grain damaged by Erichtho's progress at Luc. *Ph.* 6.521),
or on something too valuable to be stepped on (gems, Sen. *Ep.* 86.7; onyx, Luc. *Ph.*
10.117; Mart. 12.50.4). A related notion of damaging progress along a path seems to
emerge from Horace's use of *calcare* to describe traveling a road as a metaphor for dying
(Hor. *C.* 1. 28.15–16).

[83] Compare Baldwin (1911) on 152.

activity of producing the poem, "treading" violently on the path of poetry, congruent with the action of his character Caesar "treading" violently through the Alps.[84]

To describe the appropriate distancing of poetic discourse from ordinary speech, Eumolpus quotes the opening line of Horace's Roman odes, *"odi profanum vulgus et arceo"* ("I hate the profane crowd and I keep them away," *C.* 3.1.1), itself a powerful and prominent quotation from a programmatic epigram by Callimachus: in the epigram, Callimachus says that he hates cyclic epic poetry, a heavily traveled road, and a lover who roams about, and that he avoids the common well, and "I detest all common things" (σικχαίνω πάντα τὰ δημόσια *Ep.* 28.4 Pf.).[85] Perhaps Eumolpus is only thinking of Horace and is unaware of this phrase's Callimachean source, or perhaps he is implying a contrast between Horace's superior adaptation of Callimacheanism and the inferior neo-Callimacheans who are Eumolpus' initial target. Either way, the Callimacheanism of the Augustan poet is a mere fossil in its new post-Horatian context. But Eumolpus' quotation of this line in Eumolpus' programme allows Petronius to bring before his audience the memory of Horace's Roman odes (*C.* 3.1–6), which in their own way represent an Augustan world order – that is, they construct one version of an end for the story of civil strife at Rome; in quoting the line which marks their beginning, Petronius acknowledges that end.

Boundaries

As Aeneas and Turnus move toward their final confrontation in the *Aeneid*, Turnus picks up a huge stone which had been set up as a boundary (*limes*, 12.898) to settle disputes over land and tries to hurl it at Aeneas. At the level of literary history, the stone marks a break with the Homeric past. In the *Iliad*, Diomedes hurls a huge stone like this at Aeneas with murderous success – Aeneas is only saved by the intervention of Aphrodite (*Il.*5.302–10); this time, when Turnus re-enacts Diomedes' attack, he fails to hit the mark and Aeneas wins.[86] In the *Iliad* the stone is just a stone; in Virgil it is a boundary stone,

[84] On the conceit of identifying a poet's action with what his poem describes, see Masters (1992), 6–7, extending the lines of argument pursued by Cairns (1972), 163 and n. 6, and Lieberg (1982).

[85] On Horace's use of Callimachean terms of reference in the Roman odes see Ross (1975), 139–45.

[86] Later in the *Iliad*, Aeneas himself is about to cast the same kind of huge stone at Achilles but is rescued by Poseidon from the certain death that would result (*Il.* 20.283–91). See the excellent discussion of Virgil's multi-layered Homeric allusions by Quint (1993), 68–72.

a claim to possession of land in Italy, and the removal of a boundary marker from the landscape metaphorically clears the ground for the birth of empire *sine fine*, without limit (*Aen.*1.279). This metaphor finds a literal counterpart in the right (not always exercised) afforded to leaders who had expanded Roman *imperium* to expand the city's boundary, the *pomerium*.[87]

Boundary markers which metaphorically signify Rome and its imperial history stand in the text at the end of Lucan's and Eumolpus' civil war texts too. First Eumolpus: in her speech inciting the war, Discordia taunts Pompey, bidding him to fight for the walls of Epidamnus if he does not know how to defend Rome (*BC* 292–93):[88]

> ... nescis tu, Magne, tueri
> Romanas arces? Epidamni moenia quaere

> ... Magnus, don't you know how to protect
> the hills of Rome? Seek the walls of Epidamnus ...

Discordia's question obviously mocks Pompey's flight from the city he professes to defend,[89] while her command that Pompey go to Epidamnus looks ahead to Pompey's failure to press his advantage there, at a point where, as it was widely believed, decisive action against Caesar would have ended the war.[90] The waste of Pompey's efforts at the battle of Dyrrachium, or Epidamnus, is probably suggested in the very name of the place, long deemed inauspicious. Discordia commands: go then to Epidamnus and be damned.[91]

In its juxtaposition with *Romanas arces* (*BC* 293), the language of Discordia's command, *Epidamni moenia quaere*, alludes to Virgil. In Virgil's account of the fall of Troy, Hector appears to Aeneas in a dream and bids him to take flight and found a new city; so is born the idea of Rome (Virg. *Aen.* 2.293–95):

> sacra suosque tibi commendat Troia penatis;
> hos cape fatorum comites, his moenia quaere
> magna pererrato statues quae denique ponto.

> Troy entrusts its holy things and *penates* to you;
> take them up as companions of your fate, seek great walls for them

[87] See Tac. *Ann.* 12.23–4 on Claudius' expansion of the *pomerium*.
[88] Some of the following discussion of the final lines of the *Bellum Civile* first appeared in Connors (1994).
[89] So Collignon (1892), 197.
[90] It was Caesar himself who said this: so Suet. *Jul.* 36; Plut. *Pomp.* 65.5, *Caes.* 39.5; Appian *b.c.* 2.62; cf. Lucan *Ph.* 6.296–313 and 7.312–13; and see Caesar *Civ.* 3.70.1.
[91] For the pun on *damnum/Epidamnus* compare Plaut. *Men.* 263–64, and Pliny *Nat.* 3.145.

which you will build at last after you wander far and wide over the sea.

Discordia's command to Pompey, *Epidamni moenia quaere,* thus restates Hector's exhortation to Aeneas, *his moenia quaere.* The walls which Aeneas dreams he is to seek have yet to be built; in Virgil's poetic vision, the walls of Rome will be the eventual result of Aeneas' obedience to Hector's command. Like Aeneas, Pompey flees from a fallen city in the hope of preserving its legacy. But Aeneas' flight at Hector's command builds Rome, Pompey's flight at Discordia's command destroys it.

The parallel between Pompey and Aeneas is strengthened by the fact that Eumolpus has already represented the flight from Rome in terms which evoke Virgil's Troy.[92] This feature of Eumolpus' poem is best approached through Lucan, who casts the flight from Rome as a negation of the flight from Virgil's Troy (*Ph.* 1.484–522): the young men abandon their aged fathers and do not carry their household gods, nor even stop to pray to them, in their headlong flight from Rome (*Ph.* 1.504–09):[93]

> nullum iam languidus aevo
> evaluit revocare parens coniunxve maritum
> fletibus, aut patrii, dubiae dum vota salutis
> conciperent, tenuere lares; nec limine quisquam
> haesit, et extremo tunc forsitan urbis amatae
> plenus abit visu; ruit inrevocabile volgus.

> Now no parent weak with age
> was able to call anyone back, nor did a wife call back her husband
> with her tears, nor did their ancestral household gods keep them back
> long enough to say prayers for safety that was far from certain;
> nor did anyone hang back on the threshold, and then depart
> filled with perhaps the final sight of the beloved city; the unstoppable
> mob rushed on.

Eumolpus, however, insists on the resemblance between his Romans in flight and their ancestors in Virgil's Troy. Bramble terms Eumolpus'

---

[92] Baldwin (1911) on 218, 230–31; Stubbe (1933) on 218 ff.

[93] Cf. Fantham (1992), 8. The details of weeping, lingering over departure and religious observances, specifically denied by Lucan, are an important feature of Dio's description of the flight from Rome (41.9.2–3), which perhaps descends from Livy. Dio's long and elaborate description of the emotional state of the Romans who flee and those who remain behind (Dio 41.7–9) would suggest that Livy may have written a moving account of this unsettling "capture" of Rome comparable to his powerful description of the destruction of Rome's past in the fall of Alba Longa (Livy 1.29). Pichon (1912) discusses Lucan's possible uses of Livy throughout the *Pharsalia*; Lintott (1971) modifies Pichon's thesis, arguing that Lucan could have used other historical sources as well.

scene "a classicistic refusal to violate convention."[94] Eumolpus' Romans do the pious things which Lucan's do not, but Eumolpus does depart from his Virgilian model in a small way: he fragments the story. Aeneas carries his gods and his father, and holds his son by the hand (Virg. *Aen.* 2.721–24, 747). In Eumolpus' Rome, each man does only one of these things (*BC* 226–32, with the lacuna marked by Müller):

> ille manu pavida natos tenet, ille penates
> occultat gremio deploratumque relinquit
> limen et absentem votis interficit hostem.
> sunt qui coniugibus maerentia pectora iungant,
> grandaevosque patres ...
> ... onerisque ignara iuventus
> id pro quo metuit, tantum trahit. omnia secum
> hic vehit imprudens praedamque in proelia ducit.

> One holds his children with a trembling hand, another hides his
>   household gods
> in his bosom, and leaves behind his lamented threshold
> and destroys the absent enemy with curses.
> Some join their sorrowing breasts to their spouses,
> the ancient fathers ...
> ... the youth, unused to the burden
> carry only what they are afraid to lose. The fool carries everything
>   with him,
> and brings booty into battle.

Even here Eumolpus is eager to juxtapose the metaphorical and the literal, and contrives a rather frigid pun on *coniugibus and iungant*.

After bidding Pompey to seek the walls of Epidamnus, Discordia turns her attention to the battle of Pharsalus (*BC* 293–94):

> Epidamni moenia quaere
> Thessalicosque sinus humano sanguine tingue

> Seek the walls of Epidamnus
> and stain the Thessalian bays with human blood.

The form of line 294 is drawn from Lucan's description of the first moment of armed conflict at Pharsalus, in which the earth of Thessaly is tainted with blood: *primaque Thessaliam Romano sanguine tinxit* ("[Crastinus' lance] first stained Thessaly with Roman blood," Luc. *Ph.* 7.473).[95] The conceit of Thessalian *bays* stained with blood expands the reference further to include Lucan's account of Pompey's

---

[94] Bramble in *CHCL* 2, 548.
[95] *Ph.* 7.473 is adduced by Rose (1971), 91, and Baldwin (1911) *ad loc.*

arrival at the sea in his flight from Pharsalus after the battle: *litora con-
tigerat per quae Peneius amnis/Emathia iam clade rubens exibat in aequor*
("he [Pompey] had reached the shore where the Peneus river, now
reddening with Emathian slaughter, ran out into the sea," Luc. *Ph.*
8.33–34). The line *Thessalicosque sinus humano sanguine tingue* combines a verbal reminiscence of the beginning of bloodshed at Pharsalus
with a conceptual evocation of Lucan's description of the aftermath
of bloodshed at Pharsalus, thus embracing the beginning and end of
Lucan's narrative of Pharsalus.[96]

The simultaneously fragmentary and universalizing final line of
Eumolpus' poem, *factum est in terris, quicquid Discordia iussit* ("Whatever Discordia commanded took place on earth," 295), encompasses
all the events of the war and its telos, in effect transcending the
boundary between epic time and novel time. The immediately pre-
ceding lines (292–94) encompass all of Lucan's poem, allusively extending from Pompey's escape from Italy, to the campaign at Pharsalus, Pompey's flight from Caesar after the battle – and finally Caesar's
memory, at the end of Lucan's *Pharsalia*, of Pompey's failure to win
decisively at Epidamnus. This memory of Caesar remembering Epidamnus too, I will argue, refigures the epic telos of imperial history as
the telos of an individual life.

And so we arrive at the Epidamnian boundary which marks the end
of Lucan's poem. In the very last lines of Lucan's unfinished *Pharsalia*,
Caesar is trapped in Alexandria and recalls the success of Scaeva
against Pompey at Epidamnus (*Ph.* 10.542–end):

> captus sorte loci pendet; dubiusque timeret
> optaretne mori respexit in agmine denso
> Scaevam perpetuae meritum iam nomina famae
> ad campos, Epidamne, tuos, ubi solus apertis
> obsedit muris calcantem moenia Magnum.

> Caught by the destiny of the place he [Caesar] hangs in the balance;
>   uncertain
> whether to fear or hope to die he looked back in the close-packed
>   line of battle
> at Scaeva who already had earned a name of perpetual fame,
> at your battlefields, Epidamnus, where alone when the walls were
>   breached he besieged Magnus trampling down the ramparts.

---

[96] On techniques of alluding to different parts of a poem in order to analyze or to embrace
its structure see Hardie (1989). In a parallel fashion, Encolpius' poem on Oenothea's
household (135.8) closes with a quotation of the first line of Callimachus' *Hecale* and
a mention of sacrifice which probably recapitulates the end of Callimachus' poem.

When Caesar remembers the battle at Epidamnus, he is remembering a battle which Lucan construed as a battle for Rome itself by his descriptions of the fortifications at Epidamnus. As Lucan carefully explains, Epidamnus is fortified not by walls built by men, but by its natural position (*Ph.* 6.19–23). In the *Pharsalia*, the space enclosed by Pompey's fortifications at Epidamnus is explicitly defined with distances measured by Roman landmarks: the extent of his walls is equivalent to the distance between Rome and Aricia, or to the distance the Tiber would flow to reach the sea if it flowed in a straight line from Rome (Luc. *Ph.* 6.73–77). In the *Pharsalia*, the fortifications erected by Pompey become a figure for the walls of Rome, and thus suggest that because Pompey could have ended the war here but failed to do so, the battle of Dyrrachium is the battle for Rome. Like Lucan, Eumolpus represents the walls of Epidamnus as a figure for the walls of Rome, but where Lucan relies on detailed enumeration of distances to equate the walls at Epidamnus with the walls at Rome, Eumolpus evokes the *Aeneid*'s initial "construction" of the walls of Rome in his quotation of the phrase *moenia quaere*.

Eumolpus tells us that his poem is unfinished (*nondum recepit ultimam manum*, "it has not received the final touches," 118.6); it breaks off just as the narrative of war has begun, and its end alludes precisely to the Epidamnian walls which form the boundary of Lucan's real unfinished *Pharsalia*. Why did Petronius end his poem with an allusion to the end of Lucan's? Again, as was the case for the Troy poem, his purpose surely had nothing to do with allowing us to date the composition of his novel or its parts.

As a production of Eumolpus, the *Bellum Civile* is unfinished and its end is accidental. As a production of Petronius, though, the poem is finished and its end is deliberate. The allusion to Epidamnian walls at the end of Lucan's poem at the end of the *Bellum Civile* is framed as both accidental and intentional, and in this way it reproduces the tension between chance and design which is already perceptible at the end of Lucan's poem. Breaking off with Caesar in trouble at Alexandria seems accidental, the result of Lucan's forced suicide in the aftermath of the Pisonian conspiracy. Yet accidental and abrupt as it is, there are ways in which Lucan's ending without ending can be read as an expression of artistic intention.

The *Pharsalia* has two sorts of telos: by its national status as the narrative of the emergence of empire it tells the tale whose end is Nero; by its fragmentation and incompleteness it tells the story of the death of its author. The tidy Bakhtinian boundaries between epic's imperial narratives and novels' stories of individual lives are compromised when epic texts bear the traces of the deaths of their authors. And other epics were said to bear such traces. The composition of the *Aeneid* was known to have been interrupted by the death of Virgil, who ordered that it should be burned because he had not yet given it the final touches (*summam manum*).[97] The half-lines which remained in the text were clear signals of the ultimately unfinished state of the poem. It has been argued that when Ovid claims at *Tristia* 1.7 to have burned his *Metamorphoses* because it was unfinished when he went into exile, he is modelling his account of his poetic career on Virgil's deathbed scene.[98] So too, Lucan's *Pharsalia* was interrupted by the death of its author; stories circulated that Lucan gave instructions for some revisions at his death (Suetonian Life 333.15–16), or that the first seven lines were added by a literary executor (Voss codex 337.20–22). To describe the unfinished state of the *Pharsalia*, the Vaccan Life quotes a line from Ovid's proposed addition to the beginning of the *Metamorphoses*: *emendaturus, si licuisset, erat* ("he was going to make changes, if it had been possible," 336.16–17, cf. *Tr.* 1.7.40).

It is here at the end that Lucan's poem has the clearest signs of fragmentation, as the narrative breaks off abruptly with Caesar surrounded by unrest in Alexandria. Caesar's own account of his war, his *de bello civili*, breaks off at a very similar point, with unrest at Alexandria, and the parallel has prompted Haffter to argue that the end of Lucan's poem is not accidental but intentional.[99] Henderson's reading of the *Pharsalia*'s last lines has suggested how deeply connected Caesar's memory of Scaeva is to the poem's larger themes and patterns.[100] He describes Lucan's Epidamnian walls, and their final position in the *Pharsalia*, as a negation of the *Aeneid*'s wall-building narrative: "This poem [the *Pharsalia*] will not have told of the raising of its culture's *moenia*, which is the *Aeneid*'s burden, those *altae moenia Romae* which are the *telos* of Virgil's programme sentence ('the walls of sublime Rome,' 1.7), but of their razing, in the pursuit of Caesarian 'greatness': *as it happens*, Lucan's text ends with *calcantem moenia Magnum* ('Pompey stamping down the walls,' 10.546)."[101] Masters agrees with Haffter that the poem's end is deliberate; through an analysis of the poem's representation of the endlessness of the war he argues that even if Lucan had not been forced to commit suicide he could

---

[97] See Suetonius/Donatus *Vit. Virg.* 35–42, Servius *Vita* 27–42; *Vita Probiana* 22–28.
[98] Grisart (1959).
[99] Haffter (1957).
[100] Henderson (1988), 125–28; and see too Marti (1966).
[101] Henderson (1988), 144, his emphasis.

have intended to end the poem as abruptly as this to reflect the chaotic nature of the subject of the Civil War and its imperial legacy: "for a poem whose premise is the impossibility of its resolution, the only possible ending is one which cuts us off at that moment where nothing is resolved."[102] Whether Lucan's ending was the product of chance or design may not be possible to determine, but within Roman conventions for viewing an epic poem as interrupted by the death of its author, after the uncovering of the Pisonian conspiracy it could make sense for Lucan to have brought the *Pharsalia* to this particular end. In the knowledge that his own poem would be read as a text brought to its end by the death of its author, Lucan could use an abrupt ending at Alexandria to suggest that he reads Caesar's own civil war story as a text like his own which was brought to an end by the death of its author. It is within this chain of readings of finished-yet-unfinished, accidental-but-intended, ends that Petronius' positioning of an allusion to Lucan's endless end takes place. Petronius' poem reads Lucan's poem as a text brought to an end by the death of its author.

Shipwreck

To argue that the abrupt end of the *Bellum Civile* holds such a dense knot of allusions to Virgil's visions of imperial order and Lucan's visions of imperial disorder may exert a lot of interpretive pressure upon its final lines. But the novelistic frame draws attention to the poem's end in a way which encourages such high-stakes readings. That is, when Eumolpus begins his *Bellum Civile* with the apology that it is not finished yet (118.6), the implication is that the poem we are about to hear is the one which he was writing as Lichas' ship was sinking (115.2–3).[103] Like the unfinished end of Lucan's poem, the unfinished end of Eumolpus' poem was produced near the boundary between life and death. Thus, the framing of the *Bellum Civile* reads the poet Lucan's death in the end of the *Pharsalia*.

In a juxtaposition of the figurative and the real that has become familiar, scenes on board Lichas' ship exploit conventional figures of the ship of state and the ship of poetry. Allegorical ships of state are a commonplace; a famous example is Horace *Odes* 1.14, as discussed by Quintilian (*Inst.* 8.6.44). Shipboard dispute on Lichas' ship is represented as a civil war: the travellers are divided up into "factions"

---

[102] Masters (1992), 253.
[103] Stubbe (1933), 68–69; Rose (1966), 298; Cameron (1970), 415; Gagliardi (1980), 113, n. 69.

(*partes*), and the helmsman threatens to abandon the rudder (108.8).[104] The figuring of the conflict as civil strife is reinforced too when Tryphaena delivers her hexameter rebuke (*Sat.* 108.14). Her opening question *quis furor . . . pacem convertit in arma?* alludes to the beginning of Lucan's account of the causes of the Civil War: *quis furor, o cives, quae tanta licentia ferri?* ("What madness, O citizens, what outrageous license of the sword?" Luc. *Ph.* 1.8), which follows his seven-line proem. Eumolpus uses the figure of the ship of state in his poem when he compares the flight from Rome to sailors abandoning their ship (*BC* 233–37, cf. Luc. *Ph.* 1.498–504). In the *Bellum Civile* then, the shipwreck simile is both literary topos and a reflection of the experience of the poet in the frame at the novelistic site of composition.

While Lichas' ship founders, so does the ship of poetry, for as the storm rages, Eumolpus spends what might well have become his final moments writing a poem on a huge piece of parchment.[105] The fragmentation of the ship in the storm "causes" the civil war poem's incompleteness. After the ship begins to break up, Encolpius and Giton hear loud cries emanating from the captain's cabin. It sounds like a beast trying to escape, but when they open the door they find Eumolpus crying out in a fever of composition (*Sat.* 115.1–5):

audimus murmur insolitum et sub diaeta magistri quasi cupientis exire beluae gemitum. persecuti igitur sonum invenimus Eumolpum sedentem membranaeque ingenti versus ingerentem. mirati ergo quod illi vacaret in vicinia mortis poema facere, extrahimus clamantem iubemusque bonam habere mentem. at ille interpellatus excanduit et "sinite me" inquit "sententiam explere; laborat carmen in fine". inicio ego phrenetico manum iubeoque Gitona accedere et in terram trahere poetam mugientem.

We heard an unusual sound and groan from the captain's cabin, as if of a beast trying to escape. So we followed the sound, and we found Eumolpus sitting there pouring out verses on a huge piece of parchment. We were amazed that he had time to write poetry with death so close at hand, and we dragged him out shouting, and we told him to be sensible. But he was furious at having been interrupted, and said, "let me finish my thought; my poem is in trouble at its end." I laid hands on the maniac, and I told Giton to help drag the bellowing poet to land.

---

[104] Cf. Zeitlin (1971a), 67; a connection between civil strife in the *BC* and on Lichas' ship is made in passing by Slater (1990), 16.

[105] On the figure of the ship of poetry in the Greek tradition, see Rosen (1990). Examples of the ship of poetry in Roman literature include: Virg. *Georg.* 2.39–45, 4.116–17; Prop. 3.3.22–24, 3.9.3–4; Stat. *Theb.* 12.809; Juv. 1.149, with the note *ad loc.* of Courtney (1980); and compare Quint. *Inst.* 12.10.37. The figure is especially frequent in Ovid: see e.g., *Ars* 3.26, *Fasti* 1.4, and other instances collected at Kenney (1958), 206. Davis (1989) offers a reading of Horace's ship (*C.* 1.14) as the ship of poetry.

Eumolpus' poetic composition is interrupted not only by the storm but by the intractability of the poem itself. Eumolpus uses the verb *laborare* to signify the difficulties of his poem; it can be used of a foundering ship as well.[106] The explicit and literal wreck of Lichas' ship is matched by the implicit and metaphorical shipwreck of Eumolpus' poem.[107]

In his poetic programme too Eumolpus takes up the ship of poetry figure. He mocks the bad poets who imagine that they can escape the strains of public life by finding a safer harbor in poetry (118.2):

sic forensibus ministeriis exercitati frequenter ad carminis tranquillitatem tamquam ad portum feliciorem refugerunt, credentes facilius poema extrui posse quam controversiam sententiolis vibrantibus pictam.

In this way people vexed by their public duties often have fled to the serenity of poetry as though to a safer harbor, believing that a poem can be more easily put together than a declamation adorned with quivering epigrams.

The complex of water imagery was a rich source of programmatic images, and Eumolpus chooses another water figure to express the depth of literary learning a poet requires (*Sat.* 118.3):[108]

ceterum neque generosior spiritus vanitatem amat, neque concipere aut edere partum mens potest nisi ingenti flumine litterarum inundata.

But a nobler spirit abhors what is insubstantial, and the mind cannot conceive or bring forth anything unless it has been flooded with a huge river of literature.

Just as his poetic road imagery rejects the Callimachean aesthetic of the untouched path, Eumolpus' metaphor of the big river rejects Callimachean programmatic imagery in which bad poetry is compared to a big river while good poetry is compared to the drops of fine spray gathered by bees at a pure fountain.[109] And as we have seen, Encolpius figures Eumolpus as source of flowing words in closing off his narrative of the poem: *cum haec Eumolpos ingenti volubilitate verborum effudisset, tandem Crotona intravimus* ("When Eumolpus had poured forth this poem with a huge flow of words, finally we entered Croton," 124.2). Seizing the river image from Eumolpus, Encolpius describes a flooded path of poetry along the road to Croton.

---

[106] Cic. *Nat. Deor.* 3.89; Caes. *Civ.* 2.6.5; Ov. *Pont.* 2.6.22.

[107] Ovid stages an analogous scene at the end of his first book of poems from exile, which he says he has written at sea (*Tr.* 1.11.1–2). During a storm, the sea splashes his poetic page (*Tristia* 1.11.39–40). Ovid dramatizes his resistance to the interruption, but in fact the poem and the book break off within a few lines.

[108] On water imagery in poetic programme, see the examples collected at Wimmel (1960), 222–33.

[109] Call. *Hymn* 2.105–12.

In the comparison between Eumolpus and a wild beast it is possible to see an allusion to Horace's picture at the end of his *Ars Poetica* of the poet who is a victim of his own inability to control his inspiration by the application of *ars* (technical skill). Such a one gets caught in a frenzy of composition and plunges into a well or a pit unawares (Hor. *Ars* 457–59), and rages (*furit*) like a bear trying to break out of its cage (472–73).[110] Yet, as Labate observes, Eumolpus' own participation in the novelistic fiction frees him from the dangers which beset Horace's mad poet: rescued by his fellow characters, he survives the "shipwreck" of his poem, and the wreck of Lichas' ship, and goes on to contrive the fictional mime (*mimum componere*, 117.4) that he is wealthy, ill, and childless – ripe for the attentions of the legacy hunters of Croton.[111] Encolpius and Giton place themselves under Eumolpus' authority by swearing to be burned, bound, beaten, and killed (117.5). By posing as their wealthy master, Eumolpus surrenders for the time being his identity as a poet. But since such an oath is sworn by men who bind themselves over as gladiators, "*auctorati*," there is a joke here too about Eumolpus' role as the source or authority (*auctor*) for the mime.[112] At the same time as it makes a self-consciously literary joke about authority, the gladiatorial language ironically foreshadows events at Croton. Gladiators fight in deadly spectacles; Eumolpus, having staged the spectacle by deploying Encolpius and Giton as his "gladiators," himself becomes the deadly spectacle when the Crotonians become suspicious. Was his pretense at Croton really "fatal"? Probably he survived, though the staged death of Trimalchio and the real death of Lichas each offer patterns which the Croton episode could have followed, so there is no way of knowing whether Eumolpus "really" perished in Croton or not.

In various ways, the *Satyricon*'s professional poet Eumolpus is a figure of metaliterary dimensions, reflecting Petronius' own enterprise in crafting the novel. Within the *Satyricon*, Eumolpus is a foil for Petronius as author, for he creates plots for Encolpius to participate in passively (as Quartilla, Trimalchio, and Circe also do). Just as Demodocus, the poet in the *Odyssey*, is a self-conscious representation of the role of the poet in Homeric society, so too Eumolpus embodies the

---

110 So Slater (1990), 192–94.
111 Labate (1995), 175.
112 For the oath, cf. Horace *Sat.* 2.7.58–59 with Ps. Acro *ad loc.*, Sen. *Ep.* 37.1, and compare Pliny's description of a pivoting theater provided by Curio (whom he calls its *auctor*) which while pivoting put the audience in more danger than the gladiators (*ipsum magis auctoratum populum Romanum circumferens*, Pliny *Nat.* 36.117). On the oath, see further Ville (1981), 246–52.

production of literature in his age. Madly scribbling away in the teeth
of the storm, Eumolpus struggles with the unfinished epic poem that
reads and remembers the unfinished ending of Lucan's *Pharsalia*. At a
time when the emperor had so much invested in developing and displaying his poetic skill, whatever the truth about the way that Lucan's
relationship with Nero deteriorated into conspiracy, the story will
easily have slipped into telling that the poet fell victim to the emperor's
literary jealousy. Such a context can lend resonance to Petronius' story
of a poet less revered than Demodocus and his crisis of composition
and closure. Walking along the road to Croton, just after having become the "*auctor*" of the mime, Eumolpus performs his poem on the
Civil War before suppressing his poetic identity to play his role in the
mime. Once the impersonation is under way, a "professional" poetic
performance could give the whole game away: here too, as on the sinking ship, poetry has the potential to place the poet in danger. As the
scheme unravels, Eumolpus' stipulation that the beneficiaries of his
will can inherit his property if they consume his body (141.2) mirrors
the novel's own "consumption" of inherited poetic forms: Eumolpus'
testament lays out a mocking challenge for the future of prose fiction.

Of course, Eumolpus is not the only poetic presence in the novel;
many of the major characters engage in some poetic performance, and
the presences of poetry are felt in one way or another on virtually every
page of the *Satyricon*. Thus one way to describe the *Satyricon* would
be to say that it is "flooded" with literature: its prosimetric narrative
includes elements modelled on or parodying epic, tragedy, oratory,
philosophy, satire, Milesian tales, and mime, and this literary abundance makes the *Satyricon* unique among ancient fiction known to
date. This variety has been diagnosed as crisis: it can be said to constitute disorder, chaos, anarchy, or uninterpretability. By contrast,
Conte's encyclopedic history of Roman literature views the varied literary texture of the *Satyricon* within a conceptual structure that is more
comprehensive than disorderly or fragmented, characterizing Petronius
as "the author of a kind of literary encyclopedia of imperial Rome."[113]
As we have seen, on numerous individual points Pliny's *Natural History*
can be profitably adduced to sketch a more detailed cultural context
for individual elements of the novel; but as this formulation suggests,
the relationship between the *Natural History* and the *Satyricon* can be
construed more broadly. Although Pliny's completeness and order are
utterly opposed to Petronius' tales of happenstance and disarray, these
are both literary projects of inclusion which assemble the substance of

---

[113] Conte (1994a), 464; Barchiesi (1991), 238.

empire and reframe it in a newly arresting and accessible manner. Pliny aspires to an accurate account of the physical world as it is now and everywhere. Pliny's world even encompasses Petronius himself: in his concluding book as he discusses gems and gemstones, Pliny notes that Petronius smashed a valuable myrrhine ladle to prevent Nero from claiming it from his estate (*Nat.* 37.20). In Petronius' novel, the narrating voice does not seem to consider anything off limits: as Encolpius says (132.15.4), "whatever people do, my lucid tongue reports." Turning away from epic's practice of constructing the here and now as the undescribed end of the stories which make the world what it is, both Pliny and Petronius reproduce the present in all its particularity. Unlike epic's inscriptions of *imperium Romanum*, describing a world and a cosmos which is uniformly and generally Roman, these works privilege individual persons and objects, carrying their variety and distinctness along in a flood of prose. The *Natural History* positions itself as a replacement for epic's cosmic and imperial structures by beginning with the world (*mundus*, 2.1) and closing with the superiority of Italy over all of Nature's regions (*Nat.* 37.201). Petronius' competition with the epic world order is piecemeal, played out in the way his characters and their poems evoke the certainties of poetry and then confront in prose the realities that *fortuna* produces. Over and over again, in becoming a poet Petronius acknowledges the limits of the poetry he leaves behind.

Epilogue

Like all books of criticism, this one fragments and reassembles its object of study. Prying Petronius' novel apart to see how verse fits into prose may leave it in more fragments than many people would like.

I began by asking why Petronius spends time being a poet while writing his novel. At the most basic level, ancient prose fiction has generic boundaries loose enough to include verse; a professional poet is a useful character; and the ability to produce competent verse defines Encolpius (and of course Petronius) as someone who has had an education. Yet to choose a genre, even one as loosely defined as prose fiction, is to reject all the others. The inclusion of verse insistently keeps performing this rejection: by producing verse within his fictional prose, Petronius sets his novel in a self-consciously agonistic relationship with the literary genres which he has repudiated. The *Satyricon* turns epic's national heroism into private obscenities, expands satiric characters and epigrammatic situations to lengthy episodes, and stages mimes in the privacy of its own pages. How might the *Satyricon* have measured up against such Greek novels as could have been in circulation? It would parody an idealizing, romantic plot, and might have overturned the idealizing novels' affirmation of the social order in the marriage and homecoming of the hero and heroine. If, as is likely, Greek criminal-satiric fiction was already a going concern, the *Satyricon* might differ mainly in not making the Roman empire invisible: racy Greek fiction would not have consumed, as the *Satyricon* did, Roman satire's pungent Italian inventions, nor would it have parodically imitated and debased the imperial monuments of Roman epic.

Defining the *Satyricon* against many genres enacts an extreme form of a strategy which we see at work elsewhere in ancient fiction. Though prose fiction's generic limits seem not to have been named or formally defined in themselves, novelists could project an identity for their fictions by evoking any number of other forms and being what those forms were not. So, among the Greek idealizing novelists, Chariton is busy not being a historian, Achilles Tatius is busy not being a philosopher,

Longus is busy not being a bucolic or lyric poet, Heliodorus is busy not being an epic poet. Apuleius is busy on one hand not telling a short self-contained Milesian tale and on the other not recounting a straightforward religious conversion. Petronius takes on the ambitiously circular task of rejecting everything that is not what he is producing, and in becoming a poet, he self-reflexively stages the *Satyricon*'s contests with poetic genres. But all of this is not meant to lock Petronius the mad scientist away in the genre lab. The *Satyricon* is not the oddly compelling book that it is simply because it self-reflexively stages for us the problems and challenges of its own composition. Rather, its self-reflexive strategies of representation are interesting and important because its unique form and exceptionally vivid content are bound up in the Neronian matrix – in which representation is power and power is representation. Observing the peculiar alignments of verse and prose in the novel sharpens the outlines of the *Satyricon*'s fragments and their relation to those other fragments we call ancient Rome.

Bibliography

Adams, J. N. (1982). *The Latin Sexual Vocabulary*. London.

Ahl, F. M. (1976). *Lucan: An Introduction*. Ithaca and London.

(1985). *Metaformations: Soundplay and Wordplay in Ovid and Other Classical Poets*. Ithaca and London.

Andrews, A. C. (1941–42). "The Silphium of the Ancients: A Lesson in Crop Control," *Isis* 33:232–36.

Anton, C. G. (1781). *Titi Petronii Arbitri Satyricon quae supersunt*. Leipzig.

Arrowsmith, W. (1959). *Petronius Arbiter: The Satyricon*. Ann Arbor.

(1966). "Luxury and Death in the *Satyricon*," *Arion* 5: 304–31.

Astbury, R. (1977). "Petronius, P.Oxy. 3010, and Menippean Satire," *CP* 72: 22–31.

(1977a). "Varroniana," *RhM* 120: 173–84.

(1985). ed. *M. Terentii Varronis Saturarum Menippearum Fragmenta*. Leipzig.

Auerbach, E. (1953). *Mimesis*. Princeton.

Austin, R. G. (1964). *P. Virgili Maronis, Aeneidos Liber Secundus*. Oxford.

Avery, W. T. (1960). "*Cena Trimalchionis* 35.7: *hoc est ius cenae*," *CP* 55: 115–18.

Bacon, H. H. (1958). "The Sibyl in the Bottle," *Virginia Quarterly Review* 34: 262–76.

Bakhtin, M. (1981). *The Dialogic Imagination: Four Essays by M. M. Bakhtin*. M. Holquist, ed. Translated by C. Emerson and M. Holquist. Austin.

Baldwin, B. (1971). "Trimalchio's Poetry," *CJ* 66: 254–55.

(1973). "Trimalchio's Corinthian Plate," *CP* 68: 46–47.

(1976). "Petronius' Tryphaena," *Eranos* 74: 53–57.

(1987). "Hannibal at Troy: The Sources of Trimalchio's Confusion," *PSN* 17: 6.

(1995). "Roman Emperors in the Elder Pliny," *Scholia* 4: 56–78.

Baldwin, F. T. (1911). *The Bellum Civile of Petronius*. New York.

Barchiesi, A. (1984). "Il nome di Lica e la poetica dei nomi in Petronio," *MD* 12: 169–75.

(1991). "Il romanzo," in *La prosa latina: Forme, autori, problemi*, 229–48 ed. F. Montanari. Rome.

(Forthcoming) "*Extra legem*: consumo di letteratura in Petronio, Arbitro."

Barchiesi, M. (1981). "L'orologio di Trimalchione (struttura e tempo narrativo in Petronio)," *I Moderni alla Ricerca di Enea*, ed. F. Della Corte, 109–46. Rome.

Barnes, E. J. (1971). "Further on Trimalchio's Poetry," *CJ* 66: 255.

— (1971a). *The Poems of Petronius*. Diss. Toronto.

Barton, T. (1994). *Power and Knowledge: Astrology, Physiognomics and Medicine under the Roman Empire*. Ann Arbor.

Bartsch, S. (1989). *Decoding the Ancient Novel: The Reader and the Role of Description in Heliodorus and Achilles Tatius*. Princeton.

— (1994). *Actors in the Audience: Theatricality and Doublespeak from Nero to Hadrian*. Cambridge, Mass.

Beagon, M. (1992). *Roman Nature: The Thought of Pliny the Elder*. Oxford.

Beare, W. (1939). "Masks on the Roman Stage," *CQ* 33: 139–46.

— (1964). *The Roman Stage*. 3rd edn. London.

Beck, R. (1973). "Some Observations on the Narrative Technique of Petronius," *Phoenix* 27: 42–61.

— (1975). "Encolpius at the *Cena*," *Phoenix* 29: 271–83.

— (1979). "Eumolpus *poeta*, Eumolpus *fabulator*: A Study of Characterization in the *Satyricon*," *Phoenix* 33: 239–53.

— (1982). "The *Satyricon*: Satire, Narrator, and Antecedents," *MH* 39: 206–14.

Bendz, G. (1941). "Sprachliche Bemerkungen zu Petron," *Eranos* 39: 27–55.

Bettini, M. (1982). "A proposito dei versi sotadei, greci e romani: con alcuni capitoli di 'analisi metrica lineare,'" *MD* 9: 59–105.

Bodel, J. P. (1984). *Freedmen in the Satyricon of Petronius*. diss. University of Michigan.

— (1992). "*Captatio* at Croton: Petronius and Horace," *Abstracts of the American Philological Association Annual Meeting*. Atlanta, Georgia.

— (1994). "Trimalchio's Underworld," James Tatum, ed., *The Search for the Ancient Novel*, 237–59. Baltimore.

Bonaria, M. (1965). *Romani Mimi*. Rome.

Borghini, A. (1991). "*unda ... minor* (Petr. *Satyr.* LXXXIX v. 31)," *Latomus* 50: 164–75.

Bowersock, G. W. (1994). *Fiction as History: Nero to Julian*. Berkeley.

Boyd, B. W. (1987). "The Death of Corinna's Parrot Reconsidered: Poetry and Ovid's *Amores*," *CJ* 82: 199–207.

Boyle, A. J. ed. (1988). *The Imperial Muse: Ramus Essays on Roman Literature of the Empire*. Berwick, Victoria, Australia.

Bramble, J. C. (1982). "Lucan," *CHCL* 2, 533–57.

Brandis, T. and Ehlers, W. (1974). "Zu den Petronexzerpten des *Florilegium Gallicum*," *Philologus* 118: 85–112.

Branham, R. B. (1989). *Unruly Eloquence: Lucian and the Comedy of Traditions*. Cambridge, Mass.

Brooks, P. (1984). *Reading for the Plot: Design and Intention in Narrative*. New York.

Bryson, N. (1990). *Looking at the Overlooked: Four Essays on Still Life Painting*. Cambridge, Mass.

Bücheler, F. ed. (1862). *Petronii Arbitri Satirarum Reliquiae Adiectus est Liber Priapeorum*. Berlin.

Burman, P. (1743). *Titi Petronii Arbitri Satyricon quae supersunt*. 2nd edn. Amsterdam. repr. Hildesheim 1974.

Cairns, F. (1972). *Generic Composition in Greek and Roman Poetry*. Edinburgh.

Callebat, L. (1974). "Structures Narratives et Modes de Représentation dans le *Satyricon* de Pétrone," *REL* 52: 281–303.

Cameron, A. (1970). "Myth and Meaning in Petronius: Some Modern Comparisons," *Latomus* 29: 397–425.

Cèbe, J.-P. (1966). *La caricature et la parodie dans le monde romain antique des origines à Juvénal*. Paris.

———— (1972). *Varron: Satires ménippées*: Édition, Traduction et Commentaire. Collection de l'École Française de Rome 9. Rome.

Ciaffi, V. (1955). *Struttura del Satyricon*. Torino.

Coffey, M. (1957). "Seneca Tragedies 1922–1955," *Lustrum* 2: 113–86.

———— (1989). *Roman Satire*. 2nd edition. Bristol.

Coleman, K. M. (1993). "Launching into History: Aquatic Displays in the Early Empire," *JRS* 83: 48–74.

Colker, M. L. (1975). *Analecta Dublinensia: Three Medieval Latin Texts in the Library of Trinity College, Dublin*. The Mediaeval Academy of America no. 82. Cambridge, Mass.

———— (1992). "New Light on the Use and Transmission of Petronius," *Manuscripta* 36: 200–09.

Collignon, A. (1892). *Étude sur Pétrone*. Paris.

———— (1900). "Notes sur l''Euphormion' de Jean Barclay I: Explication de P. Abram," *Annales de l' Est* 14: 497–530.

———— (1901). "Notes sur l''Euphormion' de Jean Barclay II: Les Emprunts au 'Satiricon' de Pétrone," *Annales de l' Est* 15: 1–39.

———— (1905). *Pétrone en France*. Paris.

Connors, C. (1992). Review of E. Courtney, *The Poems of Petronius*. *CP* 87: 274–77.

———— (1994). "Famous last words: authorship and death in the *Satyricon* and Neronian Rome," in Elsner and Masters (1994), 225–35.

———— (1995). "Beholding Troy in Petronius' *Satyricon* and John Barclay's *Euphormionis Lusinini Satyricon*," *Groningen Colloquia on the Novel* 6: 51–74.

Conte, G. B. (1966). "Il proemio della *Pharsalia*," *Maia* 18: 42–53.

———— (1986). *The Rhetoric of Imitation: Genre and Poetic Memory in Virgil and Other Latin Poets*, translated from the Italian, edited with a foreword by C. Segal, Ithaca and London.

———— (1987). "Petronius, *Sat.* 141.4," *CQ* 37: 529–32.

———— (1987a). "Una correzione a Petronio (Sat. 89 v. 31)," *RFIC* 115: 334.

———— (1994). *Genres and Readers: Lucretius, Love Elegy, Pliny's Encyclopedia*, G. W. Most, trans. Baltimore and London.

———— (1994a). *Latin Literature: A History*, J. B. Solodow, trans., revised by D. Fowler and G. W. Most. Baltimore and London.

Cotrozzi, A. (1979). "Enotea e il fiume di pianto (Petronio 137; frg. LI Ernout)," *MD* 2: 183–89.

Courtney, E. (1962). "Parody and Literary Allusion in Menippean Satire," *Philologus* 106: 86–100.

———— (1970). "Some Passages of Petronius," *BICS* 17: 65–69.

———— (1980). *A Commentary on the Satires of Juvenal*. London.

———— (1987). "Petronius and the Underworld," *AJP* 108: 408–10.

(1988). "Problems in the Text of Petronius," *Eranos* 86: 74–76.

(1988a). "Theocritus, Virgil, and Petronius," *AJP* 109: 349–50.

(1991). *The Poems of Petronius*. Atlanta, Georgia.

(1993). *The Fragmentary Latin Poets*. Oxford.

Culler, J. ed. (1988). *On Puns: The Foundation of Letters*. Oxford.

Curtius, E. R. (1953). *European Literature and the Latin Middle Ages*, trans. by W. R. Trask. London.

Dalby, A. (1996). *Siren Feasts: A History of Food and Gastronomy in Greece*. London.

Davis, G. (1989). *"Ingenii cumba?* Literary *aporia* and the rhetoric of Horace's *O navis referent* (*C.* 1.14)," *RhM* 132: 331–45.

Dewar, M. (1994). "Laying it on with a Trowel: the Proem to Lucan and Related Texts," *CQ* 44: 199–211.

DeWitt, N. J. (1941). "Rome and the 'Road of Hercules,'" *TAPA* 72: 59–69.

Di Simone, M. (1993). "I fallimenti di Encolpio, tra esemplarità mitica e modelli letterari: una ricostruzione (*Sat.* 82, 5; 132,1)," *MD* 30: 87–108.

Diels, H. and Kranz, W. eds. (1951–2). *Die Fragmente der Vorsokratiker*. 6th edn. Berlin.

Dronke, P. (1994). *Verse with Prose from Petronius to Dante: The Art and Scope of the Mixed Form*. Cambridge, Mass.

Duckworth, G. E. (1967). "Five Centuries of Latin Hexameter Poetry: Silver Age and Late Empire," *TAPA* 98: 77–150.

Dupont, F. (1977). *Le plaisir et la loi*. Paris.

(1985). *L'Acteur-Roi ou le théâtre dans la Rome antique*. Paris.

Earl, D. C. (1961). *The Political Thought of Sallust*. Cambridge.

Eden, P. T. (1984). *Seneca: Apocolocyntosis*. Cambridge.

Edwards, C. (1993). *The Politics of Immorality in Ancient Rome*. Cambridge.

(1994). "Beware of Imitations: Theatre and the Subversion of Imperial Identity," in Elsner and Masters (1994), 83–97.

Eliot, T. S. (1922). *The Waste Land*. New York.

Elsner, J. (1993). "Seductions of Art: Encolpius and Eumolpus in a Neronian Picture Gallery," *PCPS* 39: 30–47.

Elsner, J. and Masters, J. eds. (1994). *Reflections of Nero: Culture, History and Representation*. London.

Emanuele, D. (1989). *"Aes Corinthium*: Fact, Fiction, and Fake," *Phoenix* 43: 347–58.

Erbse, H. (1969). *Scholia Graeca in Homeri Iliadem*. Berlin.

Ernout, A. (1923). *Pétrone: Le Satiricon*, texte établit et traduit. Paris.

Fantham, E. (1989). "Mime: The Missing Link in Roman Literary History," *CW* 82: 153–63.

(1992). *Lucan: De Bello Civili II*. Cambridge.

Fedeli, P. (1981) "Petronio: il viaggio, il labirinto," *MD* 6: 91–117.

(1987). "Petronio: Crotone o il mondo alla rovescia," *Aufidus* 1: 3–34.

(1988). "Encolpio – Polieno," *MD* 20–21: 9–32.

Feeney, D. C. (1991). *The Gods in Epic: Poets and Critics of the Classical Tradition*. Oxford.

(1993). "Towards an Account of the Ancient World's Concepts of Fictive Belief," in C. Gill and T. P. Wiseman eds., *Lies and Fiction in the Ancient World*, 230–44, Austin.

Ferri, R. (1988). "Il Ciclope di Eumolpo e il Ciclope di Petronio: *Sat.* 100. ss.," *MD* 20–21: 311–15.

Fisher, N. (1996). "Laser-Quests: Unnoticed Allusions to Contraception in a Poet and a Princeps?" *Classics Ireland* 3: 73–97.

Fleming, D. A. ed. (1973). *John Barclay Euphormionis Lusinini Satyricon* 1605–1607. Bibliotheca Humanistica and Reformatorica 6. Nieuwkoop.

Flores, E. (1982). "Petronio e lo *schedium Lucilianae humilitatis,*" *Prosimetrum e Spoudogeloion*, Università di Genova Facoltà di Lettere, Instituto di Filologia Classica e Medievale. Genova.

Fowler, D. P. (1991). "Narrate and Describe: The Problem of Ekphrasis," *JRS* 81: 25–35.

Fraenkel, E. (1957). *Horace*. Oxford.

Friedländer, L. (1906). *Petronii Cena Trimalchionis*. 2nd edn. Leipzig.

Frueh, E. (1988). *Problems of Discourse and Representation in the Satyricon*. Diss. Columbia.

Frye, N. (1957). *Anatomy of Criticism: Four Essays*. Princeton.

Furneaux, H. (1907). *The Annals of Tacitus*. vol. 2. 2nd edition, revised by H. F. Pelham and C. D. Fisher. Oxford.

Gagliardi, D. (1980). *Il comico in Petronio*. Palermo.

Galinsky, K. (1972). *The Herakles Theme: The Adaptations of the Hero in Literature*. Oxford.

Garrido, I. M. (1930). "Note on Petronius *Satyricon* 135," *CR* 44: 10–11.

Gemmill, C. L. (1966). "Silphium," *Bulletin of the History of Medicine* 40: 295–313.

Getty, R. J. (1951). "East and West in Lucan 1.15 and Elsewhere," *CP* 46: 25–31.

George, P. A. (1974). "Petronius and Lucan *De Bello Civili*," *CQ* n.s. 24: 119–33.

Goddard, J. (1994). "The Tyrant at Table," in Elsner and Masters (1994), 67–82.

Goldhill, S. (1991). *The Poet's Voice: Essays on Poetics and Greek Literature*. Cambridge.

Gowers, E. (1993). *The Loaded Table: Representations of Food in Roman Literature*. Oxford.

(1994). "Persius and the Decoction of Nero," in Elsner and Masters (1994), 131–50.

Gowing, A. M. (forthcoming). "Cassius Dio on the Reign of Nero," *ANRW* 2.34.3.

Gresseth, G. K. (1957). "The Quarrel between Lucan and Nero," *CP* 52: 24–27.

Griffin, M. T. (1976). *Seneca: A Philosopher in Politics*. Oxford.

(1985). *Nero: The End of a Dynasty*. New Haven and London.

Grimal, P. (1977). *La Guerre Civile de Pétrone dans ses rapports avec la Pharsale*. Paris.

(1982). "Le *Bellum Civile* de Pétrone dans ses rapports avec la *Pharsale*," J.-M. Croisille and P.-M. Fauchère, eds., *Neronia 1977*, Clermont-Ferrand.

Grisart, A. (1959). "La publication des *Métamorphoses*: une source du récit d' Ovide," in E. Paratore, ed., *Atti del convegno internationale ovidiano II*, 125–56.

Grondona, M. (1980). *La religione e la superstizione nella Cena Trimalchionis.* Brussels.

Gruen, E. S. (1990). *Studies in Greek Culture and Roman Policy.* Leiden.

Guido, G. (1976). *Petronio Arbitro. Dal "Satyricon": Il "Bellum Civile".* Bologna.

Haffter, H. (1957). "Dem schwanken Zünglein lauschend wachte Cäsar dort," *MH* 14: 118–26.

Hägg, T. (1983). *The Novel in Antiquity.* Oxford.

Hardie, P. R. (1986). *Virgil's Aeneid: Cosmos and Imperium.* Oxford.

(1989). "Flavian Epicists on Virgil's Epic Technique," *Ramus* 18: 3–20.

(1993). *The Epic Successors of Virgil: A Study in the Dynamics of a Tradition.* Cambridge.

Harth, H. ed. (1984). *Poggio Bracciolini Lettere,* vol. 1–2. Florence.

Haskins, C. E. (1887). ed. *M. Annaei Lucani Pharsalia,* with an introduction by W. E. Heitland. London.

Häussler, R. (1978). *Studien zum historischen Epos der Antike II: Das historische Epos von Lucan bis Silius und seine Theorie.* Heidelberg.

Heinze, R. (1899). "Petron und der Griechische Roman," *Hermes* 34: 494–519.

Helm, R. (1906). *Lucian und Menipp.* Leipzig and Berlin.

Henderson, J. G. W. (1988). "Lucan / The Word at War," in Boyle (1988), 122–64.

(1991). "Statius' *Thebaid* / Form Premade," *PCPS* 37: 30–80.

Herter, H. (1932). *De Priapo.* Religionsgeschichtliche Versuche und Vorarbeiten 23. Giessen.

Heseltine, M. and Rouse, W. H. D. (1987). *Petronius Satyricon and Seneca Apocolocyntosis,* revised by E. H. Warmington, Loeb Edition. Cambridge, Mass., and London.

Highet, G. (1941). "Petronius the Moralist," *TAPA* 72: 176–94.

Hinds, S. E. (1987). *The Metamorphosis of Persephone: Ovid and the Self-Conscious Muse.* Cambridge.

(1988). "Generalising about Ovid," in Boyle (1988).

Hollis, A. S. (1970). *Ovid: Metamorphoses Book VIII.* Oxford.

(1990). *Callimachus: Hecale.* Oxford.

Hopkinson, N. (1988). *A Hellenistic Anthology.* Cambridge.

Hosius, C. ed. (1913). *M. Annaei Lucani de Bello Civili Libri Decem.* Leipzig.

Householder, F. W. (1944). "ΠΑΡѠΔΙΑ," *CP* 39: 1–9.

Housman, A. E. (1926). ed. *M. Annaei Lucani Belli Civilis Libri Decem.* Oxford.

Huet, P. D. (1670). *Zayde Histoire Espagnole, par Monsieur de Segrais. Avec un traité de l'Origine des Romans, par Monsieur Huet.* Paris.

Hunter, R. (1983). *Eubulus: The Fragments.* Cambridge.

Hutcheon, L. (1985). *A Theory of Parody: The Teachings of Twentieth-century Art Forms.* New York and London.

Huxley, H. H. (1970). "'Marked Literary Inferiority' in the Poems of the *Satyricon,*" *CJ* 66: 69–70.

Innes, D. C. (1979). "Gigantomachy and Natural Philosophy," *CQ* n.s. 29: 165–71.

Jal, P. (1963). *La Guerre civile à Rome.* Paris.

Johnson, W. R. (1987). *Momentary Monsters: Lucan and his Heroes*. Ithaca and London.

Johnston, P. A. (1993). "Love and *Laserpicium* in Catullus 7," *CP* 88: 328–29.

Jones, C. P. (1987). "*Stigma*: Tattooing and Branding in Graeco-Roman Antiquity," *JRS* 77: 139–55.

(1991). "Dinner Theater," in W. J. Slater, ed. *Dining in a Classical Context*, 185–98. Ann Arbor.

Jory, E. J. (1996). "The Drama of the Dance: Prolegomena to an Iconography of Imperial Pantomime," in W. J. Slater, ed. *Roman Theater and Society*, 1–27. Ann Arbor.

Kaibel, G. (1887–90). *Athenaeus Dipnosophistae*. Leipzig.

Keith, A. M. (1992). *The Play of Fictions: Studies in Ovid's Metamorphoses Book 2*. Ann Arbor.

Kennedy, D. F. (1993). *The Arts of Love: Five Studies in the discourse of Roman Love Elegy*. Cambridge.

Kenney, E. J. (1958). "*Nequitiae poeta*," pp. 201–09, in N. I. Herescu, ed. *Ovidiana*. Paris.

Kershaw, A. (1991). "In Defense of Petronius 119, verses 30–32," *AJP* 112: 262.

Kindt, B. (1892). "Petron und Lucan," *Philologus* 51: 355–60.

Kirk, E. P. (1980). *Menippean Satire: An Annotated Catalogue of Texts and Criticism*. New York.

Klebs, E. (1889). "Zur Composition von Petronius *Satirae*," *Philologus* 47: 623–35.

Kragelund, P. (1989). "Epicurus, Priapus and the Dreams in Petronius," *CQ* 39: 436–50.

Kraus, C. S. (1994). " 'No Second Troy': Topoi and Refoundation in Livy, Book V," *TAPA* 124: 267–89.

Labate, M. (1990). "Note petroniane," *MD* 25: 181–89.

(1995). "Eumolpo e gli altri, ovvero lo spazio della poesia," *MD* 34: 153–75.

Lakoff, G. and Johnson, M. (1980). *Metaphors We Live By*. Chicago and London.

Lapidge, M. (1979). "Lucan's Imagery of Cosmic Dissolution," *Hermes* 107: 345–70.

Leach, E. W. (1988). *The Rhetoric of Space: Literary and Artistic Representations of Landscape in Republican and Augustan Rome*. Princeton.

LeLièvre, F. J. (1954). "The Basis of Ancient Parody," *G&R* n.s. 1: 66–81.

Lieberg, G. (1982). *Poeta Creator*. Amsterdam.

Lintott, A. W. (1971). "Lucan and the History of the Civil War," *CQ* n.s. 21: 488–505.

Loporcaro, M. (1984). "Il Proemio di Eumolpo. Petronio, *Satyricon* 83,10," *Maia* 36: 255–61.

Luck, G. (1972). "On Petronius' *Bellum Civile*," *AJP* 93: 133–41.

Maass, E. (1925). "Eunuchos und Verwandtes," *RhM* 74: 432–76.

Marmorale, E. (1948). *La Questione petroniana*. Bari.

Marti, B. (1966). "Cassius Scaeva and Lucan's Inventio," L. Wallach, ed., *The Classical Tradition: Literary and Historical Studies in Honor of Harry Caplan*, 239–57. Ithaca and London.

Martin, J. (1979). "Uses of Tradition: Gellius, Petronius, and John of Salisbury," *Viator: Medieval and Renaissance Studies* 10: 57–76.

Martindale, C. A. (1976). "Paradox, Hyperbole and Literary Novelty in Lucan's *de Bello Civili*," *BICS* 23: 45–54.

——— (1993). *Redeeming the Text: Latin Poetry and the Hermeneutics of Reception.* Cambridge.

Masters, J. (1992). *Poetry and Civil War in Lucan's Bellum Civile.* Cambridge.

McCarthy, B. P. (1934). "Lucian and Menippus," *YCS* 4: 3–55.

——— (1936). "The Form of Varro's Menippean Satires," *University of Missouri Studies* 9.3: 95–107.

McKeown, J. C. (1989). *Ovid: Amores. Text, Prolegomena and Commentary, vol. 2: A Commentary on Book One,* Leeds.

Melville, A. D. (1986). *Ovid, Metamorphoses,* with introduction and notes by E. J. Kenney. Oxford.

Morford, M. P. O. (1967). *The Poet Lucan: Studies in Rhetorical Epic.* Oxford.

Morgan, J. R. (1993). "Make-believe and Make Believe: The Fictionality of the Greek Novels," in C. Gill and T. P. Wiseman eds., *Lies and Fiction in the Ancient World,* 175–229, Austin.

Mössler, J. G. (1842). *Commentatio de Petronii Poemate De Bello Civili.* Breslau.

——— (1857). *Quaestionum Petronianarum specimen, quo poema "De bello civili" cum "Pharsalia" Lucani comparatur.* Hirschberg.

——— (1865). *Quaestionum Petronianarum specimen alterum.* Hirschberg.

——— (1870). *Quaestionum Petroniarum specimen tertium.* Hirschberg.

——— (1891). "*Quaestionum Petronianarum specimen novissimum,*" *Philologus* 50: 722–30.

Most, G. (1987). "The 'Virgilian' *Culex,*" in Whitby et al. (1987), 199–209.

——— (1992). "*disiecti membra poetae*: the Rhetoric of Dismemberment in Neronian Poetry," *Innovations of Antiquity,* R. Hexter and D. Selden, eds., pp. 391–419. New York and London.

Müller, K., ed. (1995). *Petronius Satyricon Reliquiae.* Stuttgart and Leipzig.

Müller, K. and Ehlers, W. (1983). *Petronius Satyrica: Lateinisch – Deutsch.* Munich.

Myers, K. S. (1990). "Ovid's *tecta ars: Amores* 2.6, Programmatics, and the Parrot," *ECM* 34 n.s. 9: 367–74.

Mynors, R. A. B., ed. (1969). *P. Virgili Maronis Opera.* Oxford.

Néraudau, J. P. (1985). "Néron et le nouveau chant de Troie," *ANRW* 2.32.3: 2032–45.

Newton, R. M. (1982). "Trimalchio's Hellish Bath," *CJ* 77: 315–19.

Nicolet, C. (1991). *Space, Geography, and Politics in the Early Roman Empire.* Jerome Lecture Series 19. Ann Arbor.

Nicoll, A. (1931). *Masks, Mimes, and Miracles: Studies in the Popular Theatre.* London.

Nisbet, R. G. M. (1962). Review of K. Müller, *Petronii Arbitri Satyricon* (Munich 1961), *JRS* 52: 227–38.

Nisbet, R. G. M. and Hubbard, M. (1970). *A Commentary on Horace: Odes Book I.* Oxford.

——— (1978). *A Commentary on Horace: Odes Book II.* Oxford.

Nodot, F. (1693). *Titi Petronii Arbitri, equitis Romani, Satyricon: cum fragmentis albae Graecae recuperatis ann. 1688. nunc demum integrum*. London.

Panayotakis, C. (1994). "A Sacred Ceremony in Honour of the Buttocks: Petronius, *Satyrica* 140.1–11," *CQ* n.s. 44: 458–67.

(1994a). "Quartilla's Histrionics in Petronius, *Satyrica* 16.1–26.6," *Mnemosyne* 47: 319–36.

(1995). *Theatrum Arbitri: Theatrical Elements in the Satyrica of Petronius*. Leiden.

Paratore, E. (1933). *Il Satyricon di Petronio*. Florence.

Parsons, P. (1971). "A Greek *Satyricon?*" *BICS* 18: 53–68.

(1974). *The Oxyrhynchus Papyri*, vol. 42 [*POxy.* 3010 = pp. 34–41]. Egypt Exploration Society. London.

Pease, A. S. (1955–58). *M. Tulli Ciceronis De Natura Deorum*. 2 vols. Cambridge, Mass.

Pellegrino, C. (1975). *Petronii Arbitri Satyricon*. Rome.

Pelling, C. B. R. (1979). "Plutarch's Method of Work in the Roman Lives," *JHS* 99: 74–96.

Perry, B. E. (1952) *Aesopica* I. Urbana.

(1967). *The Ancient Romances: A Literary-Historical Account of Their Origins*. Berkeley.

Perutelli, A. (1986). "Enotea, la capanna e il rito magico: l'intreccio dei modelli in Petron. 135–36," *MD* 17: 123–43.

Petrone, G. (1988). "*Nomen/omen*: poetica e funzione dei nomi (Plauto, Seneca, Petronio)," *MD* 20–21: 33–70.

Pfeiffer, R., ed. (1949–53). *Callimachus* 2 vols. Oxford.

Pichon, R. (1912). *Les sources de Lucain*. Paris.

Pohlenz, M. (1965). *M. Tullius Cicero, Tusculanae Disputationes*. Stuttgart.

Powell, J. U. (1925). *Collectanea Alexandrina: reliquiae minores poetarum graecorum aetatis ptolemaicae, 323–146 A.C., epicorum, elegiacorum, lyricorum, ethicorum*. Oxford.

Preston, K. (1915). "Some Sources of Comic Effect in Petronius," *CP* 10: 260–69.

Purinton, J. S. (1993). "Epicurus on the *telos*," *Phronesis* 38: 281–320.

Quint, D. (1993). *Epic and Empire: Politics and Generic Form from Virgil to Milton*. Princeton.

Raith, O. (1963). *Petronius ein Epikureer*. Nuremberg.

Rankin, H. D. (1966). "Petronius, Priapus and Priapeum LXVIII," *C&M* 27: 225–42.

Rauk, J. (1989). "The Parrot and Poetry in Ovid *Amores* 2.6," *Abstracts of the American Philological Association Annual Meeting*. Atlanta, Georgia.

Rawson, E. (1987). "*Speciosa locis morataque recte*," in Whitby et al. (1987), 79–88.

(1993). "The Vulgarity of Roman Mime," *Liverpool Classical Papers* 3: 255–60.

Reardon, B. P., ed. (1989). *Collected Ancient Greek Novels*. Berkeley.

(1991). *The Form of Greek Romance*. Princeton.

Reeve, M. (1983). "Petronius," in L. D. Reynolds, ed., *Texts and Transmission: A Survey of the Latin Classics*, pp. 295–300. Oxford.

Reich, A. (1903). *Der Mimus*, 2 vols. Berlin.

Relihan, J. C. (1987). "Vainglorious Menippus in Lucian's Dialogues of the Dead," *ICS* 12: 185–206.

——— (1993). *Ancient Menippean Satire.* Baltimore.

Reynolds, R. W. (1946). "The Adultery Mime," *CQ* 40: 77–84.

Richardson, N. J. (1974). *The Homeric Hymn to Demeter.* Oxford.

——— (1983). "Recognition Scenes in the *Odyssey* and Ancient Literary Criticism," *Papers of the Liverpool Latin Seminar* 4: 219–35.

Richardson, T. W. (1980). "The Sacred Geese of Priapus? (Satyricon 136, 4f.)," *MH* 37: 98–103.

Richlin, A. (1992). *The Garden of Priapus: Sexuality and Aggression in Roman Humor.* 2nd edn. New Haven and London.

——— (1993). "Materiality of the Cinaedus and the Roman Law against Love between Men," *Journal of the History of Sexuality* 3: 523–73.

Riddle, J. M. (1992). *Contraception and Abortion from the Ancient World to the Renaissance.* Cambridge, Mass.

Riese, A. (1865). *M. Terenti Varronis Saturarum Menippearum reliquiae.* Leipzig.

——— (1894–1906). *Anthologia Latina.* Leipzig.

Riikonen, H. K. (1987). *Menippean Satire as a Literary Genre with special reference to Seneca's Apocolocyntosis.* Commentationes Humanarum Litterarum 83. Societas Scientarum Fennica. Helsinki.

Robinson, E. S. G. (1927). *Catalogue of the Greek Coins of Cyrenaica.* London.

Rohde, E. (1914). Der griechische Roman und seine Vorläufer. 3rd edition. Leipzig.

Romm, J. S. (1992). *The Edges of the Earth in Ancient Thought: Geography, Exploration and Fiction.* Princeton.

Rosati, G. (1983). "Trimalchione in scena," *Maia* 35: 213–27.

Rose, K. F. C. (1966). "Problems of Chronology in Lucan's Career," *TAPA* 97: 379–96.

——— (1966a). "The Petronian Inquisition: An Auto-da-fé," *Arion* 5: 275–301.

——— (1971). *The Date and Author of the Satyricon,* Mnemosyne Supplement no. 16. Leiden.

Rose, M. A. (1993). *Parody: Ancient, Modern, and Post-Modern.* Cambridge.

Rosen, R. M. (1990). "Poetry and Sailing in Hesiod's *Works and Days*," *CA* 9: 99–113.

Rosenblüth, M. (1909). *Beiträge zur Quellenkunde von Petrons Satiren.* Berlin.

Rosenmeyer, P. A. (1991). "The Unexpected Guests: Patterns of *Xenia* in Callimachus' 'Victoria Berenices' and Petronius' *Satyricon*," *CQ* n.s. 41: 403–13.

Ross, D. O. (1975). *Backgrounds to Augustan Poetry: Gallus, Elegy, and Rome.* Cambridge.

——— (1975a). "The *Culex* and *Moretum* as Post-Augustan Literary Parodies," *HSCP* 79: 235–63.

Rouse, R. H. (1979). "*Florilegia* and Latin Classical Authors in Twelfth-century Orléans," *Viator: Medieval and Renaissance Studies* 10: 131–60.

Rudich, V. (1993). *Political Dissidence under Nero: The Price of Dissimulation.* London and New York.

Russell, D. A. (1964). *"Longinus" On the Sublime.* Oxford.

Sage, E. T. (1915). "Atticism in Petronius," *TAPA* 46: 47–57.

Saint-Denis, E. de (1965). "La parodie dans la littérature latine de Plaute à Sénèque," *L'information littéraire* 17: 64–75.

Sandy, G. (1969). "*Satire in the Satyricon*," *AJP* 90: 293–303.

——— (1974). "Scaenica Petroniana," *TAPA* 104: 329–46.

——— (1976). "Publilius Syrus and *Satyricon* 55.5–6," *RhM* 119: 286–87.

——— (1994). "New Pages of Greek Fiction," in J. R. Morgan and Richard Stoneman, eds., *Greek Fiction: The Greek Novel in Context*, 130–45. London.

Sanford, E. M. (1931). "Lucan and his Roman Critics," *CP* 26: 233–57.

Saylor, C. (1987). "Funeral Games: the Significance of Games in the *Cena Trimalchionis*," *Latomus* 46: 593–602.

Schissel von Fleschenberg, O. (1913). "Die Technik des Bildeinsatzes," *Philologus* 72: 83–114.

Schmeling, G. L. (1991). "The *Satyricon*: The Sense of an Ending," *RhM* 134: 352–77.

——— (1992). "Petronius 14.3: Shekels and Lupines," *Mnemosyne* 45: 531–36.

——— (1994). "*Quid attinet veritatem per interpretem quaerere? Interpretes* and the *Satyricon*," *Ramus* 23: 144–68.

——— (1994/5). "*Confessor Gloriosus*: A Role of Encolpius in the *Satyrica*," *Würzburger Jahrbücher für die Altertumswissenschaft Neue Folge* 20: 207–24.

Schmeling, G. L., and Stuckey, J. H. (1977). *A Bibliography of Petronius*. Leiden.

Seager, R. (1979). *Pompey: A Political Biography*. Oxford.

Selden, D. L. (1994). "Genre of Genre" in J. Tatum and G. Vernazza, eds., *The Search for the Ancient Novel*, 39–64. Baltimore.

Shackleton Bailey, D. R. (1965–70). *Cicero's Letters to Atticus*. 7 vols. Cambridge.

——— (1977). *Cicero: Epistulae ad Familiares*. 2 vols. Cambridge.

——— (1982). *Anthologia Latina*, vol. 1. Stuttgart.

——— (1987). "On Petronius," *AJP* 108: 458–64.

——— (1987). "Against Interpretation: Petronius and Art Criticism," *Ramus* 16: 165–76.

——— (1987a). "*Satyricon* 80.9: Petronius and Manuscript Illustrations," *CJ* 82: 216–17.

Slater, N. W. (1990). *Reading Petronius*. Baltimore and London.

Smith, K. F. (1913). *The Elegies of Albius Tibullus*. New York.

Smith, M. S. (1975). *Petronii Arbitrii, Cena Trimalchionis*. Oxford.

Snyder, J. M. (1980). *Puns and Poetry in Lucretius' De Rerum Natura*. Amsterdam.

Sochatoff, A. F. (1962). "The Purpose of Petronius' *Bellum Civile*: A Reexamination," *TAPA* 93: 449–58.

——— (1970). "Imagery in the Poems of the *Satyricon*," *CJ* 65: 340–44.

Solodow, J. B. (1988). *The World of Ovid's Metamorphoses*. Chapel Hill and London.

Soverini, P. (1985). "Il problema delle teorì retoriche e poetiche di Petronio," *ANRW* 2.32.3, 1706–79.

Starr, R. J. (1987). "The Circulation of Literary Texts in the Roman World," *CQ* n.s. 37: 213–23.

—— (1987a). "Trimalchio's *Homeristae*," *Latomus* 46: 199–200.

Steele, R. B. (1920). "Literary Adaptations and References in Petronius," *CJ* 15: 279–93.

Stephens, S. A., and Winkler, J. J., eds. (1995). *Ancient Greek Novels: The Fragments*. Princeton.

Stolz, W. (1987). *Petrons Satyricon und François Nodot*. Stuttgart.

Stramaglia, A. (1992). "Prosimetria narrativa e 'romanzo perduto': P Turner 8 (con discussione e riedizione di PSI 151 [Pack ed.2 2624] + PMil Vogliano 260," *ZPE* 92: 121–49.

Strelitz, A. (1879). "*Emendationes Petronii Satirarum*," *Jahrbücher für classische Philologie* 119: 629–34, 844–45.

Stubbe, H. (1933). *Die Verseinlagen im Petron*, Philologus Suppl. 25. Leipzig.

Sullivan, J. P. (1967). "Petronius, Artist or Moralist?" *Arion* 6: 71–88.

—— (1968). "Petronius, Lucan and Seneca: A Neronian Literary Feud?" *TAPA* 99: 453–67.

—— (1968a). *The Satyricon of Petronius: A Literary Study*. Bloomington, Ind., and London.

—— (1985). *Literature and Politics in the Age of Nero*. Ithaca & London.

—— (1986). *Petronius: the Satyricon, Seneca: the Apocolocyntosis*, trans. with introduction and notes. Revised edition. London.

Thomas, É. (1902). *Pétrone: l'envers de la société Romaine*. 2nd edn. Paris.

Trampe, E. (1884). *De Lucani arte metrica*. Berlin.

Ullman, B. L. (1928). "Tibullus in the Mediaeval *Florilegia*," *CP* 23: 128–74.

—— (1930). "Petronius in the Mediaeval *Florilegia*," *CP* 25: 11–21.

Ville, G. (1981). *La gladiature en Occident des origines à la mort de Domitien*, Bibliothèque des Écoles Françaises d'Athènes et de Rome 245. Rome.

Walbank, F. W. (1957). *A Historical Commentary on Polybius* vol. I. Oxford.

Walsh, P. G. (1968). "Eumolpus, the *Halosis Troiae*, and the *de bello civili*," *CP* 63: 208–12.

—— (1970). *The Roman Novel*. Cambridge.

—— (1974). "Was Petronius a Moralist?" *G&R* 21: 181–90.

—— (1980). Review of Grimal (1977), *Gnomon* 52: 172–74.

Watt, W. S. (1986). "Notes on Petronius," *C&M* 37: 173–84.

Webb, C. C. J. (1909). *Ioannis Saresberiensis episcopi Carnotensis Policratici sive de nugis curialium et vestigiis philosophorum libri viii*, 2 vols. Oxford.

West, M. L. (1972). *Iambi et Elegi Graeci*, vol. 2. Oxford.

Whitby, M., Hardie, P. and Whitby, M., eds. (1987). *Homo viator: Classical Essays for John Bramble*. Bristol.

Williams, G. D. (1994). *Banished Voices: Readings in Ovid's Exile Poetry*. Cambridge.

—— (1994a). "Nero, Seneca and Stoicism in the Octavia," in Elsner and Masters (1994), 178–95.

Williams, G. (1978). *Change and Decline: Roman Literature in the Early Empire*. Berkeley.

Wimmel, W. (1960). *Kallimachos in Rom. Hermes Einzelschriften* 16.

Winkler, J. J. (1985). *Auctor & Actor: A Narratological Reading of Apuleius's Golden Ass*. Berkeley.

(1990). *The Constraints of Desire*. New York and London.

Wiseman, T. P. (1974). "Legendary Genealogies in Late Republican Rome," *G&R* 21: 153–64.

(1985). *Catullus and his World: A Reappraisal*. Cambridge.

Wright, J. (1976). "Disintegrated Assurances: The Contemporary American Response to the *Satyricon*," *G&R* 23: 32–9.

Zeitlin, F. I. (1971). "Petronius as Paradox: Anarchy and Artistic Integrity," *TAPA* 102: 631–84.

(1971a). "Romanus Petronius: A Study of the *Troiae Halosis* and the *Bellum Civile*," *Latomus* 30: 56–82.

(1990). "The Poetics of Eros: Nature, Art and Imitation in Longus' *Daphnis and Chloe*," in D. M. Halperin, J. J. Winkler, F. I. Zeitlin, eds., *Before Sexuality: The Construction of Erotic Experience in the Ancient Greek World*, Princeton.

Index of passages discussed

Index of subjects